MEN OF THE SHIRES
THE SHIRE HORSE,
AND THE MEN
WHO SHAPED THE BREED

JAMES F. GALLIMORE

Cover picture

The cover picture shows a pair of black Shire geldings at work during a ploughing match at Flintham Show, Nottinghamshire, in September 2016.
The photograph of *Jack* (*Cwmsymlog Crackerjack*), a seven-year -old and *Sergeant* (*Shirland Resolution*), a five -year -old, is shown here by courtesy of their owner, **Mr. Kevin Morris of Warwick**.

Acknowledgements:

- The author wishes to acknowledge the help and support of the **Shire Horse Society**.

- **Newspaper images** are reproduced here with thanks to the **British Newspaper Archive** (www.britishnewspaperarchive.co.uk)

  Newspaper images (c) The British Library Board. All rights reserved.

Published by **James Gallimore**

ISBN 978-1514302002

Foreword

by Victoria Clayton, Secretary of the Shire Horse Society

Forty years have passed since the commissioning and publication of *'The Shire Horse'*. The book which was written by Keith Chivers, became the definitive work, giving a detailed account of the history and development of the Breed.

More recent publications about the Shire horse have inevitably drawn on the work and information contained in Mr Chivers' book, and *'Men of the Shires'* does that, but it provides a further, different insight.

The author of *'Men of the Shires'* is not a Shire breeder, but a person with a keen interest in heavy horses. James Gallimore became intrigued by references made by Keith Chivers to several significant early horses called *Gallemore*.

During his research, Mr Gallimore found evidence of a stud having existed, owned by a Staffordshire yeoman called Samuel Gallimore. With the help of the Shire Horse Society, contact was made with Mr Chivers. Both were keen to discover the identity of a human 'Gallimore', after whom these horses may have been named.

Through the passage of time new information has become available which now demonstrates the role Samuel Gallimore played as an owner and breeder in the early years of the Shire horse.

'Men of the Shires' is a unique book, meticulously researched, which expands to give an account of the work carried out by a large number of other owners and breeders of the evolving Shire horse who lived in the English Midland Counties.

This book goes a long way towards filling in gaps and adding to current knowledge of the early period not covered in 'The Shire Horse', due to information constraints.

'Men of the Shires', is complementary to *'The Shire Horse'*, and is a recommended read for anyone wishing to learn more about the early history of this majestic animal.

It is hoped that by adding to the long history of the Shire a superior value may be placed upon the importance of the survival of this much-loved but at-risk heavy horse breed.

SHIRE STALLION—"GAER CONQUEROR"

Photo. Parsons

SHIRE MARE—"DUNSMORE CHESSIE"

Photo. Babbage

Plate 1: Some examples of show-winning Shires from the early 20th Century:
Gaer Conqueror (owned by Abraham Grandage) – London Champion
Stallion in 1910 & 1911 and
Dunsmore Chessie (owned by Sir Walpole Greenwell) - London Champion
Mare in 1912 & 1913.

Introduction

No one who encounters a Shire horse for the first time can fail to be impressed by the magnificence of such an animal. Shires are gentle giants which were once as much a part of everyday life as motor vehicles are today. Now they are few - a rare breed, and owe their survival to dedicated breeders and owners who proudly parade them in the show-ring.

Today's Shire horses are given individual names and each can be clearly identified by a registration number in the breed stud-book. Pedigree details may also reveal an ancestry which goes back many generations.

The Shire horse has a long history, and like other types of heavy horse it emerged as a distinct breed sometime during the second half of the eighteenth century.

Published information about the breeding history of the heavy horses which existed in those early days is however limited, fragmentary and sometimes unreliable. Written evidence has been lacking or not readily available.

This book traces the early breeding history of the Shire horse by using new information obtained from written sources which have now become more accessible. The descent of individual horses which played a significant part, and the identities of the men who shaped the breed are now revealed. These men, equally proud of their horses, gave them names and advertised their pedigrees.

Keith Chivers, in his authoritative work 'The Shire Horse' [6], written for the Shire Horse Society, referred to a number of important named stallions and their breeders or owners, but was unable to shed much light on the earliest period of Shire history. The development of the Internet has provided access to new information which was not easily available to Keith Chivers when his book was first published in 1976. It is now much easier to locate relevant documents in county archives, and in particular, old newspapers, now 'on-line', have been a valuable resource in researching this book.

I corresponded with, and also met Keith Chivers in the 1990s. I had been intrigued by references in his book to a series of stallions named *Gallemore*, which he indicated had been significant in the early development of the Shire Horse. He was extremely keen to identify the **human** Gallemore [or Gallimore] family after which these early 'Shires' were presumed to have been named.

Investigations into my own family history had revealed evidence of the horse-breeding activities of a Staffordshire yeoman called Samuel Gallimore. He had died in 1750; but the earliest of the *Gallemore* stallions was recorded in volume 1 of the Shire Horse stud-book as having been foaled in about 1780.

No link could be established at the time between Samuel Gallimore and these stallions, and this problem remained unresolved until 2011 when I uncovered the existence of earlier *Gallemore* stallions. These horses included '*Galymoor*', and on current evidence he is the earliest-known named 'Shire'. There are also clear indications that this stallion was once owned by Samuel Gallimore.

Additionally, evidence is presented here to support the suggestion that *Galymoor* was the sire of the famed *Packington Blind Horse*, often portrayed as the foundation sire of the early Shires.

No doubt there were others who were active in breeding the ancestors of today's Shire horse in the years before 1750. Evidence of the work of these other breeders may yet be discovered, but the link between Samuel Gallimore and the stallion *Galymoor* makes his contribution of particular interest.

Important as it has been to the early beginnings of the Shire breed, the part played by Samuel Gallimore is but the starting point to this book which expands to provide a comprehensive account of the breeding history of the Shire horse, beginning in the 1750s and continuing into the first half of nineteenth century.

From the 1750s onwards much more information became available as breeders and owners began to advertise their stallions via newspapers, notably in Leicestershire, Derbyshire and Staffordshire, and later in Lincolnshire.

Plate 2: ***Edingale Mascot*** – a celebrated Shire horse of the more modern era
[pictured with groom George Duggins]
This stallion was owned by E. J. Holland of Edingale, Tamworth, Staffordshire.
He was sold to an American buyer for 8000 guineas, in advance of a sale in April 1984
when the entire Edingale Stud was dispersed.

The research material accumulated by Keith Chivers, as the basis for his book 'The Shire Horse', known as the Chivers Collection, and housed at the Museum of Rural Life in Reading [23], does not provide us with any indication that he made use of old newspapers in his work. This is not surprising as they would have been difficult to access at the time.
By making extensive use of information in such newspapers, in my book I have produced a work which complements that of Chivers.
Regrettably, Keith Chivers is no longer alive.
It is in part, in tribute to him, that this account has been written.

James Gallimore 2018

Contents

Note: References within the text are given by number in superscript. These identify newspaper advertisements and notices which are referred to within this book e.g. 1772^{38} is for a newspaper extract from the year 1772, and listed 38, the extracts being numbered chronologically. Newspaper extracts <u>reproduced</u> in this work have additional referencing e.g. 1803^{149De} .
[For an explanation - See the introduction to:

PART 2. BREEDERS AND OWNERS OF THE 'SHIRE' HORSE [page 33]

GREY SPARK 43426. CHAMPION STALLION, DERBY SHOW, 1945.
EXHIBITED BY MESSRS. JAMES FORSHAW AND SONS.

ALTHORPE TRUMP CARD 43873. CHAMPION STALLION, DERBY SHOW, 1947.
EXHIBITED BY MESSRS. J. & W. WHEWELL.

Plate 3: Some examples of show-winning mid - 20th Century Shires, including a stallion owned by the Forshaw family, famous breeders and dealers from the late 19th century, and into the middle of the 20th century.

Illustrations

Tables

BOWER WINALOT 40672. Champion Stallion, London Show, 1939.
Exhibited by Mr. James G. Runciman.

126610 BATTY GRACE DARLING. Champion Mare, London Show, 1939.
Exhibited by Messrs. C. & M. Barker.

Plate 4: Some further examples of show-winning 20th Century Shires

PART 1. ORIGINS AND CONNECTIONS

CHAPTER 1: THE RISE OF THE SHIRE

The horse in its various forms has long been exploited by man; it could be ridden, and also used as an instrument of war. The ability of lighter horses to gallop at speed gave rise to the thoroughbred or race horse. Other types were found to be useful for carrying goods, becoming pack horses, while some were equiped to became draught animals, having the size and strength to pull a chariot, coach, cart, plough or harrow.

The Shire horse, said to be descended from the medieval Great War Horse is one of several breeds of heavy, draught, or cart horse whose power was made use of in helping to drive the revolutions in agriculture and industry.

In medieval England the dominant draught animal used in farming the land, especially for ploughing was not the horse, but the ox. Horses existed alongside oxen, and could be used for some tasks e.g. harrowing where their greater speed resulted in the soil being broken down more efficiently. At this time, horses used for working the land would have been smaller animals called common cart horses. The larger, powerful Great Horse, otherwise called the War Horse was too valuable to be used for farm work, being in use for, of course, waging war! For centuries oxen were preferred for farm work. They were cheaper to feed and maintain, and had a resale value as beef when their working life was over. On the other hand, fewer horses were required for the work than oxen (in the ratio of about 1 : 2), and they could be purchased more cheaply [4]. It is also likely that regional variations developed, in some areas, the horse becoming preferred for agricultural purposes, while at the same time, in other places the the ox still reigned supreme.

The Great War Horse had ceased to be useful in battle by the end of the seventeenth century. It was now that it was available for hauling rather than being ridden, and employed increasingly as a carriage horse or as a draught animal. No longer used in war, it joined the common cart horse on the farm and could be crossed with it to produce something which was better equiped. It was during the eighteenth century that the horse came into widespread use as a draught animal in English agriculture.

Land enclosure, which had begun in some regions in Tudor times, was occurring with greater frequency through Enclosure Acts in the late eighteenth century. Medieval open field systems were being replaced by smaller enclosed fields. This change alone is considered to have contributed significantly to the decline in the use of oxen and a consequently increased use of the heavy horse. A plough team of 6 or 8 oxen had difficulty in ploughing into the corners of the smaller fields, a task easily managed by a smaller team of 2 or 3 horses.

A further factor which favoured the horse was the improvement and greater usage of roads. Oxen were less well suited to the roads with their new metalled surfaces. The horse was faster and had always been more versatile. It was possible to ride a horse, use it to carry goods, or pull a cart, everyday tasks which an ox could not do well or not at all. Ploughing was also only seasonal work. It now made more practical and economic sense to keep heavy horses only, as they could perform both farm work in the fields, and in addition haul goods on the roads to and from the farm. [Some lighter, faster types of horse were increasing employed for long distance road travel, as coach horses.] Cattle breeding also became focused on selecting animals most suited to dairying or beef production rather that their ability to pull a plough. This contributed further to the demise of the draught ox [4].

In considering why and when the heavy horse, and in particular the Shire horse rose to prominence, then the above factors are relevant. However, the heavy horse did more than just replace the ox; there were new and increasing demands for its services during the eighteenth century.

The 1750s onwards saw the beginning of the use of newspaper advertising by horse owners and breeders (many examples of which are given in this book); a trend which probably reflects an increasingly important role for the heavy horse.

A number of factors contributed to a significantly increased role for the Shire. These factors need to be seen within the context of changes taking place at a regional, national and international level.

The Enclosure Acts resulted in smaller, compact blocks of land which could be managed more efficiently (particularly, by horses). Enclosure was accompanied by an increase in the value of the land. Common land and areas of land formerly regarded as waste e.g. swampy, undrained land was also taken into cultivation for the first time. Landowners and tenant farmers employed better farming practices to increase the crop yields and the livestock productivity of their holdings for greater profit. An expanding agriculture was dependent upon a ready supply of horses which were also suited to the task.

The eighteenth century also saw the invention of new farm machinery. Jethro Tull's seed drill depended on horse power, as did his later horse-drawn hoe. Also at a national level, British agriculture had to sustain the supply of food needed to meet the requirements of the rapidly expanding population.

Robert Bakewell, other enterprising gentlemen, and members of the nobility who had developed an interest in farming, sought to improve the quality of their cattle and sheep through selective breeding, with the consequent increased value of their improved stock. The same practice was applied to the evolving 'Shire' horse. More men were entering into the business of breeding heavy horses with the desired qualities. A big, strong stallion with an impressive pedigree, and proven to have produced progeny of quality, could command high cover fees, and itself a high price if sold. The increasing value of horses would have encouraged more farmers, gentlemen and graziers to become breeders to meet demand.

During the eighteenth century, Britain prospered as an increasingly important world power. Agricultural production was however subject to changes in national and international circumstances e.g. war, the general economic climate, and disease (of crops, livestock and the human population). Importation of food from abroad would have benefited the poor, but vested interests of the landowners and farmers ensured this was restricted to ensure that prices were maintained at home. High food prices supported a confident British agriculture, which in turn would have been supported by a strong supply of draught horses such as the evolving Shire. Most notably during the period of the Napoleonic wars [1803 -1815] grain imports into Britain were blocked. Farming was then particularly lucrative due to sustained high grain prices. As war ended, a flood of imported grain, with a consequent fall in price was prevented by the 1815 Corn Law, which again favoured the farmer and his landlord.

High demand for the services of the heavy horse should not however be seen to have come solely from an expanding and profitable farming sector. Increasingly, and partly as a result of land enclosures, many of the once rural population now lived in the expanding towns and cities. Other industries were developing which employed many former farm labourers. The 'Shire' was in great demand here in the urban setting, helping to build houses, factories and infrastructure and for all manner of tasks where carriage and heavy hauling was required. The horse had become the essential means of transportation on the roads. Notably, it also had a new role. Construction of canals during the second half of the eighteenth century transformed transport systems in Britain. The Shire horse was the ideal animal to use as a barge horse, pulling canal boats along the waterways, as well as hauling waggons, carts and drays.

CHAPTER 2: FLANDERS AND FRISIAN CONNECTIONS

The use of the term 'Shire' indicates an inextricable link with the English (more specifically, Midland) Shire counties. But how English is the Shire horse?

The answer seems to be - not as much as is generally supposed!

Chivers provided some evidence of 'foreign blood' having being introduced from continental Europe at various times in centuries past [6].

In 1066 the Normans invaded and conquered with their heavy war horses.

In about 1200 King John imported 100 stallions from the Low Countries, for breeding purposes, with the aim of improving the size, strength and numbers of the 'English Great War Horse'. These are thought to have included black, hairy-legged stallions from Flanders; now regarded to be a highly significant contribution to the foundation the Shire breed. Further importations of Great Horses occurred in subsequent reigns, notably from Flanders (the northern part of Belgium), and from Friesland (in the Netherlands). It is believed that Friesian horses were in great demand as war horses throughout continental Europe. Some indication of their qualities may be seen within the modern Friesian horse (also Frisian), an all black breed of 15-17 hands. These present-day Frisians are powerfully built and agile with a thick mane and tail, and feather on lower legs [11].

In later centuries there was legislation to limit the export of war horses. In the time of Henry VIII, in order to ensure a continuing supply of large, powerful Great War horses, and prompted by declining quality, new laws were introduced to control breeding. Only horses meeting certain size criteria were to be allowed to be bred.

By the time of the Civil War, lighter cavalry horses were being employed. However, the fact that the heavy war horse was still much in demand is revealed by a letter written in 1644 by the future Parliamentary leader, Oliver Cromwell. Cromwell referred to a 'Black' (a term which by this time was synonymous with Great Horse) won at Horncastle (in Lincolnshire) which he was very keen to acquire for his son, and for which he was prepared to pay a high price. According to Chivers this was almost certainly a Frisian horse [6]. Parliamentary forces were strongest in eastern counties, and Chivers speculated that they may have benefited from having access to the biggest and best horses which were descended from Flemish and Frisian stock imported earlier in the seventeenth century. These horses were introduced as a work force by the Dutch engineer Vermuyden who was employed in an ambitious (but largely failed) project to drain the Fens (in Cambridgeshire, Lincolnshire and Northamptonshire). From these origins the Shire variant, the Lincolnshire Black is presumed to have developed (page 101).

It is to the Flanders horse that the modern Shire horse owes most of its ancestry [6]. However, the Frisian had an important secondary role, and the importation of some of these horses in the first half of the 18th century may be of some significance.

In the 1790s William Marshall [21] stated that it was generally understood that the development of the improved breed of black cart-horse followed the importation of six 'Zealand' mares, sent over from The Hague by the late Lord Chesterfield (i.e. Philip Dormer Stanhope, the 4th Earl) [1694 - 1773] when he was an ambassador (i.e. 1728 -1732). The final destination of these mares is said to have been at the Earl's seat at Bretby (near Burton-on-Trent), Derbyshire. Chivers was of the opinion that these mares were a diplomatic gift and likely to have been Frisians. To what extent these mares may have been used as breeding material around Bretby and beyond is not known, but according to Wykes [33], Robert Bakewell (the celebrated agriculturalist) was said to have been so impressed by the progeny he saw 20 or 30 years later that he travelled to Holland and part of Flanders with his friend George Salisbury of Heather, returning with six mares to improve his own stock. Marshall [21] was of the opinion that the initial improvement in the breed took place in Derbyshire, but also that it was breeders in Leicestershire, including Robert Bakewell who took the lead in bringing about further improvement.

Plate 5: Representations of the **Black Horse**, the slow, inferior **common cart horse**, and the **improved cart-horse** with its greater size, strength, activity and vigour- by Thomas Bewick 1807 (although he was of Newcastle upon Tyne, not the Midlands).

'Shire' breeding was certainly established in the Bretby area when in 1758[4], Mr. 'Falconer' (Faulkner) of Bretby advertised a *'Black Horse of the Heavy Breed'* to cover. In 1750, Mr. Faulkner of Bretby, and *'a man from Bratby Hall'* were both recorded (page 126) in the 'leaping' records of Samuel Gallimore as customers for his stallions [19].

Chivers also referred to the contribution thought to have been made by Francis Hastings [1729-1789], who succeeded as 10th Earl of Huntingdon in 1746. He resided at Castle Donington, only about ten miles east of Bretby. Francis Hastings travelled extensively in Europe, and according to George Culley (Bakewell's friend and pupil) *'he brought a set of coach-horses from the Continent, mostly stallions and prevailed upon his tenants by the Trent side to put their mares to them'*. Chivers stated that the horses he imported would have been Frisians [6].

The Earl of Chesterfield was mentor to the much-younger Earl of Huntingdon, both being politicians. It is unlikely that either of them would have had much time for cart horses, although Hastings must have had some interest in horses generally; in 1760 he held the office of *Master of the Horse* under George III. The Earl of Huntingdon was however, in 1788, with Robert Bakewell, one of the founder members of the Leicestershire Agricultural Society.

Historically, the Hastings family, Earls of Huntingdon were based in Ashby-de-la-Zouch, and still held lands (and therefore had tenants) in the area at this time, including, notably, at Packington (a nearby village, the significance of which will become apparent).

Chivers recorded that according to Culley's account, Robert Bakewell, 'many years later' travelled to the continent, accompanied by George Salisbury, and returned with Dutch and Flemish mares, and *'Bakewell then used some of the imported mares to improve the old black breed of the Leicestershire cart horse'* [6]. Culley's use of the term *'many years later'* has to be unreliable, unless he was referring to the time of the Earl of Chesterfield's importation of mares, rather than when horses were imported by the Earl of Huntingdon. Chivers suggested that the Earl of Huntingdon may have imported his stock around 1755-1760, although this would seem to be closer to the time when Bakewell introduced his mares. It was certainly no later for Bakewell, given that an advertisement (page 58) was placed in 1763[10Le] for Mr. Salisbury's well-bred Black Horse to cover at Barrow, near Loughborough which *'came out of a fine Flanders Mare'*.

CHAPTER 3: THE GALLIMORE CONNECTION

The origins of what was to become the Shire horse breed are obscure, but a horse known as *the Packington Blind Horse* (owned by Mr. Hood of Packington, near Ashby-de-la-Zouch, Leicestershire) is often regarded as the foundation stallion.

Keith Chivers, in his book 'The Shire Horse' has made it clear that this is a simplistic view, and an exaggeration. He does however acknowledge that *the Packington Blind Horse*, a stallion which is believed to have been serving mares from about 1755 to about 1770, was a great sire in his day, and is still of historical interest.

A more complex picture of early Shire history is emerging. Apart from the mysterious Mr. Hood, other breeders were involved, not only in Leicestershire, but also, particularly in Derbyshire and Staffordshire. Chivers pointed out the difficulties faced by the compilers of the first Stud-book of the Shire Horse Society in obtaining reliable information about the past [6]. He referred to a story, which he says was related in 1875, by an old stud groom who had said his grandfather had worked for a famous stud, within two miles of Calwich Abbey (in Staffordshire, but near Ashbourne, Derbyshire) owned by a family called 'Gallemore'. The old man's grandfather had apparently told him that in 1745, as the Scottish army of Bonnie Prince Charlie marched towards Derby, he had to take the stallions into hiding. Sir Walter Gilbey [12] gave a similar account although both these writers seem to have extracted the account from Biddell et al [3], as follows:

> *'Unfortunately for the present generation, Derbyshire records are somewhat involved in the mysteries of the past. Traditions once handed down with some semblance of care have, in a great measure, been lost and forgotten, till now apparently only a few fragments remain. Only within the last year or so there went over to the great majority one of the oldest links between the present and the past, in the shape of an old stud groom, whose grandfather in his day was at the head of a famous stud owned by people of the name of Gallemore, who for generations had a celebrated Shire stud within two miles of Calwich Abbey. At the time when Prince Charlie marched on Derby in the famous '45 (1745), this old retainer was forced to take refuge from the invaders, and place the stallions of this stud in a place of safety. This he successfully did, and if curious readers will take the trouble to investigate Volume 1 of the Stud book, they will find several of the original Derbyshire stallions named Gallemore, having been doubtless in the first place christened after the owners. The stud was stabled at Croxden Abbey, and from its courtyard the horses went into hiding. Though it cannot be stated as an absolute fact, all the evidence points to the famous Packington Blind Horse having been begotten at this same place'.*

Recollections of events long past become blurred, and errors and elaboration can be introduced, but often they have a core of truth. The old stud groom may be out by a generation or two, but members of a family called Gallimore were living in 1745 in the small village of Wootton, which **is** within two miles of Calwich Abbey.
[Note: Croxden Abbey and Calwich Abbey are both in Staffordshire, although close to the Staffordshire border with Derbyshire.] Interestingly, Calwich Abbey itself was the location of a famous Shire stud, but this was much later, established by the Duncombe family after

1842. The celebrated Shire horse *Harold* (**Plate 12**, page 83) ancestor of the modern breed was owned by A. C. Duncombe of Calwich Abbey in the 1880s.

Chivers noted that a series of six 'genuinely historical' stallions was recorded in the first Studbook of the Shire Horse Society between 1780 and 1839. A link between these horses and a **human** Gallemore (or Gallimore) has not been made, until now. New evidence has emerged from documents associated with the will of Samuel Gallimore (1697-1750), a Staffordshire yeoman [19]. After his death his executors sold off his goods and livestock which included a total of forty horses (stallions, mares, colts, fillies etc.) (Appendix 1, page 119).

The executors also had the task of collecting 'leaping money' i.e. money paid for a stallion to cover a mare. It is evident that Samuel Gallimore's executors identified 'customers' using records 'in his book'.

The following map (**Plate 6**, page 17) shows that Samuel Gallimore's many 'customers' were located all over north Staffordshire, into Derbyshire and beyond. Each spot plotted is for one entry, identifying the place where a 'customer' lived.

[The key for this map is included in Appendix 3 (page 128). A copy of the inventory from which this information has been extracted is given in Appendix 2 (page 122). The inventory also named Samuel Gallimore's 'customers'.]

Chivers also suggested (in a letter to me) that the mapping of the places indicated where the stallions served mares, and each stallion may have walked a weekly route, leaving home on Monday and returning Friday or Saturday. This, he said, would be the earliest evidence of this method of breeding. [Examples of this type of practice from the 1920s and 1930s, using cards to advertise the route to be taken by travelling stallions are provided in Appendix 4 (page 131)].

Court records of the Diocese of Lichfield reveal Samuel Gallimore's personal circumstances and events leading up to his death [19]. The records exist because he committed suicide, and also it seems because his will was contested; with the implication that he was not of sound mind when writing his will.

He farmed on a large scale with several farms producing…………..

*'considerable quantities of corn and grain ………and did also stock the same with great numbers of Horned cattle for Feeding and with considerable numbers of other Horned cattle for Dairying and Breeding and with Numbers of young horned cattle of different sorts for rearing. 'And with **Stallions, Geldings, Mares, Colts** and Sheep.'*
*'But by undertaking for many years before his Death, more Farms than he could personally manage, And in order to stock the same, And afterwards to **buy in several stallions of High Price** some of which for several years before his death he kept **at his own House** and **stationed others in different parts of the Country** and to support many labourers and Servants for the several purposes before specified, And **large expenses in High Housekeeping, keeping Company abroad and in making extravagant Entertainment calculated to support his Esteem and Influence** in the Neighbourhood of Wootton aforesaid and to **promote Custom to his Stallions'**.*

The documents reveal that Samuel Gallimore was judged to be sane, but troubled in mind, in particular about debt. The above supports evidence that amongst other things he was involved in the breeding, buying and selling of horses of high value and quality. Samuel Gallimore's financial concerns were caused in part by the loss of cattle to distemper (cattle plague) which was having a devastating effect countrywide at this period. [The inventory for his will contains relatively few cattle (which he was also breeding), compared with the great/considerable number indicated above.]

Gallimore had bought several stallions for which he had paid high prices, and kept some of these at his home in Wootton. He is said to have kept others elsewhere, which perhaps suggested he was also a stallion-letter.

Plate 6:

Leaping Record for horses of Samuel Gallimore of Wootton, Staffs [died 1750]

Samuel Gallimore's debt problems were evidently partly due to travel, and the lavish entertainment he provided to attract custom for his stallions. On a more personal level, Samuel had two illegitimate children, but no legitimate heirs, his wife also having left him. He was also suffering some incapacity, having hurt his shoulder in a fall from his horse. On 20 July 1750, after having written his will, he committed suicide by hanging himself [16]. From 21 July 1750 Samuel Gallimore's executors began to sell his goods, produce and livestock, and collect outstanding debts, including 'leaping money' from 'customers' recorded in his book (page 122). Perhaps the most significant name in this list of 'customers', is that of John Massey (of Birchwood Moor, in the neighbouring Derbyshire village of Norbury). His purchase included a mare and foal for £8 - 17s - 6d, but more importantly, on 30 July 1750, only about a week after Samuel Gallimore's death, he bought (page 122) a stoned horse (stallion) for £47 - 16s - 6d (equivalent to a substantial sum, in excess of £4000 today). This was clearly a stallion of high quality and value.

Samuel Gallimore had travelled (presumably to fairs and markets) and entertained to attract customers for his stallions, but during the 1750s breeders of horses 'of the heavy kind', or what were to become 'Shires' were beginning to use newspaper advertisements for this purpose. One of the earliest of these advertisements appeared, in the Derby Mercury in 1757[1De].

'The **Famous Black HORSE**, call'd
GALYMOOR
Is in the hands of *THOMAS MASSEY* at Little Ireton,
Near DERBY, and will leap this next Season, at
*Twelve Shillings and Sixpence a Mare; if Barren Five Shillings
and Sixpence*
*N.B. His Colt got by the above Horse, will Leap this
next Season at Swarkeston Hall near DERBY: To be
there the 20th Day of April, and will Leap at Half a guinea
a Mare; if Barren, Five Shillings and Sixpence.*

The above advertisement (page 86) was placed by Thomas Massey (brother of John Massey of Norbury). This is possibly the earliest known newspaper advertisement featuring a named 'Shire' stallion. Thomas Massey advertised GALYMOOR (or GALLYMOOR) in the Derby Mercury several times up until 1762[9].

[The important contribution to the development of the Shire horse made by the Massey family is discussed in later chapters [81,86]].

An advertisement (page 98) was for cover by Joseph Glossop in 1777[64De], 'got by that noted Horse OLD GALLIMORE, otherwise MASSEY'. This appears to be a reference to Thomas Massey's 'Galymoor'.

These advertisements indicate that there were at least two generations of stallions called GALLIMORE before the first entries in the Stud-book.

An advertisement in the Derby Mercury in 1803[51], and similarly in 1804[152De], featured a horse called GALLIMORE, late the property of Mr. Moore of Winshill (near Burton-upon-Trent). This horse is identifiable as Gallemore 903, the earliest Gallimore stallion to be listed in the first Stud-book [29]. Interestingly, the sire of Gallimore was given as old Manseter (Manseter 1476), and not Kirby 1286 as the compilers of the first Stud-book [29] suggested.

In 1803[50] a cover advertisement was placed for Young Gallimore, a son of the above (Old) Gallimore, and bred by Mr. Falkner (Faulkner) of Bretby. A similar advertisement (page 93) followed in 1804[156De] when Young Gallimore was said to be rising eight years old.

'Young Gallimore' can be identified, with some confidence as Gallemore 904, the horse also known as Perkin's Gallemore (**Table 1**, page 22) which the Stud-book [29] records as having been owned and bred by Perkins of Whitgreave of Stafford (page 78).

The Stud-book records *Bulstrode 349* (foaled 1806) as having been owned and bred by Isaac Bennet, and sired by *Perkin's Gallemore 904* [29]. Isaac Bennett advertised (page 91) his two year old colt *Bulstrode* in 1808[202De], and similarly in 1812[230]. *Bulstrode* was said to have been sired by *Gallimore* and bred by Mr. Faulkner of Bretby. It was further claimed that *Gallimore*, was sired by *Old Gallimore* that formerly covered at Winshill (*Gallemore 903*, owned by John Moore of Winshill). This is evidence firstly, that Faulkner, not Perkin, bred *Gallemore 904*, and secondly that Perkin acquired the stallion *Gallimore* some time before 1806.

In 1811[243], another *Young Gallimore*, a five year old stallion, owned by William Evans, of Birches, near Weobley, was advertised to cover in Herefordshire. He was said to have been got by *Old Gallimore*, whose sire in turn was *'that well known Horse Old Gallimore, the property of the Earl of Oxford'*. Similar advertisements were placed in 1811[218], 1812[228] and 1814[253]. It is interesting to speculate as to the identity of the horse owned by the Earl of Oxford (**Table 1**, page 22). Could this stallion have been *Gallemore 903*, the horse owned, and later sold by John Moore of Winshill? Moore's *Gallimore* (*Gallemore 903*), according to the Stud-book [29], was foaled in about 1780, although he was probably born closer to 1790.

Moore's *Gallimore* was last advertised for cover (by Mr. Abbot of Spondon) in 1806[175], in a similarly-worded advertisement to that placed (page 92) in 1804[152De]. Paul Holmes of Newton Solney, near Burton-upon-Trent had advertised Moore's *Gallimore* in 1803[151]. The stallion was already, at this time, no longer in Mr. Moore's ownership.

An auction sale advertised (page 54) to take place near Shrewsbury, Shropshire in 1811[214Le] featured a stallion called *Sweep* rising 8 years old. His dam was said to have been sister to the *'noted old Gallimore'*. In an additional comment it was stated that *Gallimore* was sold, when 18 years old for 300 guineas. He must have been a celebrated stallion to command such a high price. Could this have been a reference to the purchase of *Gallemore 903* by the Earl of Oxford, although he apparently paid 500 guineas?

In 1830[281], a 'cover' advertisement which referred back to another stallion called '*Young Gallimore*' appeared in the Hereford Journal, although he was also called '*Trumper's Young Gallimore* (**Table 1**, page 23). It was also stated that '*Trumper's Young Gallimore was got by Lord Oxford's Gallimore, which cost 500 guineas*'.

Interestingly, advertisements for *Gallimore* stallions in this later period show a shift of focus away from the traditional Shire-breeding heartland in Leicestershire, Staffordshire and Derbyshire to Herefordshire and Wales (with some detail of these provided in **Table 1** (pages 22-24). The Stud-book also reflects this trend [29]. *Gallemore 908* is recorded as having been bred by Watkin's of Abergavenny. The Stud-book also states that *Gallemore 906* was sired by *Lord Oxford's Gallimore*, and had been owned and bred by Stephens of Follington, Hertfordshire. This is however almost certainly an error, and should have been recorded as Stephens of Hollington (near Holme Lacy), Herefordshire. The stated foaling date of 1836 is also suspect, being much later than expected for a son of *Lord Oxford's Gallimore*. [Stephens of Hollington was mentioned in the above 1830[281] 'cover' advertisement as the owner of a stallion called *Hercules* which had been got by *Trumper's Young Gallimore*.

Mr. Trumper can be identified as William Trumper [1764 - 1822] of Pembridge, Herefordshire who advertised his stallion *Gallimore* (said to be a son of *Lord Oxford's Gallimore*), to cover for the season in 1814[244]. William Trumper had earlier, in 1809[203], advertised *Young Blaze*, got by the *Earl of Oxford's Gallimore* to cover at his stable in Pembridge. James Stephens [1762 - 1830] of Hollington (also known as Hollaton) Farm, Holme Lacy was brother-in-law to William Trumper, having married his sister Ann in 1785.

An 1854[299] advertisement in the Hereford Times offered a colt for sale – which had included '*Old Gallimore*' in his pedigree. This '*Old Gallimore*' was said to have been the property of the late Lord Oxford, and '*one of best horses of his day*'. A number of these later advertisements were for descendants of *the Earl of Oxford's Gallimore* in an area of Herefordshire, close to the family home of the Earls of Oxford at Brampton Byran. The Earl of Oxford mentioned in these advertisements, and the purchaser of the stallion *Gallimore*, probably some time after 1806, would have been Edward Harley [1773-1848], who succeeded to the title of 5th Earl of Oxford and Earl Mortimer in 1790. In his obituary (recorded in the Hereford Journal 3rd January 1849) [5], it was noted that as a young earl he had been attracted to the 'captivating and fashionable amusements of the turf' and became the proprietor of his own large stud of race-horses at Newmarket. I am indebted to Mr Edward Harley, the present representative of the family for instigating a search within his family's archive on my request. The 5th Earl was rather more interested in race-horses, so it is not surprising that no specific reference to the Earl of Oxford having owned a cart horse has been found, even to one for which he may have paid as much as 500 guineas!

Stallions were still being named *Gallimore* in the 1860s, over a hundred years after Thomas Massey's first advertisement (page 18) in 1757[1De]. With so many stallions having been simply called *Gallimore*, there is inevitably, much confusion.

'That well-known STALLION, Young Gallimore one of the best bred HORSES in the County' was advertised for sale in the Hereford Journal in March 1863[304]. He was clearly not the first stallion so named!

As noted earlier, Chivers was keen to identify any human Gallimore after whom the stallions listed in the first Stud-book were likely to have been named. It is now apparent that this was just one individual, Samuel Gallimore of Wootton, Staffordshire. Evidence within newspaper advertisements however enables us to take this further.

Could the *'stoned horse',* bought for £47 - 16s - 6d by John Massey in 1750 (from the executors of Samuel Gallimore, page 122) be the same horse first advertised by his brother Thomas Massey in 1757[1De]?

An advertisement (page 156) for a horse called *Conqueror* in 1804[156De] seems to provide the answer. Details are given of his pedigree, going back to *'....the original Old Gallimore that covered at Wotton'* (i.e. Wootton, where Samuel Gallimore lived).

Another advertisement (page 87), in 1833[286De] for the stallion *Derbyshire* gave a very detailed pedigree, and identified his earliest ancestor. It was claimed that his great great great great great grandam had been sired by *Mr. Massey's Gallimore of Swarkestone*.

These two advertisements also provide evidence of another point of interest; the suggestion that *the Packington Blind Horse* was sired by a *Gallimore* stallion (or more particularly by the horse we can call *Massey's Gallimore*).

The 1804[156De] advertisement continued *'....the original Old Gallimore that covered at Wotton', which Horse was supposed to be the sire of the Packington blind Horse'.*

The 1833[286De] advertisement stated, more positively, and continued *'.... his great great great great great grandam had been sired by Mr. Massey's Gallimore of Swarkestone, which was the sire of the Packington Blind Horse'.*

The many advertisements which are reproduced later in this work reveal the claims which breeders and owners made about the pedigree of their horses. Some claims are clearly exaggerated, or are inaccurate (due to mis-spelling, and other reasons). Some information may be deliberately misleading, or even lies, although reputable breeders are likely to have attempted to give a truthful account. Information passed by word of mouth, over time, inevitably leads to errors which may be unintentionally given in an advertisement.

How much credence can we give to the 1833[286De] advertisement which claims (perhaps as much as 80 years after the event) that the famed *Packington Blind Horse* was sired by the stallion *Gallimore*? The advertisement was placed by John Sims of Stanton-by-Bridge and gave an impressive pedigree for his stallion *Derbyshire*, which included horses by well-known breeders such as Wiles, Bulstrode, Knowles, Bulstrode and Faulkner, as well as Massey.

Was Sims a reputable breeder? Chivers [6], in his discussion of breeders of the county of Derbyshire, clearly thought so, mentioning him as 'a notable man', being represented by horses listed in the first Stud-book by horses foaled between 1790 and 1834.

Further to this, John Sims [1766-1843] lived at Stanton-by-Bridge, in Derbyshire where he was born into a long-established family, only about one mile away from where the Massey family lived at Swarkestone, at the other end of Swarkestone Bridge. The Massey family were still living at Swarkestone in 1833, when the advertisement was placed, and as Swarkestone and

Stanton-by-Bridge were both small communities, it would be reasonable to assume that the Massey and Sims families were well acquainted. John Sims would have been in a very good position to know the true facts. This is, of course, not proof, but the evidence that the *Packington Blind Horse* was sired (probably some time between 1755 and 1760) by *Gallimore* (then in the hands of the Massey family) is as good as it can be.

Table 1: Stallions called Gallimore

The table below gives details 'Shire' stallions named using the name or prefix *Gallimore*. This information is from newspaper advertisements. It does not include all the stallions listed in volume 1 of the Stud-book [29].

Name of horse (+ colour)	When foaled	o - owner b - breeder Ad. - advertiser	Sire	Dam	Notes/other references
1. *Massey's Gallimore* ['*Galymoor*' or '*Gallymoor*'] (Black)	Before 1747	o - Samuel Gallimore o + Ad. - Thomas Massey of Little Ireton, near Derby 1757[1De] -1762[9]			Bought by John Massey in 1750 from executors of Samuel Gallimore
2. *Glossop's Gallimore* [*Old Gallimore*] (Black)	Before 1764	o - Francis Glossop of Upper Haddon, Derbys., then o + Ad. - Joseph Glossop of Stonegravels, near Chesterfield, Derbys. 1777[64De]	1. *Massey's Gallimore* ['*Old Gallimore, otherwise Massey*']		
3. *Knowles' Gallimore* (Black)	Before 1774	o + b - William Knowles of Nelston [Nailstone], Leics. Ad. - Richard Wild of Burchill, near Bakewell 1777[67Le]			Probably a grandson of 1. *Massey's Gallimore*
4. *Young Gallimoore* (Black)	Before 1780	o + Ad. - Joseph Glossop of Stonegravels, Chesterfield 1783[81De]	2.*Glossop's Gallimore*	Mare of Mr. Knowles' of Nelson, Leics - by Mr Knowles's *Conqueror* out of his mare *Mettle*	
5. *Young Gallimore* (Black)	1789	o - Mr. Johnson of Culverthorpe, near Sleaford, Lincs.	Pycroft's old Black horse, of Donington, Lincs.	Mare of Mr Andrew's of Kyme, Lincs.	To be sold in 1793[123Li] (together with *Young Gee*) at Sleaford, Lincs.

6. **Old Gallimore [Moore's Gallimore]*** (Black)	Before 1793	o(late) - Mr. John Moore of Winshill, near Burton-upon-Trent. Ad. - Paul Holmes of Newton Solney, near Burton-upon-Trent 1803[151] Ad. - Mr. Abbott of Borrowash, Derbys. 1804[152De]-1806[175]	*Oldacres' Mansetter*		*Gallemore 903*
7. **Young Gallimore***	1796	b - Mr. Faulkner of Bretby, Derbys. Ad. - Mr. Abbott of Borrowash, Derbys. 1803[150] Ad. - Daniel Moore of Winshill, near Burton-upon-Trent 1804[156De]	6. *Old Gallimore [Gallemore 903]*	Falkner's mare - got by *Falkner's Bald Horse*; her dam by *the Packington Blind Horse*	Identified as *Gallemore 904* - same horse as 8. **Perkins Gallimore** [See below]
8. **Perkin's Gallimore***	Before 1804	Ad. - Mr. Cook of Cocknidge, Trentham. 1807[193]	*[Gallemore 903]*		*Gallemore 904* Two mares sold at farm sale in 1807[193] by Mr. Cook of Cocknidge, Trentham were by *Mr. Perkins's horse Gallimore*
9. **Earl of Oxford's Gallimore***	Before 1803				*Possibly the same horse as Gallemore 903?* In 1809[203] advert. for *Young Blaze* - got by *the Earl of Oxford's Gallimore*
10. **Old Gallimore**	Before 1805				Ref. in adverts 1811[218]-1815[253] by William Evans of Weobley. Grandsire was *Old Gallimore*, owned by the Earl of Oxford
11. **Young Gallimore** (Black)	1808	o - John Evans of Birches, near Weobley, Herefordshire Ad. - William Evans, Groom 1811[218]-1812[228]. o + Ad. - William Evans of Birches, near Weobley, Herefordshire 1814[243]-1815[253]	10. *Old Gallimore*	A black waggon mare	*Young Gallimore* was got by *Old Gallimore* - his sire was *Old Gallimore*, the property of The Earl of Oxford. His grandam was got by *the Packington Horse.*
12. **Young Gallimore**	1808	o + Ad. - Richard Hill of East	8. *Mr. Perkins's*	Mare owned by Mr. Ward of	*Bold Will* was got by *Old Gallimore*

(Brown)		Langton, Leics. 1815[255St]	*horse*, of Whitgreave, near Stafford, called *Bold Will*, son of *Old Gallimore*	Church Langton, Leics. - also got by *Old Gallimore*	
13. **Young Gallimore** (Black)	Before 1811	Ad. - at Halton, near Warrington, Cheshire 1814[245,246St]	8. *Mr. Perkin's Gallimore* of Whitgreave, near Stafford	Dam got by *Old Kirby*	
14. **Trumper's Gallimore**	Before 1811	o + Ad. - William Trumper of Pembridge, Herefordshire 1814[244]	9. *Lord Oxford's Gallimore*		In 1830[281] advert. for *Young Hercules* - *Trumper's Young Gallimore* was got by *Lord Oxford's Gallimore* which cost 500 guineas
15. **Mr. Bill's Gallimore**	Before 1820?		9. *Lord Oxford's Gallimore*		Ref. to in 1862[302] advert. for *Young Regulator* for sale in Monmouthshire
16. **Young Gallimore*** (Brown)	1829	Ad. - George Jones of Birches, near Weobley, Herefordshire 1835[287]	*Mr. Smithies' Grey Horse*	Dam by *Old Gallimore*	For sale in Herefordshire in 1835[287]
17. **Jones's Gallimore***	Before 1842		*Mr. Smithies' Grey Horse*	Dam by the *Earl of Oxford's Gallimore*	Ref. to in sale by auction in Hereford in 1850[296]
18. **Gallimore***	1842	o - John Watkins of Crasswell, Clodock, Herefordshire. Ad. - David Jones in 1849[298]			For sale by auction in Herefordshire in 1849[298]
19. **Gallimore** (Strawberry grey)	1845	o - Mr. Jones of Lyonshall Ad. - Wm. James of Hereford 1850[296]	*Regulator*, by *Young Emperor*, by *Mr. Smithies' Emperor*. *Regulator*'s dam was by *Marson*, by *the Earl of Oxford's Gallimore*	Dam by *Mr. Jones's Gallimore*, by *Mr. Smithie's Grey horse*. *Jones's Gallimore*'s dam was by *the Earl of Oxford's Gallimore*	For sale by auction in Hereford in 1850[296]
20. **Gallimore**	Before 1846	b - Mr. Merrick of Fenhampton, near Weobley, Herefordshire	*The Farmer's Glory*, property of Mr. Robert Rogers of Walterstone, Longtown	Dam by *Old Merryman*, grandam was by *Old Gallimore*, property of the Earl of Oxford	Ref. to in 1849[297] advert. - for sale by auction at Woolhope, Herefordshire. *The Farmer's*

					Glory - descended from the 'real old *Sweet William'*
21. **Young Gallimore** (Rich brown)	1848	Ad. - Mr. Edwin Alfred Price of Ross 1855[300]	*Gallimore*	Dam by *'Sweet William'*,(late belonging to Mr. Hemmings, the Vineyard), grandam by *'Crackwaggon'*	For sale by auction sale at the Sheep Fair at Ross in 1855[300]
22.**Watkins's Gallimore***	Before 1851			Dam by *Fretwell's Warwickshire Lad*	Ref. to in auction sale at Abergavenny Fair in 1867[306]
23. **Young Gallimore**	1857	Ad. - Mr. Thomas Parry of Cefnduglwyd, Llanvetherine, Abergavenny, Monmouthshire 1862[301]			For sale in Monmouthshire in 1862[301]
24.**Young Gallimore**	Before 1859	Ad. - Mr. George Pye of Hereford			For sale by auction in Hereford in 1863[304]

Note: Estimated foaling dates are based on the assumption that the sire of each stallion listed was a minimum of three years old on covering the stallion's dam.

In commenting further on stallions* listed in the above table ....
Stallions numbered 6. and 9. might have been the same horse - both *Gallimore 903*.
Similarly horses numbered 7. and 8. appear to be the same horse - listed as *Gallemore 904* in the first Stud-book. Stallions numbered 16. and 17. are also likely to have been the same horse. Stallions numbered 18. and/or 22., could have been *Watkin's Gallimore* - the horse listed in the first Stud-book as *Gallemore 908*. [John Watkin's of Craswell lived in Herefordshire, but within ten miles of Abergavenny.]
John Evans of Birches, near Weobley (re. stallions numbered 10. and 11.) can be identified as John Evans [1746 -1833]; his groom being his son William Evans [1784 -1815]. George Jones (re. stallion numbered 16.) was given the same address, a few years later. He was perhaps related to the Evans family; the Birches being a single farm.
Mr. Smithies' Grey Horse is named several times in the table, his owner having been the Rev. John R. Smythies [1778-1852], who had an estate at Lynch Court, close to Pembridge, Herefordshire. Rev. Smythies was a noted agriculturalist and livestock breeder. He was one of the founders of the Royal Agricultural Society, as well as being a member of the clergy.
The presence, in Lincolnshire of a stallion called *Gallimore* (horse numbered 5. in the table) is an interesting abberation, together with the fact that another stallion called *Gee* was on sale in 1793[123Li] together with *Gallimore*. The name *G or Gee* may possibly suggest a link back to Robert Bakewell, but, frustratingly, no pedigree details were provided.

CHAPTER 4:   A SNAPSHOT IN TIME

An interesting window into the past is provided in *'A 'General View of the Agriculture of Derbyshire'* by John Farey, published in 1817 but covering a period from about 1811[8]. He provided the names of the principal livestock breeders operating in Derbyshire (and Leicestershire) in the early years of the 19th Century.

In the section on Horses he described Derbyshire as having long been famous, ranking only behind Leicestershire for its *'stout, boney clean-legged breed of work horses, principally of a black colour'*.

OLD ENGLISH BLACK HORSE

Plate 7: A representation of an **Old English Black Horse**, typically found in Derbyshire and Leicestershire.

In his comment on Leicestershire, Farey referred to the writings of William Pitt [25] who had said that Leicestershire had long enjoyed a good breed of cart horses before the late Robert Bakewell began his celebrated improvements.

Mr. Bakewell *'went to Flanders and Holland and selected some West Frieseland Mares which he imported and crossed with stallions selected in Leicestershire'*.

In this context, Farey began by listing the most noted *'stallion letters'* or professional breeders of the improved cart-horse or work horse, **who are not resident within the County** (of **Derbyshire**), but have let their stallions into the County, (almost all of these being breeders from **Leicestershire**). They included:

Astley, Richard, of Odstone-Hall, near Market-Bosworth, Leicestershire
Bakewell, Robert, (the late), of Dishley Grange, near Loughborough, Leicestershire
Challener, _____, of Nether Thorp, in Shire Oaks, near Worksop, Nottinghamshire
Grice, Joseph, of Blackfordby, near Ashby-de-la-Zouch, Leicestershire
Hart, William, of Culloden Farm, in Norton, near Ashby-de-la-Zouch, Leicestershire
Inge, _____, of Thorpe, near Hinckley, Leicestershire
Knowles, Samuel, of Nailstone, near Ashby-de-la-Zouch, Leicestershire

Moira, Earl of, Donnington-Park, near Loughborough, Leicestershire
Stevenson, Thomas, of Snareston, near Ashby-de-la-Zouch, Leicestershire
*Wilds, _____, of Coton, near Market-Bosworth, Leicestershire

The list of the most noted Derbyshire *'Stallion letters'* of the improved cart-horse [and Nag kinds] included:

Abbot, John, of Spondon, near Derby
Arnold, John, of Radburne, near Derby
Bancroft, John, of Synfin, near Derby
Blunston, John, of Risley, near Derby
Chesterfield, Earl of, Bradby Park, near Burton-upon-Trent
Clarke, Job, of Repton, near Burton upon Trent
Cockayne, _____ of Walton, near Burton-upon-Trent
Devonshire, Duke of, Chatsworth House, near Bakewell
Edge, _____ of Quarndon, near Derby
Hassall, Thomas, of Hartshorn, near Ashby-de-la-Zouch, Leicestershire
Moore, Daniel and John, of Winshill, near Burton-upon-Trent
Morley, Joseph, of Draycot, near Derby
Orpe, William, of Birchwood-Moor, near Ashburne
Plimley, Walter, of Styd-Hall in Shirley
Robinson, John, of Weston -on -Trent, near Derby
Shepherd, Thomas, of Newton Solney, near Burton-upon-Trent
Shirt, Robert, of Beighton, near Sheffield
Sitwell, Sir Sitwell Bart. (the late), Renishaw, Chesterfield
Smith, Edward, of Draycot, near Derby
Smith, James, of Aston in Sudbury, near Uttoxeter
Smith, John, of Coton, near Burton-upon-Trent
Smith, John, of Sawley, near Derby
Smith Joseph, of Lullington, near Burton-on-Trent
Twig, Joseph, of the Common, Marston Montgomery, near Ashburne
Ward, John, of Lullington, near Burton-upon-Trent

Using supplementary notes Farey provided some further information about breeders of work - horses. He noted that Mr. Luke Ashby of Eggington kept four or five breeding mares, but no stallion. He also recorded that John Bancroft of Synfin, who kept eight breeding cart mares and a stallion for his own and his neighbours' use, had hired or used stallions of Samuel Knowles. The Earl of Chesterfield of Bradby-Park (Bretby Park) was said to possess *'two' Hanoverian stallions of the Nag kind'*, from which he bred a few colts annually, but also kept a few black cart mares which he bred from for use on his farm. Mr. Richard Harrison of Ash (Sutton on the Hill) was also said to hire stallions of Samuel Knowles. Mr. Joseph Clarke of Willesley (near Ashby-de-la-Zouch) was mentioned as keeping five breeding mares of the black kind; he had hired or used stallions of, amongst others, (his brother-in-law), Mr. William Hart (*'whose Stallions have long been in great repute in this part of Derbyshire'*) and Mr. *Wilds.
[*Wilds – can be identified as Joseph Wiles of Coton]

Animal breeders frequently bred more than one type of livestock e.g. Samuel Knowles of Nailstone was recorded as being a noted breeder of cattle and sheep as well as heavy horses. Farey also recorded the names of notable breeders of cattle and sheep in Leicestershire and Derbyshire. Listed below is a selection of these noted breeders who in some way also had a connection with heavy horse breeding.

'Bull-letters' or Professional Breeders of Cattle, of the 'Improved or new Long-Horn kind' included:

Bakewell, Robert, (the late), of Dishley Grange, near Loughborough, Leicestershire
Hacket _____, of Nailston, near Ashby-de-la-Zouch, Leicestershire
Honeyborn, Robert, of Dishley Grange (successor to Robert Bakewell), near Loughborough, Leicestershire
Knowles, Samuel, of Nailstone, near Ashby-de-la-Zouch, Leicestershire
Paget, Thomas (late), of Ibstock, near Ashby-de-la-Zouch, Leicestershire
Chesterfield, Earl of, Bradby Park, near Burton-upon-Trent, Derbyshire
Smith, William, of Foremark Park & Swarkstone Lowes, Derbyshire
Greaves, Robert Charles, of Ingleby, Derbyshire

Tup breeders (of the 'New Leicester kind') included:

Bakewell, Robert, (the late), of Dishley Grange, near Loughborough, Leicestershire
Knowles, Samuel, of Nailston, near Ashby-de-la-Zouch, Leicestershire
Paget, Thomas (late), of Ibstock, near Ashby-de-la-Zouch, Leicestershire
Bancroft, William, of Barrow, near Derby
Bowyer, Thomas, of Waldley in Cubley, Ashburne, Derbyshire
Greaves, Robert Charles, of Ingleby Hall, near Derby, Derbyshire
Smith, William, of Swarkstone Lows, near Derby, Derbyshire

Thomas Bowyer [1759 -1824], according to Farey, was for several years a pupil and assistant to Mr. Bakewell of Dishley. An earlier Mr. (Thomas) Bowyer of Waldley (Marston Montgomery) the father or grandfather of Thomas Bowyer, had used the services of Samuel Gallimore's stallions, and was recorded (page 126) in his 'leaping 'records of 1750.
Another interesting reference was to Robert Charles Greaves [1748 -1823] of Ingleby Hall, an earlier Mr. Greaves of Ingleby (page 126), possibly his father William Greaves [1714 –1781] having been one of Samuel Gallimore's customers.
William Smith [c1768 - 1843] of Foremark Park and Swarkstone Lows was a prominent agriculturalist, a breeder of cattle and sheep, and agent to Sir Henry Harpur Crewe, Bart. of Calke. More significantly, his obituary (Derby Mercury 1 February 1843) recorded that *'in 1817 he succeeded the family of Mr. Bakewell, at Dishley'* [5]. This would have followed the death of Robert Bakewell's nephew, Robert Honeyborn, who had died in 1816. William Smith's son, Henry is also said to have succeeded his father at Dishley. Henry Smith also married Selina Bancroft, daughter of William Bancroft of Sinfin (page 94). Farey referred to William Smith as a friend. William Smith was also related by marriage to the Massey family of Norbury and Swarkstone, his daughter Sarah having married Sampson Massey at Swarkstone in 1813.
William Orpe [1782-1859] was a grandson of John Massey [1709 -1799] and appears to have succeeded his uncle, Bartholomew Massey at Birchwood Moor (page 86).
'Hacket' of 'Nailston' (page 50) was another Massey relative.
Philip Stanhope, 5th Earl of Chesterfield [1755 -1815], unlike the 4th Earl (his distant cousin), resided at the family seat at Bretby and took great interest in agricultural matters and improving farming practices. He seems to have experimented with the breeding of all manner of livestock, although less so with horses.

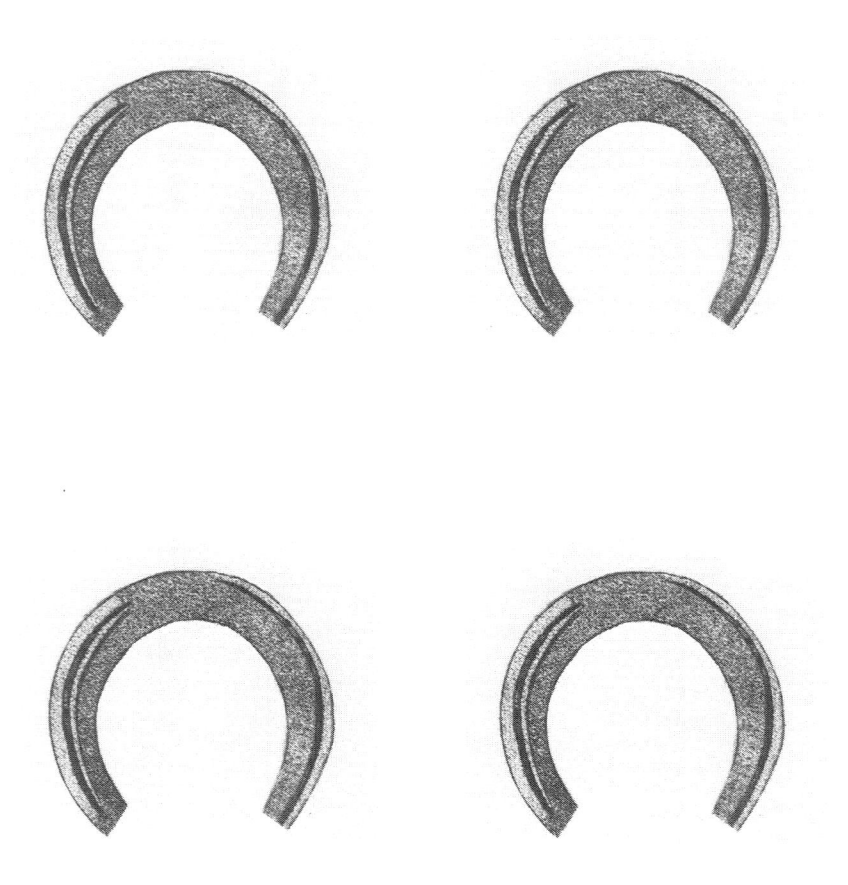

CHAPTER 5: THE FIRST STUD-BOOK AND GENEALOGICAL TABLE

The first Shire Horse Stud-book [29], published in 1880 (and then called the English Cart horse Stud-book: Volume 1) contains the pedigrees of 2381 stallions foaled prior to 1 January 1877. The compilers of this work had to dig deep into the past to unearth detailed information about each of the individual stallions listed.

They had a very difficult task, given the length of time which had elapsed, using what written evidence they could find, and memories passed down through the generations by word of mouth. Inevitably, despite their best efforts, and apparently cautious approach we cannot rely upon some of the information supplied. Obvious errors were also included which they could not resolve.

Also bound within the Stud-book, a genealogical table was provided which claimed to give several generations of the more immediate descendants of the *Packington Blind Horse*.

According to Chivers [6] the table was compiled in 1834. It is not known who compiled the table, although Chivers gave the names of some possible candidates. Presumably the genealogical table was included to provide an indication that the 'Shire' breed had some degree of antiquity (comparable with the Suffolk breed). However, the information it contains often contradicts that given in the individual pedigrees presented within the Stud-book.

No attempts were made to cross-reference by e.g. adding Stud-book numbers to the table. Chivers described the table as 'utterly useless'; stating that the Stud-book had to be accepted as the only authentic information.

The wealth of information now available from newspaper sources, dating from the 1750s, and covering the period of time during which the descendants of the *Packington Blind Horse* were in existence, enables us to view the genealogical table in a new light. The information given in the table, which Chivers thought to be of little value, is now, in many instances, found to be supported by evidence provided by these newspaper sources. Consequently, some of the information given in individual Stud-book entries, rather than in the genealogical table, is in doubt.

The following table (**Table 2 ,** pages 30-31) is a reproduction of the above-mentioned genealogical table, which accompanied the first Stud-book.

Table 2

Genealogical Table	
OF	
THE MORE IMMEDIATE DESCENDANTS	
OF	
THE PACKINGTON BLIND HORSE	
With the dates of their birth ascertained in instances marked *, and inferred in the remainder.	

Little John (Oldacre's), 1793. . . . .

Samson (Shaw's), 1793 . . . .

Old Gallemore (Moore's), 1790 . . . .

Mansetter (Oldacre's), 1780 . . . .

Dam of Fray's Horse.

Dam of Donnisthorp's Horse

Grandam of Blaze (Cockayne's).

Merryman (Massey's), 1793 . . . .

Merryman (Harp's), 1795 . . . .

Blaze (Hart's), 1790 . . . .

Old Kirby (Oldacre's), 1773 . . . . .

THE PACKINGTON BLIND HORSE, ... 1760.

Ball ( ), 1785 . . . .

Tinker (R. Horsefield's), 1788 . . . .

Hean's Black Horse, 1790 . . . .

Bald Horse (Bulstrode's), 1778 . . . .

Mellor's Black Horse, 1795

Blaze (Radford's), 1788 . . . .

(Massey's), 1790 . . . .

Ragman (Eaton's), 1790 . . . .

Kirby (Kettle's), 1795 . . . .

*Farmer (Brown and Davies'), 1817
*Nelson (Shaw's), 1809
*Kirby (Wright's), 1810

Old Merryman, 1770 . . . .

Grandam of Marston (Chadwick's),

Grandam of Bulstrode (Chadwick's),

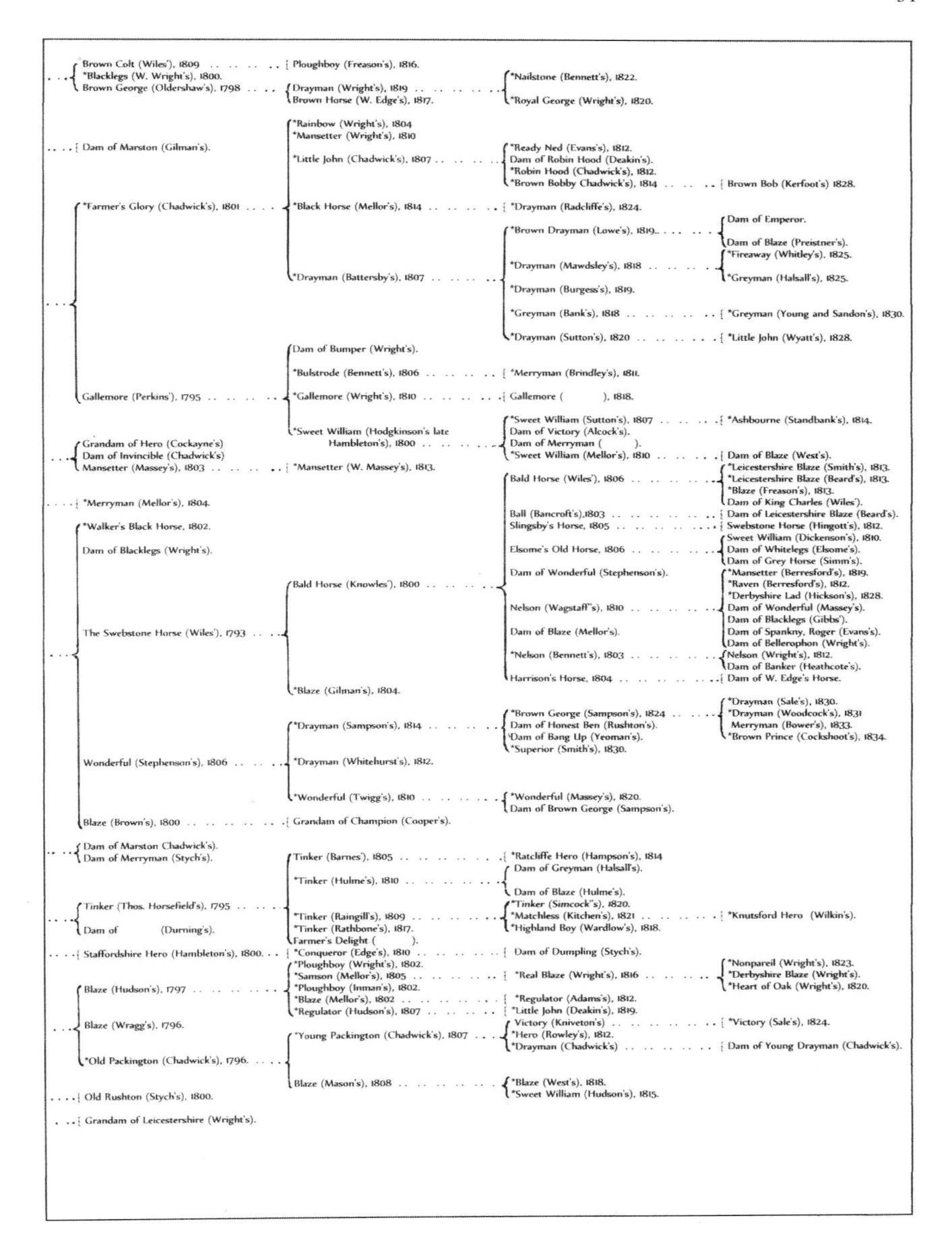

Brown Colt (Wiles'), 1809 . . . . { Ploughboy (Freason's), 1816.

*Blacklegs (W. Wright's), 1800.

Brown George (Oldershaw's), 1798 . . . . { Drayman (Wright's), 1819 . . . . { *Nailstone (Bennett's), 1822.
Brown Horse (W. Edge's), 1817. { *Royal George (Wright's), 1820.

. . . { Dam of Marston (Gilman's).

*Rainbow (Wright's), 1804
*Mansetter (Wright's), 1810

*Little John (Chadwick's), 1807 . . . . { *Ready Ned (Evans's), 1812.
Dam of Robin Hood (Deakin's).
*Robin Hood (Chadwick's), 1812.
*Brown Bobby Chadwick's), 1814 . . . . . . { Brown Bob (Kerfoot's) 1828.

*Farmer's Glory (Chadwick's), 1801 . . . . { *Black Horse (Mellor's), 1814 . . . . { *Drayman (Radcliffe's), 1824.

*Brown Drayman (Lowe's), 1819.. . . . . . { Dam of Emperor.
Dam of Blaze (Preistner's).

*Drayman (Mawdsley's), 1818 . . . . { *Fireaway (Whitley's), 1825.
*Greyman (Halsall's), 1825.

*Drayman (Battersby's), 1807 . . . . { *Drayman (Burgess's), 1819.

*Greyman (Bank's), 1818 . . . . { *Greyman (Young and Sandon's), 1830.

*Drayman (Sutton's), 1820 . . . . { *Little John (Wyatt's), 1828.

Dam of Bumper (Wright's).

*Bulstrode (Bennett's), 1806 . . . . { *Merryman (Brindley's), 1811.

Gallemore (Perkins'), 1795 . . . . . { *Gallemore (Wright's), 1810 . . . . { Gallemore ( ), 1818.

*Sweet William (Sutton's), 1807 . . . . { *Ashbourne (Standbank's), 1814.
Dam of Victory (Alcock's).
*Sweet William (Hodgkinson's late
Hambleton's), 1800 . . . . { Dam of Merryman ( ).

Grandam of Hero (Cockayne's)
Dam of Invincible (Chadwick's)
Mansetter (Massey's), 1803 . . . . . { *Mansetter (W. Massey's), 1813.

*Sweet William (Mellor's), 1810 . . . . . { Dam of Blaze (West's).
*Leicestershire Blaze (Smith's), 1813.

Bald Horse (Wiles'), 1806 . . . . { *Leicestershire Blaze (Beard's), 1813.
*Blaze (Freason's), 1813.
Dam of King Charles (Wiles').

. . . . . { *Merryman (Mellor's), 1804.

*Walker's Black Horse, 1802.

Ball (Bancroft's),1803 . . . . { Dam of Leicestershire Blaze (Beard's).

Slingsby's Horse, 1805 . . . . { Swebstone Horse (Hingott's), 1812.
Sweet William (Dickenson's), 1810.

Dam of Blacklegs (Wright's).

Elsome's Old Horse, 1806 . . . . { Dam of Whitelegs (Elsome's).
Dam of Grey Horse (Simm's).

Dam of Wonderful (Stephenson's).

Bald Horse (Knowles'), 1800 . . . . . . { *Mansetter (Berresford's), 1819.
*Raven (Berresford's), 1812.

Nelson (Wagstaff's), 1810 . . . . { *Derbyshire Lad (Hickson's), 1828.
Dam of Wonderful (Massey's).

The Swebstone Horse (Wiles'), 1793 . . . {

Dam of Blaze (Mellor's).

Dam of Blacklegs (Gibbs').
Dam of Spankny, Roger (Evans's).
Dam of Bellerophon (Wright's).

*Nelson (Bennett's), 1803 . . . . { Nelson (Wright's), 1812.
Dam of Banker (Heathcote's).

*Blaze (Gilman's), 1804.

Harrison's Horse, 1804 . . . . { Dam of W. Edge's Horse.

*Drayman (Sampson's), 1814 . . . . { *Brown George (Sampson's), 1824
Dam of Honest Ben (Rushton's).
Dam of Bang Up (Yeoman's).
*Superior (Smith's), 1830.

*Drayman (Sale's), 1830.
*Drayman (Woodcock's), 1831
Merryman (Bower's), 1833.
*Brown Prince (Cockshoot's), 1834.

Wonderful (Stephenson's), 1806 . . . . . { *Drayman (Whitehurst's), 1812.

*Wonderful (Twigg's), 1810 . . . . { *Wonderful (Massey's), 1820.
Dam of Brown George (Sampson's).

Blaze (Brown's), 1800 . . . .{ Grandam of Champion (Cooper's).

Dam of Marston Chadwick's).
Dam of Merryman (Stych's).

Tinker (Barnes'), 1805 . . . .{ *Ratcliffe Hero (Hampson's), 1814
Dam of Greyman (Halsall's).

*Tinker (Hulme's), 1810 . . . . { Dam of Blaze (Hulme's).

Tinker (Thos. Horsefield's), 1795 . . . . {

Dam of ( ) (Durning's).

*Tinker (Raingill's), 1809 . . . . { *Tinker (Simcock's), 1820.
*Matchless (Kitchen's), 1821 . . . . { *Knutsford Hero (Wilkin's).
*Tinker (Rathbone's), 1817. *Highland Boy (Wardlow's), 1818.
Farmer's Delight ( ).

Staffordshire Hero (Hambleton's), 1800. . . { *Conqueror (Edge's), 1810 . . . . { Dam of Dumpling (Stych's).
*Ploughboy (Wright's), 1802.
*Samson (Mellor's), 1805 . . . . { *Real Blaze (Wright's), 1816 . . . . . . { *Nonpareil (Wright's), 1823.
*Derbyshire Blaze (Wright's).
*Heart of Oak (Wright's), 1820.

Blaze (Hudson's), 1797 . . . . { *Ploughboy (Inman's), 1802.
*Blaze (Mellor's), 1802.
*Regulator (Hudson's), 1807 . . . . . . { *Regulator (Adams's), 1812.
*Little John (Deakin's), 1819.

Blaze (Wragg's), 1796.

Victory (Kniveton's) . . . . { *Victory (Sale's), 1824.

*Young Packington (Chadwick's), 1807 . . .{ *Hero (Rowley's), 1812.
*Drayman (Chadwick's) . . . . { Dam of Young Drayman (Chadwick's).

*Old Packington (Chadwick's), 1796 . . . .{

Blaze (Mason's), 1808 . . . .{ *Blaze (West's), 1818.
*Sweet William (Hudson's), 1815.

. . . . { Old Rushton (Stych's), 1800.

. . . { Grandam of Leicestershire (Wright's).

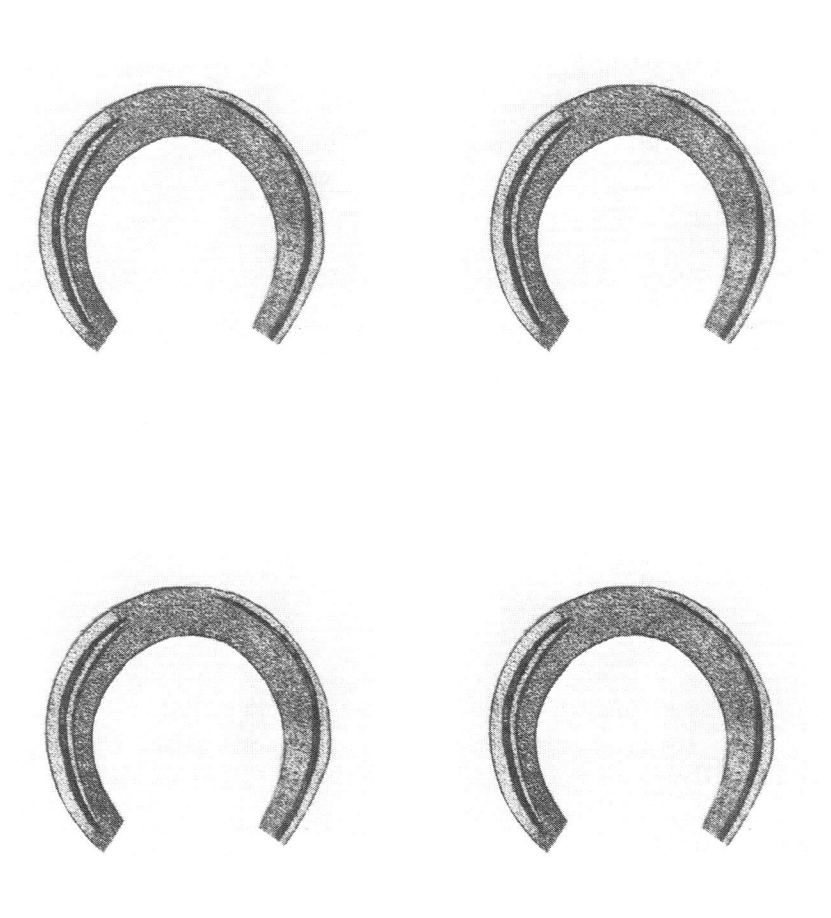

PART 2. BREEDERS AND OWNERS OF THE 'SHIRE' HORSE

Specific individuals who have made a significant contribution to the early development of the Shire horse are identified here.

By the middle of the 18th century breeders and owners of working horses had begun to advertise those with the necessary or desired qualities. Apart from describing their stallions in terms of their age, colour (always black in the earliest advertisements) and size (generally between 16 and 17 hands), they claimed that their horses were e.g. *'uncommonly wide'*, *'short legg'd'*, *'remarkably full of bone'*, and sometimes *'beautiful'* ! Most importantly, a stallion may have also been described as *'well-bred'*, *'a sure foal-getter'*, or that *'his stock are exceedingly good'*.

Those men who advertised the early 'Shires' included country gentleman, but also prosperous yeoman, farmers and graziers. Advertisers also included men who were not owners but had horses hired out to them by owners known as 'stallion-letters' (some of whom from around the beginning of the 19th century were named by Farey [8] in Chapter 4 (page 25).

Initially stallions were unnamed, or only named in a way which indicated their present or former ownership as e.g. *Hood's horse, Donnisthorp's horse, Massey's horse.* Some names such as *Blaze* or *Bald* described their appearance while e.g. the *Packington horse* indicated where a stallion originated or was at stud. Unspecific naming of horses means that tracing their ancestry with any degree of certainty is difficult. The pedigrees of horses with unusual names such as *Bulstrode* or *Gallimore* are easier to trace, but it was not until the development of numerical registration in the late 19th century that naming became trully specific.

During the second half of the 18th century, there was a movement within some circles, notably amongst Leicestershire gentlemen, to invest in their farms and populate them with specimen cattle, sheep and horses which they could show off, and make exchanges with their neighbours, relatives and acquaintenances.

The increasing demand for heavy, working horses also stimulated the development of horse-breeding as a business. It became a useful source of income; and a lucrative one for some. Written forms of advertising via newspapers began to be used, and this has provided useful documentary evidence. Stud cards were to come later, but much of this account is drawn from information provided by early newspapers in which the 'cover' or 'leaping' services of stallions, or sales of horses were advertised.

Reynolds, in his *History of the English Cart-Horse*, published within Volume 1 of the Stud-book [29], made reference to records which indicated that the earliest heavy English draught horses were located in Leicestershire, and the contiguous counties of Staffordshire and Derbyshire. This is supported by evidence in early newspapers, with a picture emerging of early breeding activity having taken place primarily within these three Midland shire counties.

Reynolds was also of the opinion that Lincolnshire, Cambridgeshire, and perhaps several other counties had made an early contribution, although he intimated that records were lacking. Lincolnshire has certainly made a highly significant contribution, although indications are that this came later. It is for this reason that evidence of 'Shire' breeding in Lincolnshire, as well as in the counties of Leicestershire, Staffordshire and Derbyshire (and also Shropshire) is documented here.

The earliest 'cover' or 'leaping' advertisements and sale notices recorded in newspapers for the evolving Shire horse breed date from the 1750s. They were few, with only six newspaper entries found in the period up to 1760. Advertising steadily increased, with twenty three entries in the decade 1761-1770, and forty nine entries found during the years 1771-1780.

An attempt has been made to include all informative early newspaper advertisements and notices from the 1750s onwards, up to about 1820. (Some newspaper entries lacking names of breeders or owners, names of horses, or pedigree details having been ignored).

Beyond 1820, only some of the later 19th century entries are included, being selected on the basis that they contain significant information which links back to that given in earlier records. The *Derby Mercury* has been by far the most important source of this information, having a circulation which covered the very area where the 'Shire' had its origins in Derbyshire, North Leicestershire, and into Staffordshire. Other newpapers which have been particularly useful sources include *the Leicester and Nottingham Journal (later the Leicester Journal)* , and *the Stamford Mercury*. Important information has also been provided by *the Northampton Journal, the Northampton Mercury, Staffordshire Advertiser, Hereford Journal and Hereford Times,* amongst others.

This part of the book is divided into chapters on each of the above mentioned counties. Within each chapter, important breeders and owners associated with that county are identified and the significance of their contribution to the development of the Shire horse breed discussed.

Evidence for this information is provided by over 300 referenced newspaper entries, of which almost 100 have been reproduced and inserted within each of the following chapters depending on the county and individual to which they have most relevance (although, of course, many demonstrate links to more than one county and individual breeder or owner).

Newspapers sources which have been reproduced can be located by additional reference information e.g. 1768[18Li] indicates that it is from a newspaper dated 1768 which is listed 18 in the reference section at the back of this book (page 135). The additional reference 'Li' indicates that it has particular relevance to Lincolnshire.

Similarly, for other newspaper entries reproduced (which can be found within each relevant chapter), 'Le' is the reference used for Leicestershire, 'De' for Derbyshire. 'St' for Staffordshire, and 'Sh' for Shropshire.

CHAPTER 6: LEICESTERSHIRE BREEDERS AND OWNERS

Leicestershire had a primary role to play in the early history of the Shire horse with a number of breeders and owners making an important contribution. They resided principally between Ashby-de-la-Zouch and Loughborough, in an area which also extended south to Market Bosworth.

Plate 8:
Ploughing scene featuring three Leicestershire heavy horses

This depiction, carved in local slate, can be seen on the side of the tomb (dated 1745) of Sir Joseph Danvers and his wife Frances, in the churchyard of Swithland, Leicestershire.
[Swithland is approx. four miles south of Loughborough]

The above plate gives an early illustration of the type of horse which worked on the land in the middle of the 18th century in Leicestershire. It cannot be concluded that the use of horses for ploughing was then typical, but much of the land in Leicestershire was already enclosed, a process linked to the decline in the use of oxen for this task. Also, the reputation that this county acquired for producing a distinctive type of heavy horse - the 'Leicestershire Black' seems well established by this date.

Almost any reference to Shire horse history makes mention of the village of Packington, (just south of Ashby-de-la-Zouch), and the **Packington Blind Horse**, claimed to be the foundation shire. The *Packington Blind Horse* features in the pedigrees of many of the earlier horses, although Chivers has made clear that his role has been over-emphasized, certainly in terms of a connection with the modern Shire breed. A lack of information about other stallions is considered, in part, the reason for this. Packington is certainly of significance however; as several breeders had links with the parish of Packington (parts of which also used to be in Derbyshire).

Hood - of Packington, Leicestershire …….. and the Packington Blind Horse

The identity of Mr. Hood (who was the owner, but not necessarily the breeder of the *Packington Blind Horse*) has not been established. It has been suggested that Mr. Hood was probably John Hood of Bardon Hall [near Coalville], a likely associate of Robert Bakewell, as a fellow Presbyterian [33]. There is however no evidence that this wealthy London barrister ever spent much time in Leicestershire, and no links between this Hood family and Packington have been discovered. It seems unlikely that this Mr. Hood would have had an interest in breeding cart horses! As there were several individuals with the surname Hood living at Packington at the relevant period, it seems more likely that we do not need to look for candidates outside the village. These candidates include: John Hood [1686? -1757], and, more probably, his sons (baptised at Packington), John Hood [1726-1795] and William Hood [1723-1806]. The fact that he was always referred to as Mr. Hood probably indicates that he was a gentleman; John Hood, senior and his sons all being of that rank [17].

According to Gilbey [12], *the Packington Blind Horse* was '*in full vigour from 1755 to 1770'*. The genealogical table (**Table 2,** page 30-31), included within Volume 1 of the Stud-Book [29] which gives what were thought to have been his immediate descendants, inferred that the *Packington Blind Horse* was foaled in about 1760.

Also, an article on 'The Rise of the Shire Horse' published in the Derby Mercury in 1891[309] claimed that the stallion was foaled in 1760, but this can only be a guess.

Apart from his assumed blindness, no direct description of *the Packington Blind Horse* seems to exist. Reynolds [29] was of the view that he was 'black in colour, with a white face and markings, or that he was destitute of hair upon lips, muzzle and eyelids' – these later inferences being deduced fron the fact that some of his near descendants were known as '*Ball*', *Ball'd* or '*Bald*'.

Mr. Hood seems to have left no evidence that he himself or anyone else advertised his famous horse. Also, no cover advertisements have been found in newspapers which feature him before 1769[22], when some colts were advertised claiming to have *Mr. Hood's Old Horse* (otherwise known as *the Packington Blind Horse*) in their pedigree. Mr. Hood clearly had no difficulty in finding customers. For many later horses, descent from *the Packington Blind Horse* was claimed. Mr. Hood's horse was also, it seems, able to command a price 'above the going rate'.

An 1805[172Le] advertisement (opposite) featuring a horse called *Kirby*, bred by Abijah Hill, a wealthy gentleman of Warwickshire, gave detail of his descent from Oldacres' *Kirby*, who was, in turn, a son of *the Packington Blind Horse*. It was also stated that *the Packington Blind Horse* covered at three guineas a mare. However, advertisements in 1812[228], 1814[243] and 1827[277] all stated that the stallion covered at five guineas a mare. [Stallions at this period were generally advertised to cover at a price between half a guinea and 15 shillings.]

In 1771[36De], John Massey of Cockshuthill (near Muggington, Derbyshire) advertised (page 87) his black horse called *Fair Leaper*. He was said to have been '*got by 'Mr. Hood's famous old Horse of Packington, commonly call'd the Blind Horse'*.

To COVER, this Season, 1805, At the GRIFFIN INN, SOUTHAM,

THAT noted Horse, KIRBY; bred by Mr. ABIJAH HILL, of Offchurch Grounds, in the County of Warwick, at One Guinea a Mare, and Half-a-Crown the Man.

KIRBY is nine Years old, got by Mr. John Moore's Horse, Packington; his Grand-dam by Mr. Hood's old blind Horse, of Packington, in Leicester-shire, which covered at three Guineas each Mare, till he was twenty-two Years old; Kirby's Dam was got by the old Kirby Horse; the old Kirby Horse was got by Mr. Hood's old blind Horse, which got Packington's Grand-Dam.—Kirby is a sure Foal-getter, and no Horse gets better Stock.

The Mares barren last Year to be covered at half Price.—Kirby will always stand at Home.

The Money to be paid at Midsummer next.

172. **Northampton Mercury** - Saturday 27 April 1805

Similar claims were made in 1771[34] by Mr. Adams at Etwall, Derbyshire for his black colt called *Cobler,* and by George Malin of Duffield, Derbyshire for the black horse called *Plough-Boy, also* advertised (page 37) in *1771*[37Le].

Thomas Johnson of Derby advertised (page 37) his horse called *the Packington Black Horse* in 1769[19Le], 1770[24] and 1771[32]. He advertised this horse again in 1774[49] when he stated that it had been bred by Mr. Hood of Packington, and '*got'* i.e. covered by *the Old Packington Horse*. We tend to assume that there was only one horse associated with the name of Hood, but these advertisements (and those which follow) indicate that Mr. Hood himself bred at least one offspring from *the Packington Blind Horse* (here referred to as *the Old Packington Horse*).

In his 1769[19Le] advertisement (below) Thomas Johnson said this horse *'is seven years old this Grass'*, suggesting he was foaled in 1762.

This is to inform the Public,

THAT the noted BLACK HORSE, late the Property of Mr. *Hood*, of *Packington* in *Leicefterſhire*, is now in the Hands of Mr. THOMAS JOHNSON, in *Derby*: He is ſeven Years old this Graſs, 16 Hands one Inch, free from all Blemiſhes, remarkable for getting good Stock, and is thought by moſt Judges, to be as compleat a Horſe as any in the Kingdom. He will Cover this Seaſon in *Friar-Gate*, DERBY, at *One Guinea* a Mare, and *One Shilling* the Man.

☞ The above Horſe will be ſhewn at *Aſhby* Fair on *Satur-day* the 25th Inſt. and at DERBY the *Friday* following.

☞ Good Graſs for Mares, and proper Care taken of them

To COVER this SEASON, 1771.

AT Mr. GEORGE MALIN's at the *King's-Head* in *Duffield*, a Black Horſe, of the Cart Kind, call'd

PLOUGH-BOY;

at *Ten Shillings* and *Six-pence* a Mare; the Money to be paid at *Midſummer* next, or at the Time of Covering.

He is five Years old, ſtands ſeventeen Hands high, and was got by Mr. *Hood's* old Horſe, at *Packington*; his Dam by Mr. *Boulſtridge's* old Horſe, at *Iſley-Walton*, which Horſes got the beſt Stock in *Leiceſterſhire*. He is a very ſure Foal getter.

In 1772[43De], John Massey of Birchwood Moor advertised (page 87) *'The Blind Horse'* which he claimed was bred by Mr. Hood of Packington. This seems to be another horse which Mr Hood had bred. He is confusingly named, but as he was said to have covered *'four of the last years'*, he cannot have been Mr. Hood's original *Old Packington Horse*, but a later generation.

Much later, in 1803[151] a cover advertisement was placed for a horse called *Young Packington*, who, it was claimed had been bred by Mr. Hood of Packington, *'from the nearest blood to his Blind Horse'*, his '*dam by Mansetter'* and his '*grandam by the Blind Horse'*.

In 1807[192St], John Chadwick advertised (page 73) his horse *Young Packington* as being available for cover, but from the pedigree information it is clear that this was a different *Young Packington*!

Whatever the relevance of *the Packington Blind Horse* to the Shire horse breed today he was clearly a celebrity who had many descendants, so that even well into the 19th century he was referred to in pedigrees, as for example in an 1833[286De] advertisement (page 86) for the colt called *Derbyshire*.

As late as 1874[307Li] it was still considered a useful selling point to claim that a stallion had descent from *the Packington Blind Horse*. An auction sale, which was advertised (page 110) at Sandiacre, Derbyshire featured *Lincolnshire Lad*, together with a stallion called *Young Crown Prince*. The pedigree of this horse was given in some detail, including reference to the celebrated *William the Conqueror*, *Old Black Legs*, *the Swebstone horse*, *Mansetter*, *Old Kirby* and *the Packington Blind Horse*.

It is of some debate as to whether *the Packington Blind Horse* was actually blind?

Reynolds [29] had inferred that the stallion was either totally blind, or that more probably, one of his eyes was defective. It seems somewhat strange that a stallion which may have had some disability should have been so successful. There are later references to other famous horses such as *the Wiltshire Blind horse*, although there does not appear to be enough evidence to suggest that their 'blindness' was due to any genetic defect. It seems more likely that these were cases where blinding was accidental, or even caused deliberately.

The following interesting account appeared in the *Farmers Magazine* in October 1836 [9]:

'Mr. Hood of Packington (Leicestershire) was in possession of a stallion of the Dishley Breed, which became very celebrated for the superiority of his stock; but also became so unmanageable and so dangerous, that his eyes were either purposely put out, or he lost the

sight of them in his mischievous struggles with his grooms or attendants. Even in this state, it was highly dangerous to approach him; he lived till he was eighteen years old, and continued to be as vicious as possible to the last.'

We cannot be sure that the above description is of the original *Packington Blind Horse*, nor can we rely on its accuracy. However, it does suggest that this famous horse really was blind. The reference to '*the Dishley Breed'* is intriguing. Robert Bakewell of Dishley is said to have used *Mr. Hood's 'Old Blind Horse'* , the alleged sire of Bakewell's celebrated horse 'G' [33]. Would that in a sense make Mr. Hood's horse '*of the Dishley Breed'*, or could Mr Hood have acquired his horse from Bakewell? We can only speculate!
[Evidence is presented later (page 43) to indicate that *G* was sired, not by *the Packington Blind Horse*, but by a stallion called *Sampson*.] Another interesting point relates to the age given for this horse as eighteen years. The 1805[172Le] cover advertisement, already referred to (page 36), featuring a horse called *Kirby* tells us that his ancestor, *Mr. Hood's Old Blind Horse* covered mares until he was twenty-two years old. These two accounts differ, but *the Packington Blind Horse* evidently had a long productive life. Some of his supposed sons are recorded in **Table 3.**

Table 3: Sons of the Packington Blind Horse

The following table details stallions which are claimed to have been sired by him.
All details are from 'cover' advertisements, unless stated otherwise.

Name of horse or description (+colour)	When foaled	o - owner b - breeder Ad. - advertiser	Identity of horse's dam	Notes/ other references
Packington Black Horse (Black)	1762	o + b - Mr. Hood of Packington, Leics. Ad + o - Thomas Johnson of Derby 1769[19Le] - 1774[49]		
Plough-boy (Black)	1765	Ad. - George Malin of Duffield, Derbys. 1770[28] - 1775[55]	dam by *Mr Boulstridge's old horse* at Isley Walton, Leics.	
Fair Leaper (Black)	1765	o + b - Timothy Clarkson of Ashby-de-la-Zouch, Leics. Ad. - John Massey of Cockshuthill, Muggington, Derbys. 1771[36De] -1772[41]		Let to John Massey for two years
Blaze	Before 1766	o - Robert Bakewell of Dishley, Leics.	dam by the *old Basingfield Horse*	In 1774[50] advert. for a black horse called *Merryman*, and in 1775[60Le] advert. for *Bonsar's Blaze*
Mr. Avarnes's Ball	Before 1766	o - Mr. Avarne of Breedon, Leics.		In 1772[40] advert. for a black colt whose dam was by *Mr. Avarne's horse*
Brown colt (Brown)	Before 1767	b - Mr. Frost of Stanhope Ad. - John Wagstaff of Atlow, Derbys. 1769[22De]		
Black horse	1767	b - Mr. Avarne of		

		Breedon, Leics. Ad. - Joshua Bowmer at Shottle, Derbys.1771[35]		
(Black)				
Mr. Allestry's horse	Before 1768	o – Mr. Allestry of Alvaston, Derbys.		In 1775[58] advert. For a black horse got by *Mr. Allestry's horse*
Fair Leaper (Black)	1768	Ad. - John Radford of Denby, Derbys.1772[39De]	Mr. Garner's of Packington	
Cobler (Black)	1768	b - Mr. Smith of the Ash, Derbys. Ad. - Thomas Adams of Etwall, Derbys.1770[25] - 1771[34]	mare of Mr. Smith's of the Ash	
Black stallion (Black)	1768	o - Thomas Salisbury of Higham [near Nuneaton] Ad. - Daniel Wagstaff of Nuneaton, Warks. 1774[45]		Advertised for sale
Black colt (Black)	1768	o - John Radford of Denby, Derbys.1770[26]	Mr. Garner's of Packington	
Merryman (Brown)	1769	o - Mr. Wagstaff of Atlow, Derbys., then, o + Ad. - Thomas Marsden of Hilton, Derbys. 1774[51De] - 1775[56]	brown mare of Mr. Frost's of Stanhope [Alstonfield, Staffs]	
Blaze (Black)	Before 1772	b - John Bonsar of Coats [Cotes, Loughborough] Ad. - William Berridge of Syston, Leics. 1775[60Le]		In 1775[60Le] advert. for a cart colt by *Mr. Bonsar's Blaze*
Black colt (Black)	1770	o + Ad. - John Massey of Cockshuthill, Muggington, Derbys. 1772[41]	dam by *Old Gallimore* [i.e. *Massey's Gallimore*]	
Merryman	Before 1775	b - John Capp of Loughborough, Leics. Ad. - John Wagstaff of Atlow, Derbys 1788[97]	dam - a full sister to *Blaze*	Also in 1778[72] advert. by John Capp for two aged horses: *Merryman* and *Blaze*
Kirby	Before 1780 [Could be 10 or more years earlier]	o - Thomas Oldacres of Market Bosworth, Leics.		
Mr. Oldacres Old Bennet	Before 1780 [Could be 10 or more years earlier]	o - Mr. Oldacres		In 1793[129] advert. for a black horse called *Waggoner*
R.T.	Before 1787 [as much as 20 years earlier is possible]	o - John Patrick of Thorney Fen, Cambs.		In 1797[139Li] advert. as sire of Young Farmer's Glory

Reynolds [29] stated that the more immediate scions of the Packington Blind Horse had appeared (unsurprisingly) in Leicestershire. In particular he named Mr. Oldacre (Oldacres) of Peatling Lodge, Mr. Bulstrode of Isley Walton and Mr. Bakewell of Dishley as breeders and/or owners. All of these men were frequently named in records, and are referred to below.

Bakewell - of Dishley, Loughborough, Leicestershire

Robert Bakewell [1725-1795] of Dishley Grange, near Loughborough is one of the best known names in livestock breeding, being credited with making improvements, particularly in sheep and cattle, but also in horses.

It is unfortunate that little written evidence of his activities appears to exist. Bakewell must have produced copious records which seem not to have survived. It has been suggested by Pitt [25] that he was secretive about his work and methods, although, if true, this may be understandable. He would have been wary of possible criticism of his inbreeding experiments. Robert Bakewell's greatest achievements are considered to have been with sheep, but the earliest evidence of his work is with horses. According to Chivers [6], the 'Leicestershire Blacks' were already regarded as being of high quality, but Bakewell had thought he could make improvements. Mention has already been made of his travels abroad and the importation of Dutch and Flemish mares to use in breeding with local Leicestershire stock.

To Cover this Season
At Five guineas each mare, at Robert Bakewell's
At Dishley near Loughborough, Leicestershire.
A BLACK COLT of the Cart Kind, rising two years,
His Dam the Clifton Mare, his Sire the
Late Isley Walton old Horse.

Grass for mares & proper care taken

8. **The Leicester and Nottingham Journal** - Saturday 17 March & Saturday 3 April 1762

The earliest evidence of his work seems to be in 1762[8Le] when he advertised (above) a black colt, rising two years old to cover at Dishley at five guineas a mare. The colt's dam was said to have been the *Clifton Mare* (presumably from Clifton, south of Nottingham), and his sire, the late *Isley Walton old horse*. [Isley Walton, a village about five miles north-west of Dishley has links with another breeder, John Bulstrode, page 57]. Bakewell's early success, at least locally, is indicated in a report of the Annual Show of Foals at Ashby-de-la-Zouch in 1765[14Le] (shown opposite).

Tuesday : Annual Show of Foals at Ashby - de - la - Zouch

Committee chosen to adjudicate the premiums were:

Mr Carter of Grooby, Leicestershire
Mr Flavell of Hogthrift, Staffordshire
Mr Baker of Stanton of said county
Mr Millwood of Offield in the Dale in the said county
Mr Brownhill of Aston in Derbyshire
Mr Scott of Newton in Derbyshire and
Mr Choice of Normanton in Leicestershire

Premiums for which they were Shown and the Number of Votes were as follows:

Premium of 2L – 10s

Mr Bakewell's of Dishley	(Mare foal)	7
Mr Salt's of Newton	ditto	0
Mr Rose's of Ofgathorpe	ditto	0
Mr Hall's of Ashly Old Par.	ditto	0
Mr A…… of W….ley	ditto	0

Premium of 5L

Mr Hill's of Stretton	(Horse foal)	5
Mr Bakewell's of Dishley	ditto	2
Mr Berrington's of Odstone	ditto	0
Mr Falkner's of Bratby, Derbys	ditto	0
Mr Bakewell's of Dishley	ditto	0

Mr Baker being on this Committee, on Account of his connexions & intimacy with Mr Hill, whose Foal was adjudged the Premium; and for determining the Prize Mr Hacket of Nelson in Leicestershire was chosen in his stead.

Premium of 5L
Mr Bakewell's Mare foal of Dishley
(none against it)

Premium of 10L

Mr Bakewell's of Dishley	(Horse foal)	5
Joshua Grundy Esq. of Thornton	"	2
Mr Frott's of Stanhop in Staffordshire		0

14. **The Leicester and Nottingham Journal**
- Saturday 23 November 1765

It is interesting that such an organised body promoting heavy horse breeding should have existed at this date. Bakewell had horses in all four categories; he won the premiums in three of these and was placed second in the other category.

In 1768[20], Bakewell advertised another black colt to cover at Dishley, again at five guineas a mare. Bakewell's prices, also for cattle, and particularly sheep always seem to have been high. Bakewell apparently justified this by saying that the only way to improve the breed of anything was to keep up the price of the male so that farmers would only send their best females.

In 1769[21] the cover services of two 'famous black horses', bred by Mr. Bakewell of Dishley, but now the property of Joseph Webster were advertised; at 10s - 6d for the old horse and 8s - 6d for the young one. One might well suppose that Bakewell would not have approved of these relatively cheap rates.

In 1771[31Le] (opposite) the Stamford Mercury advertised a 'Black Draft Horse' bred by Robert Bakewell of Dishley, to cover for the season at Stamford (Lincolnshire) and Uppingham (Rutland). More interestingly however, a black horse called *Merryman* was also advertised to cover. It was also stated that *Merryman* had provided cover in 1765,1766 and 1767 in Oxfordshire, at Clipstone (Clipston, near Market Harborough), Northamptonshire in 1768 and 1769, and the last season in Rutland. This is the earliest reference known for a named horse associated with Bakewell, and also an indication that he was already sending stallions into other counties.

To COVER this Season,
At One Guinea a Mare, and One Shilling the Man,
At Uppingham and Stamford,
A Black Draft HORSE,
Bred by Robert Bakewell, of Dishley, Leicestershire.

Also at Two Guineas a Mare and One Shilling the Man, at Oakham and Market-Harborough, A Black Horse, called MERRYMAN, which Horse cover'd in the Years 1765, 1766, and 1767, at Oxon, and in 1768 and 1769 at Clipstone, Northamptonshire, and last Season in Rutland.

N. B. The Days of the Week each Horse will be at the above-mentioned Places will be fixed when they come, and made known by a future Advertisement.

31. **Stamford Mercury** - Thursday 28 March 1771

In 1771[33] Richard Denshire of Belgrave, Leicester advertised three colts to cover which were said to have been got by Mr. Bakewell's horse called *Blaze*. This is another early reference to a named horse associated with Bakewell, and also the first known (of many) for a horse to be called *Blaze*. [Bakewell's *Blaze* pre-dates *Blaze* 183, associated with the name of William Hart]. [Many more stallions, notably in Derbyshire as well as Leicestershire have been called *Blaze*, a name associated with the presence of white facial markings.]

Also in 1771[30Le] (opposite), and with similar advertisements in 1772[42] and 1775[57], Bakewell's *Blaze* was mentioned again as the sire of a black colt advertised by Thomas Bott of Toadhole Furnace (near Alfreton, Derbyshire). This colt was said to have been out of a *Gallimore* mare (possibly a daughter of *Massey's Gallimore*). Bakewell is known to have been a stallion-letter, hiring out stallions for the season. This extended his influence, not just locally but also much further afield. Stallions may have been let to Thomas Bott by Bakewell. Bakewell's wider influence is also indicated by a 1774[52] advertisement for a black horse, rising six years old to cover in Oxfordshire. This horse was said to have been got by *Ball*, a stallion bred by Bakewell. The advertisement also claimed that *Ball* had covered one hundred mares in

TO Cover this Season, at Fifteen Shillings a Mare, at Mr. Thomas Bott's, of Toad-Hole Furnace, near Mr. Jonathan Kendall's, 14 Miles on the Road from Derby to Chesterfield, a BLACK COLT, rising three Years old; he was bred by Mr. Robert Bakewell, of Dishley, Leicestershire; got by Blaze, out of a Gallemore Mare.

Good Grass for Mares, and proper Care taken of them.

The Money to be paid at the Stable Door, or at Midsummer next.

30. **Derby Mercury** - 22 March 1771

Gloucestershire during the previous two seasons.

In 1774[50] Richard Denshire advertised a black horse by Bakewell's *Blaze* (which seems likely to have been one of the same animals he advertised in 1771[33]) but this time gave him the name *Merryman*. [Bakewell's *Merryman* was also later mentioned as the sire of the dam of the ten year old black stallion *Conqueror*, advertised in 1785[88] to cover at Stamford.]

In 1775[60Le] another cover advertisement (opposite) was placed for a horse called *Blaze*. This horse was bred by Mr. Bonsar of Coates (Cotes), near Loughborough and got by *Mr. Hood's Old Horse of Packington*. This advertisement, however is helpful in making it clear that this was a <u>different</u> *Blaze* by mentioning that *Mr. Bakewell's Blaze* was also sired by Mr. Hood's horse i.e. *the Packington Blind Horse*.

In 1777[66] Thomas Bott of Toadhole Furnace advertised again (presumably for a horse let to him by Bakewell). This time it was for a strong black horse belonging to Mr. Bakewell, rising six years old got by his famous horse *G*. A similar advertisement for a rising three year old colt by *G* (and out of a *Gallimore* mare) appeared in 1778[70Le] (below).

Also in 1778[73St] William Cantrell advertised (page 81) a black colt, rising three years old to cover, in Derbyshire. It was claimed that the colt had been got by Mr. Massey's Horse of Birchall-Moor, and that this stallion, had in turn, been got by Mr. Bakewell's noted horse *G*. These advertisements are interesting as Bakewell's *G 890*, the horse most associated with him, is recorded in the Stud-book as having been foaled in 1775. It is clear that G was foaled at an earlier date.

Robert Bakewell was declared bankrupt in 1776 (as a result of, it is suggested, various extravagances). A sale of some stock was advertised in 1777[63], although not all was sold. Bakewell was clearly able to somehow retain stock for years beyond this date, and overcome this setback. Robert Honeyborn [c1762-1816], Bakewell's nephew took over at Dishley after Bakewell's death in 1795, but in 1776 was far too young to have had a role.

To cover this season
At fifteen shillings a mare and one
a shilling a man, at William Berridge's of
Syston, LEICS.
That famous noted Black horse known by the name
of BLASE.
He was bred by Mr John Bonfar of Coats and
got by Mr Hood's Old Horse of Packington, which
horse was the sire of Mr Bakewell's BLASE
which covered at five guineas; his Dam by
The old noted Bafingfield Horse.
Such Gentlemen, Graziers and Farmers that chose to
Send their mares to be covered by the said
Horse may depend on due care being taken of them
By their humble servants
W. Berridge and W. Bonfar

60. **The Leicester and Nottingham Journal** - 20 April & 27 April 1775

To COVER this Seafon, 1778,
At THOMAS BOTT's at Toadhole Furnace, near Mr.
Jonathan Kendall's, Derbyfhire.

A Beautiful Black COLT, of the heavy Kind, rifing Three Years old; very ftrong and bony. He was bred by Mr. Robert Bakewell, of Difhley, Leicefterfhire; and got by his noted Horfe G. that now covers at Five Guineas a Mare; and out of a Gallimore Mare.
He will cover at Mr. Sadler's, at Alleftry, near Derby, every Wednefday and Thurfday, and the reft of the Week at Thomas Bott's aforefaid, at fo low a Price as 12s. 6d. a Mare if with Foal, and 5s. if barren.
N. B. He will ftop at Mr. Frearfon's at Heage, every Wednefday Morning.

70. **Derby Mercury** - 10 April 1778

In 1778[71] the horse *G* was advertised to cover at Dishley at what seems to have been Bakewell's usual rate of five guineas a mare, having covered six seasons at the same price and in the same place. Bakewell was not mentioned by name, presumably because of his bankruptcy.

Also in 1778[75Le], (pages 43) at Hoton (near Loughborough), John Chamberlain advertised a black colt, sired by *Bakewell's G*. The advertisement identified the sire of *G* as a stallion called *Sampson*, and his dam as a daughter of (presumably Bakewell's) *Blaze*.

In 1779[76] Thomas Sisson of Pickworth, Rutland advertised a black stallion, rising five years old to be either let or sold. He was said to have been got by Mr. Bakewell's horse *Sampson*.

Chivers [6] recorded that in 1774, a cover advertisement was placed in the Edinburgh Courant (featuring a black horse bred by Bakewell) and another in the Edinburgh Advertiser (referring to a four year old black horse which he owned), both indicating that Robert Bakewell's fame and influence had reached Scotland. The second horse, owned by Bakewell was called *Young Sampson.* If there was a *Young Sampson,* then there must have been an *Old Sampson.* It seems reasonable to speculate that *Young Sampson* and *G* were brothers. John Chamberlain's 1778[75Le] advertisement contains another

To cover this season at John Chamberlain's
of Hoton at 10s 6d a foal, and 5s barren,
a black colt rising 2 years old.
He was got by Mr Bakewells's G.
G was got by Sampson which covered at Dishley three
seasons at 5 guineas a mare –His dam was
got by Blaze; his grandam by the Bafinfield horse.
- G covers this season at 5 guineas.
-
Note: the above Stallion will attend at Barrow every week
on a Friday at Mr Chamberlain's and at Hoton the
rest of the week.

75. **The Leicester and Nottingham Journal** - 2 May 1778

interesting piece of information. The grandam of the colt advertised was said to have been sired by *the Basingfield Horse.* This horse (also mentioned in 1775[60Le]) is another of those mysterious horses about which nothing is known. (Bassingfield is a hamlet only about three miles from the centre of Nottingham, and as such is close to Clifton, mentioned in Bakewell's 1762[8Le] advertisement).

Another son of *Bakewell's G* (and out of a daughter of *Mr. Hood's old blind Horse*) was advertised to cover at Thorpe, Staffordshire (about two miles north-west of Ashbourne, Derbyshire) in 1780[78]. This horse had been purchased by a society of gentlemen and farmers who were offering him to provide service in the neighbourhood.

Also in 1780[78], William Redfern of Mickleover, near Derby offered the services of a black horse, rising five years old who was yet another son of *Bakewell's G.*

Redfern supplied further interesting information, mentioning that full brothers of this black horse (which were therefore also sons of *G*) called *A.B.* and *A.C.* had been sold in 1779 for 300 guineas. Perhaps these horses were sold as a result of Bakewell's bankruptcy? [Bakewell's horse *A.C.* (a son of *G*) was referred to some years later, in 1792[116] as the sire of another stallion called *Blaze*, advertised together with a stallion called *Lion* to cover at Wappenham, Northamptonshire.]

In 1782 William Redfern advertised (Derby Mercury, 4 April 1782) the cover services of a six year old horse called *B* – yet another son of *G* bred by Bakewell. Also in 1782[80Le] (opposite) *Young Blaze*, bred by Bakewell and got by his famous horse *Blaze* was advertised to cover by William Kinder of Burton-upon-Trent. It was said that Bakewell had refused 1500 guineas for *Blaze*.

In 1784[84De], John Wagstaff of Atlow, Derbyshire advertised (page 89) a black horse, rising five years old called *E,* bred by Bakewell. *E* was another son of Bakewell's (old) G.

This advertisement also tells us that the dam of *E* was a mare belonging to Bakewell, which in turn had been got by his horse *K.* William Marshall was particularly impressed by *Bakewell's K,* a stallion which he believed had died in 1785, aged 19 [18].

Another indication that the 'Dishley breed' had

To COVER this Seafon, 1782,
AT William Kinder's of Burton-upon-Trent, in the County of Stafford, at FIFTEEN SHILLINGS a Mare; a fine black Horfe, of the Cart Kind, call'd
YOUNG BLAZE,
Full Sixteen Hands three Inches high, very boney, and every way in Proportion: He was bred by Mr. Bakewell of Difhley, in Leicefterfhire; got by his famous Horfe Blaze, which Horfe covered four Seafons, at Five Guineas a Mare.—Mr. Bakewell refufed fifteen Hundred Guineas for him; and the Year he died was let for One Hundred and Seventy Guineas. Young Blaze is a fure Foal Getter; and gets very boney fine Stock: Several of his getting have been fold for upwards of One Hundred Pounds each; and one the laft Seafon, for Two Hundred and Ten Pounds.
N. B. All Mares that prove barren by Blaze this Year, will be covered gratis the enfuing Seafon.
Alfo to COVER at the fame Place,
G O L D F I N D E R,
Late the Property of Sir H. Harpur,
At ONE GUINEA a Mare.

80. **Derby Mercury** - Thursday 4 April 1782

spread far and wide is shown by an advertisement (page 104) in 1797[138Li] which contains pedigree information about a son of *Bakewell's G* called *Wainfleet G*. The town of Wainfleet is close to Skegness, on the Lincolnshire coast! Bakewell's horse *G* was clearly prolific and in demand.

Interestingly, Wainfleet is where a black horse called *Biard* was advertised (page 102) to cover for the season, years earlier, in 1768[18Li]. *Biard* was said to have been got by Mr. *Dunsthorp's* (Donnisthorp's) *Black Horse* at Packington (Leicestershire), and his horse, in turn, had been got by Mr. *Bostridge's* (Bulstrode's) *Black Horse* of Easly Walton (Isley Walton). It seems that other noted Leicestershire breeders may have penetrated Lincolnshire as well as, and perhaps before, Bakewell.

In 1789[101Le] a black horse (unnamed), bred by Bakewell was advertised (opposite) to cover at Dishley; this horse having stood the previous year at Messrs Tattersall in London. He was said that '*from his form and action he is thought likely to get Horses for the Army, Coach or Road.*' He appears to have been the stallion famously reported to have been shown to George III at St. James's Palace in 1788. Chivers recorded that the horse was also taken to Tattersall's and shown to the nobility and gentry '*with great approbation*'. William Pitt [25] apparently described him as '*the famous horse G, the noblest and most complete and beautiful creature of his kind that had been seen in Europe*'. Chivers questioned whether

> To cover this season 1789
> At Dishley, near Loughborough, LEICS.
> At Five Guineas a Mare, and five shillings the man.
> A BLACK HORSE
> Bred by R. Bakewell
> Which Stood last year at Messrs TATTERSALL in London and covered several foreign mares, high bred
> Mares and others.
> – From his form and action he is thought likely to get Horses for the Army, Coach or Road.
>
> NB Good Grass for mares with proper care.
>
> 101. **The Leicester and Nottingham Journal** - 24 April 1789

this much admired creature was 'actually adapted for the labours that horses of this sort are principally designed to perform'? The other question is – was this horse really Bakewell's celebrated horse *G*? The horse *G 890*, listed in Volume 1 of the Stud-book is recorded as having been foaled in 1775. The very prolific *Bakewell's G*, whose progeny are recorded above, by contrast, cannot have been foaled later that 1767!

It seems unlikely that the horse shown in London was in excess of twenty years old.

In 1792[114] , a cover advertisement by George Bland, in Northamptonshire, for a brown cart horse called *Provident*, rising six years old, made the claim that he was got by a stallion belonging to Mr. Bakewell of Dishley which was '*shown to His Majesty and so approved of that he has gone by the name of the London Horse since that time and has covered in the County of Middlesex at Ten Guineas a mare.*'

There was no mention of the name '*G*'. In fact, another cover advertisement (opposite) in Northamptonshire in 1793[127Le] featured a black horse belonging to Robert Bakewell called *B.L.,* ('otherwise *The London Horse*'.) Also in 1793[126], a black stallion of the Dishley breed, rising six years old, and got by the *London Horse* was advertised for sale in Northamptonshire. This horse may have been Bakewell's horse *B. G.* which was advertised to cover in Northamptonshire in 1792[117].

> TO COVER, this Season, 1793, at HIGHGATE-HOUSE and WELLINGBORO'. LODGE, at Two Guineas and Half-a-Crown a Mare, A BLACK HORSE, called *B. L.* (otherwise, The LONDON HORSE), The Property of Mr. Bakewell. Particulars, as to the Time he will be at each Place, will appear in next Week's Paper.
>
> 127. **Northampton Mercury** - 20 April 1793

A reference to *Bakewell's G* appeared in a cover advertisement for a stallion called *Waggoner* in 1793[129].

In a sale by auction of a black stallion called *Merryman,* advertised (page 83) to take place at Nantwich, Cheshire in 1795[133Sh.] it was claimed that his dam had been sired by Bakewell's Gee. *Bakewell's old G* was also mentioned in the pedigree of a horse called *Farmer's Glory* advertised to cover in 1807[192].

A cover advertisement for an eight year old stallion called *Young Drayman* in 1804[154] claimed that he was got by the late Mr. Bakewell's horse called *Old Drayman*, but this seems one of the relatively few references to Bakewell after his death in 1795.

The Celebrated Cart Horse
The Property of Mr. Bakewell of Dishley 1790

Plate 9: This painting, which is attributed to John Boultbee [1753-1812] shows an unnamed horse belonging to Robert Bakewell, with Dishley Grange in the background. Is this **B.L.**, otherwise '**The London Horse**'?

Chivers [6] noted that only two Bakewell horses are listed in volume I of the Stud-book i.e. *G 890* and *Blaze 184*.

Much more information about *Bakewell 'G'* has been presented here than has previously been recorded, but if this was G 890 then the date when he was foaled (recorded as 1775) must be wrong. The suggestion that he was sired by *Blaze 183* (and out of an unknown mare) must also be incorrect. The account which supposes that the horse shown to George III in 1788 was *Bakewell's 'G'* is similarly in doubt. Chivers [6] had little to say about *Blaze 184*, the other

Bakewell horse listed in Volume I of the Stud-book [29], said to have been foaled in 1790, and sired by Blaze 185, owned by Radford of Little Eaton (page 97).

In Chivers' view [6], the lack of information about Bakewell means that there is no way that we can properly assess the effect that his activities have had on the breed. Bakewell was certainly very influential, his stallions siring offspring well beyond the county boundary of Leicestershire. We cannot, however deduce the extent to which genes of his horses have been passed on to the modern breed, or otherwise been weeded out.

There are some suggestions that Bakewell concentrated too much on appearance. The 'in - and - in' (inbreeding) methods he used, breeding together close relatives, can successfully fix visible features thought to be desirable. On the other hand, less obvious or unseen undesirable characteristics can be unwittingly selected at the same time. This 'inbreeding depression' is most evident in some pedigree dog breeds today. If there were genetic deficiencies in the 'Dishley Breed', as the following accounts suggests, Bakewell may have been unfortunate, rather than misguided. It may also help to explain why, as Chivers [6] described it, this was 'a Leicestershire line that faded'.

The Farmers Magazine Volume 5 in 1836 in an article about the Cart Horse, included a discussion about the contribution made to livestock breeding by Robert Bakewell [9]. Interestingly, whilst stating the country was indebted to Mr. Bakewell for improvements he made in sheep and horned cattle, it was by contrast critical of his 'improvements' to the heavy horse. Also, contrary to popular opinion, it reported that King George III was not impressed by the horse shown to him by Bakewell!

In referring to Bakewell it said:

'*Supposing that 'enormous bulk was indispensible to the perfection of the heavy draught breed or cart horse, he had turned his attention at the outset of his career to the ponderous, hairy-legged horse of Flanders whence he imported both horses and mares, which he crossed with the large draught animal already found in Lincolnshire as well as in the midland counties of the Kingdom, from which, about 70 years ago he produced a horse which he regarded as the best horse which had ever been seen and which he sent to Hyde Park corner for the inspection of King George III. That monarch however did not second the views of this enterprising farmer, who nevertheless succeeded in spreading this breed of heavy black horses throughout the midland counties. The appearance of these animals was extremely imposing on superficial examination; they were uncommonly large and uncommonly bulky, while their long tails and very long flowing manes aided the effect produced by the contemplation of their extraordinary size. They were well formed; but from the abundance of hair which covered their legs, they appeared unsightly in our estimation, and impressed the idea upon our minds of that lack of activity which posterior trial incontestably proved.*

However, they maintained their stand for some time, and like our racers, many of them became celebrated for the superiority of their stock. Many of them were also extremely vicious.

However, not withstanding the fame which the Leicestershire improved breed of Black or Cart horse acquired, in the course of some years it was found that in the ardour of improvement, bulk had been increased at the expense of activity, and that the very large Flemish horse, which by English management, had attained enormous size, was slow, if not sluggish in his movements or action, and not half so well calculated for the general purposes of husbandry, and the use of the farmer, as a more clean limbed and more active, yet equally strong animal, of which our embellishment presents a beautiful, if not inimitable example. The very heavy and very hairy-legged Dishley or Leicestershire horse will be found on examination defective in the metacarpal bone, or rather those bones which form the foundation of the limb between the knee and the fetlock'.

Further critical comments were made in the *Farmers Magazine Volume 8* in 1838 questioning Bakewell's judgement of the quality of stock he imported from Flanders [10]. *'He mistook bulk for strength, and thus produced animals of almost elephant-like size with small porous bone, soft tendons loose and flabby muscle'.*

It was suggested that such animals may be have been capable of pulling brewers' drays around the streets of London where distances were short, the pace slow, and with frequent stops, but not generally suited to the more demanding tasks expected of them.

By the time of his death Robert Bakewell had clearly overcome the financial difficulties he had to deal with at an earlier point in his life. His legacy in terms of the effect he had on livestock breeding is certainly considerable, though impossible to assess. In monetary terms he was clearly successful. In his will, in 1795, Bakewell left sums totalling several thousand pounds to his nephews and nieces [24].

Paget - of Ibstock, Leicestershire

Thomas Paget [1732-1814] was a celebrated breeder of cattle and particularly sheep, which commanded high prices, but he also bred heavy horses.

At the Annual Fair for foals of the black breed held at Ashby-de-la-Zouch in 1764[11Le], (opposite) Thomas 'Patchet' (Paget) of Ibstock won the £10 premium for the best horse foal.

Another reference to Paget appeared in 1769[23Le] in a cover advertisement (below) for a two year old horse owned by Robert Bakewell's friend, George Salisbury of Heather (a village in Leicestershire, about two miles north-west of Ibstock). The horse advertised was said to have been out of a mare belonging to Mr. 'Patchet' of Ibstock. Thomas Paget does not seem to have advertised any horses, presumably concentrating on the breeding of other livestock, with which he was clearly very successful.

At his sale of stock in 1793 he apparently sold 130 ewes for 3200 guineas [1]. He also sold horses at this auction, including six mares, three of them by *Dishley K*, one by *Dishley A.C.,* and two by *Mr. Avarne's blind horse.* The top price was for *Flower*, a nine year old by *Dishley K*, which had been covered by *Mr. Oldacres' best horse.* She was sold for a relatively modest 33 guineas. A yearling filley by *Mr. Hart's bald horse* was sold for 16 guineas.

Ashby-de-la-Zouch   **November 9 1764**

 Yesterday was an Annual fair for foals of the black breed

-for coach, a....y or cart
Premiums: 10L, 5L , 2L - 10s *
  10L   To Mr Patchet of Ibstock for the best horse foal
   5L   To Mr Knowles of Odston for second best.

* collected by the gentlemen, farmers & graziers
   as an encouragement for the improving &
   Increasing the breed of that noble &
   useful creature.

11. **The Leicester and Nottingham Journal** - Saturday 17
November 1764

To Cover this Season
At Samuel Priestley's at Barrow-on-Soar
A beautiful black horse, 2 Years
old, got by Mr Dexter's old horse, and a
very good mare of Mr Patchet's of Ibstock at Half
a Guinea a foal and Four and Sixpence Barren,
The Property of Mr George Sailsbury
Of Heather

23. **The Leicester and Nottingham Journal** - Saturday
15 April 1769

The only stallion in the sale, a black stallion, rising four years old, by Mr. Oldacres' *Mancetter*, and son of the mare called *Flower* was sold for 29 guineas.

The Pagets were a long-established landed family in Ibstock. Thomas Paget is said to have been Robert Bakewell's closest friend and associate in the breeding of livestock. He was also his second cousin. Robert Bakewell's grandmother was Mary Paget, sister of Thomas Paget [c1657-1699] who was Thomas Paget's grandfather.

Capp - of Loughborough, Leicestershire

In 1778[72], John Capp [1740 -1780], a grazier, advertised two aged black horses of the cart kind to cover in Loughborough, called *Merryman* and *Blaze.* Richard Denshire, a gentleman of Leicester had advertised a horse called *Merryman*, a son of *Blaze* in 1774[50]. Could this have been the same *Merryman*? Also in 1778[74] John Wagstaff of Atlow (page 88) advertised a black colt bred by Mr. Capp of Loughborough. Either this John Capp, or his father, John Capp [1707-1775], a wealthy Loughborough maltster and grazier, could have been the breeder of this colt. Ten years later, in 1788[97] John Wagstaff advertised the noted old horse *Merryman*, bred by Mr. Capp of Loughborough, and out of a full sister to *Blaze*, and got by *the Packington Old Blind Horse.* [*Bakewell's Blaze* and *Bonsor's Blaze* have both been already mentioned. It seems likely that this *Blaze* was one of those horses, both of which were said to be sons of *the Packington Blind Horse.*]
The first Stud-book [29] records that Capp of Loughborough was breeder of the dam of *Merryman 1548*, foaled in 1800, bred and owned by Massey of Birchall Moor, Staffordshire. In this case, William Capp [1751-1823], son of John Capp, junior was probably the breeder. Much later, in 1807[190], John Summerland advertised yet another horse called *Blaze*, rising four years old. His sire was said to have been by a grandson of *Hart's ball'd Horse* of Culloden House, Leicestershire, but his dam was '*by Old Merryman, Cap's sort, of Loughborough'.*

Donnisthorpe - of Packington, Leicestershire

Chivers [6] suggested that '*Donnisthorp's horse'*, recorded as a son of *the Packington Blind Horse* should have been described as 'The Donnisthorp Horse', i.e. the horse from Donnisthorp, a village near Packington. However, a young black horse, '*bred by Mr. John Donnisthorp of Packington'* was advertised (opposite) in 1757[2Le] by John Coxon of Atlow (page 88). We can therefore deduce that the original description, which implied that the horse was owned by Mr.'Donnisthorp' was correct.
'Mr Donnisthorp' can be identified as John Donnisthorpe [1701 -1773], who was baptised and buried at Packington.
Mr. *Dunsthorp's* (Donnisthorp's) *old Black Horse* at Packington was described as the sire of a '*fine Black Horse'* called *Biard,* bred

THERE is now in the Hands of JOHN COXON, at ATLOW, about Three Miles from ASHBORNE, in *Derbyshire*, a beautiful Black HORSE, goes by the Name of

The GRINN HORSE:

He was got by the old Shottle Horse, and bred by Mr. *John Chadwick.* He will cover this Season at *Half a Guinea* a Mare; and if barren, *Five Shillings.* Also his young Black Horse, bred by Mr. *John Donnisthorp* of *Packington,* near *Ashby* in *Leicestershire,* will cover this Season, at the same Price as last Season, till further Proof is made of him, being *Eight Shillings* and *Sixpence* a Mare, and if Barren *Four Shillings:*

2. **Derby Mercury** - 8 April 1757

by Mr. Ward of 'Adstone' (Odstone) Hill, Leicestershire in a cover advertisement placed in the Stamford Mercury in 1768[18Li] (pages 44, 102). Interestingly, *Biard*'s owners lived many miles away at Wainfleet, near Skegness in Lincolnshire. It seems clear that Mr. Hood's *Packington Blind Horse* was not the only horse of note with its origins in Packington.
The breeder of *Biard,* was probably Thomas Ward [1710 - 1787]. Odstone, a hamlet in Shackerstone parish, where Thomas Ward was baptised, is also where John Knowles (page 51) lived, at the same period.
In 1788[96] *Donnisthorpe's horse*, of Packington was referred to in the pedigree of a colt advertised by Paul Caulton to provide cover at Shottle (two miles west of Belper) in Derbyshire. This black colt, rising three years old, was said to have been got by Mr *Donnisthorpe's noted horse of Packington*, which in turn had been got by *Boulstridge's bald horse.*
In 1794[131], Paul Caulton (page 99) advertised another black horse, rising five years old, to cover at Shottle. This horse was also said to have been '*got by Mr Donesthorpe's best horse at*

Packington, which covered thirteen seasons at that place'.

These two later 'cover' advertisements suggest that Richard Donnisthorpe rather than his father John had owned the stallions. Richard Donnisthorpe [1728 -1790] was buried in a grand chest tomb in Packington churchyard, indicating the family to have been of some substance in the village. An auction sale of all the livestock, implements etc. of the late Richard Donnisthorpe was advertised (Derby Mercury, 31 March) to take place in April 1791, on his premises in Packington [5]. A number of horses were included in the sale; the superior quality of his cart mares being particularly noted.

In 1797[136], William Harrison, (at Little Eaton, Derbyshire) advertised his horse whose dam was said to be a daughter of the late *Mr. Donisthorpe's Ball of Packington* (and grand-daughter of *the Packington Blind Horse*). This provides further evidence that Richard Donnisthorpe was involved in 'Shire' breeding, as well as his father. This is also supported by John Chadwick's advertisement (page 75) in 1807[192St] for his *Young Packington*. Pedigree details were included which made reference to a mare of Mr. 'Donisthorpe' of Packington, and to his 'Old Horse'. Using Stud-book records [29] we can identify this stallion as *Packington 1703*, foaled in 1796, and bred by Clarkson of Breedon (below).

Clarkson - of Breedon on the Hill & Ashby-de-la-Zouch, Leicestershire

The Clarksons of Breedon Lodge were a family of gentleman farmers, said to be related to Richard Donnisthorpe of Packington.

A number of memorial tablets of the Clarkson family line the walls of Breedon church, including that of Timothy Clarkson [c1736 -1824], and his wife Judith [c1735 -1758].

Timothy Clarkson married Judith Curzon at Breedon in 1756. The Curzon family (who also have memorial tablets in Breedon church) were related to to the Curzons, Lords Scarsdale of Kedleston Hall near Derby.

In April 1771[36De], John Massey of Cockshut-Hill (Muggington, Derbyshire) advertised (page 87) the cover services of a stallion called *Fair Leaper*. He was said to have been bred and owned by Timothy Clarkson, whose address was given as Ashby-le-la-Zouch. *Fair Leaper* was advertised as having been *'got by Mr. Hood's famous old Horse of Packington, commonly call'd The Blind Horse'*. A similar advertisement was placed in 1772[41], with *Fair Leaper* now being said to be rising seven year old.

[Confusingly, what must have been another stallion called *Fair Leaper*, rising four years old, was advertised (page 96), at the same time in April 1772[39De] by John Radford of Denby (2½ miles east of Belper)! This horse, like Massey's horse seems to have been sired by *the Packington Blind Horse*.]

Chivers [6] made one reference to the Clarkson name in relation to the stallion *Packington 1703*, said to have been bred by Clarkson of Breedon (foaled in 1796), and owned by John Chadwick of Grindon. This is supported by John Chadwick's advertisements for (*Young*) *Packington* in 1807[192St] (page 75), 1808[201], 1811[221] and 1812[233St] (page 71) in which the stallion was said to have been late the property of Mr Clarkson of Breedon, having also spent eight seasons there.

Avarne - of Breedon on the Hill, Leicestershire

In 1771[35], Joshua Bowmer at Shottle, Derbyshire advertised a *'strong Black Horse of the Cart Kind, rising four Years old'*, and another similar six year old horse, both said to have been bred by *Mr. Avarnes of Breedon*.

In 1772[40], William Barker, living near Tupton, Derbyshire advertised a black colt, *'got by Mr. Avarne's BALL of Breedon in Leicestershire; which Horse was got by the Packington Old Horse'*. Little is known about John Avarne of Breedon, but a lengthy cover advertisement placed in 1783[83] for a hunter called *Herod* and a thoroughbred called *Blank* suggested that he had a greater interest in other types of horse. However, below the description giving detail of the impressive pedigree and successes he claimed for these horses, in a short note he also advertised:

'The Noted Blind HORSE, bred by Mr. Bakewell of Dishley, got by his famous Horse Blaze, and out of a Gallimore Mare'.

Also in 1783[82De], a black horse, of the cart kind, rising five years old, and advertised (page 99) to cover at Shottle in Derbyshire, was said to have been got by '*Mr. Avarne's horse of Bredon'*.

In 1786 (Derby Mercury, 14 February), a sale of the estates of John Avarne was advertised, followed, a few months later in 1786[92] by a notice advertising a meeting of his creditors [5]. It would seem he had become bankrupt. A few years later, in 1793, two mares by *Mr. Avarne's blind horse* were included in a sale of stock by Thomas Paget [1].

Garner - of Packington, Leicestershire

The Garner name first appears in 1770[26], when John Radford of Denby advertised a black colt which had been bred from a mare of Mr. 'Garnor's' of Packington.

In 1772[39De], Radford advertised (page 96) a horse called *Fair Leaper* (probably the same horse), which was out of a mare of Mr. Garner's of Packington (and got by *the Packington old Horse*). [This *Fair Leaper* was not the horse owned and bred by Clarkson (page 49).]

The Garner family lived in Packington for many generations. The stallion breeder in this case would have been Hastings Garner [1728 - 1799], a farmer and grazier, or his brother, John Garner [1729-1799], a farmer, both being of Packington.

Hackett - of Nailstone, Leicestershire

In 1759[6De] Thomas Massey of Little Ireton (in Muggington parish, but near Kedleston Hall, Derbyshire), advertised three horses, including his stallion *Gallymoor*, and a colt, '*gotten by Mr. Hacket's Horse of Nelson'* (Nailstone). Thomas Massey advertised (presumably the same animal, by then a horse) again in 1761[7] and 1762[9].

Mr Hackett was clearly a man of standing in horse-breeding circles. His role as an adjudicator at the Annual Show of Foals held at Ashby-de-la-Zouch was recorded (page 40) in a newspaper report in 1765[14Le].

The Hacketts of Leicestershire and the horse-breeding Massey family of Derbyshire were in fact, related. Ann Hackett [1738-1787], daughter of Edward Hackett of Nailstone married Sampson Massey [1723 -1764] of Swarkestone (brother of the above-mentioned Thomas Massey) at Nailstone on 9 July 1755.

'Mr. Hacket', referred to in the advertisements could have been Edward Hackett [1705 -1757], a prosperous yeoman, or his brother Thomas Hackett [1711-1795], but was probably Edward Hackett [1734 -1809], junior, a wealthy gentleman farmer, and the brother of Ann Massey. His (great) nephew, Sampson Massey was living with him in Nailstone when he died in 1809.

Knowles - of Nailstone and Odstone, Leicestershire

In 1741 (Derby Mercury, 2 April 1741) Joseph Knowles of Nelson [Nailstone] advertised '*a Beautiful Grey Horse'* which was available to provide cover [5].

This horse was said to have been brought in from Turcomania [now in Istanbul, Turkey]. He was advertised as a '*fine mover'* indicating that he was not of the heavy horse type, but it does indicate that Joseph Knowles [1693 -1759] was a horse owner, and perhaps breeder. The Knowles family apparently gained some notoriety in supporting Bonnie Prince Charlie in

1745, and lobbying support for his campaign. He is said to have met them at Nailstone, after which, as support fell away, a decision was made for the Scottish army to retreat. The Scottish army turned back at Swarkestone Bridge. A member of the Knowles family was later arrested for high treason, and condemned to hang [16]. Parish registers indicate that there was only one Knowles family at Nailstone at this time. It seems likely that Joseph, as head of the family was the condemned man, although he was later pardoned. It is interesting to speculate as to what role the Joseph Knowles and his family might have had in assisting the Young Pretender, and whether this could have included the procurement of horses, or providing information as to where they could be found.

Samuel Gallimore at Wootton, who at his death in 1750 had around 200 customers with mares receiving cover by his stallions, may have been known by the Knowles family. The Scottish army would have passed by, close to Wootton, as they made their way from Leek, via Ashbourne to Derby. Gallimore would have had even more reason to hide his horses at Croxden, if the rebels knew where horses could be found.

Joseph Knowles was the younger son of Thomas Knowles [? -1707] of Castle Donington who held the lease of Donington Park from the Earl of Huntingdon (page 14), and bequeathed it to his elder son, Thomas. Thomas Knowles, senior, however had a brother, William Knowles, a yeoman of Nailstone who left some of his extensive property to his nephew, Joseph Knowles.

Generations of the Knowles family, gentleman farmers and graziers of Nailstone and nearby Odstone, have made a significant contribution to the breeding of 'Shire' horses, as indicated by the following. An account in The Derby Mercury in 1765[13Le] (opposite) recorded that William Knowles [1724 -1782] of 'Nelson' (Nailstone) and John Knowles [1730 -1778] of Odstone (both sons of Joseph) were each awarded premiums for colts shown at Ashby-de-la-Zouch fair. John Knowles' colt was sold to Samuel Tateham (page 85).

In another account, in 1765[12] it was said that John Knowles' colt was to cover during the season at Samuel Tateham's at Tupton Hall, Northwingfield, near Chesterfield, Derbyshire. It was also reported that John Knowles had refused 100 guineas for the dam of his colt, and that he was also in possession of its sire. Mr Knowles of Odstone (presumably John Knowles) had also been awarded £5 for a second-placed foal at the Show in 1764[11Le] (page 47).

In 1766[De15], what appears to have been John Knowles' colt, now *a famous well-bred Black HORSE* was advertised (page 85) by the purchaser Samuel Tateham of Tupton Hall, south of Chesterfield, offering him to provide cover at fifteen shillings a mare. Samuel *Tateham's horse*, bred by Mr. Knowles was said to have been the sire of a colt advertised (page 89) by John Wagstaff in 1769[22De].

Also in 1766[16Le], a black colt bred by William Knowles of 'Nelson' was advertised to cover (opposite) by Daniel Roper of Toadhole Furnace (further to the south of Chesterfield, near South Wingfield). In 1774[47], a horse called *SNIP*, or otherwise *the Tupton Horse* was

13. Derby Mercury – Friday 19 April 1765
Image © THE BRITISH LIBRARY BOARD. ALL RIGHTS RESERVED
http://www.britishnewspaperarchive.co.uk/viewer/download/bl/0000189/17650419/020/0004

16. Derby Mercury - 11 April 1766
Image © THE BRITISH LIBRARY BOARD. ALL RIGHTS RESERVED
http://www.britishnewspaperarchive.co.uk/viewer/download/bl/0000189/17660411/008/0004

advertised to cover at Kirk Hallam in Derbyshire. He was said to have been bred by Mr. Knowles of 'Nelson'. John Knowles of Odstone died in 1778 and his entire stock was advertised (in the Derby Mercury, 8 January 1779) to be sold. In addition to a large number of cattle and sheep, a *considerable number of brood mares, fillies and foals of the Black* Kind were offered for sale [5]. In 1777[67Le], a black stallion called *Gallimore*, owned and bred by William Knowles of 'Nelston' was advertised (opposite) to cover near Bakewell, Derbyshire. Also in 1777[64De], Joseph Glossop had advertised his horse *Gallimore*, son of *Old Gallimore*, otherwise *Massey*. He was clearly a different horse.

Confusingly, in 1783[81De], Joseph Glossop advertised (page 98) his black stallion *Young Gallimore*. *Young Gallimore* was said to have been got by *Old Gallimore*, out of a mare bred by Mr. Knowles of Nelson (Nailstone), got by his horse *Conqueror*, and out of his noted mare *Mettle*. This is an unusual early reference to a named mare.

The name of Mr. Knowles of 'Nelson' was linked again with a stallion called *Conqueror* in 1785[88Le]. The ten year old black stallion, advertised (opposite) to cover, now the property of T. Marsden of Stamford, was formerly owned by T. Rose of Tallington, both in Lincolnshire. He was said to have been got by Mr. Knowles's *noted Black Horse*; his dam being by Bakewell's *Merryman*. As this Mr. Knowles, was of 'Nelson' he was probably William Knowles. William Knowles (of Nailstone) married Mary Massey at Lichfield Cathedral on 24 November 1753. Mary Massey was however of Barton-under-Needwood, Staffordshire and apparently unrelated to the noted horse-breeding Massey family of Derbyshire (page 86) and of Staffordshire (page 81).

A stallion advertised (opposite) for sale in Market Bosworth in 1793[122Le] was said to have been sired by a horse called *Old Derbyshire*, belonging to the late William Knowles. *Old Derbyshire*, who was awarded the £10 prize at the Ashby-de-la-Zouch Show when two years old, was also said to have sired *Conqueror*. This is an early reference to a horse called *Derbyshire*, although another stallion called *Derbyshire*, the sire of horses offered for sale by auction (page 53) in 1792[111Le] and owned by Mr. Brown (of Stretton, Warwickshire) may have pre-dated Knowles' *Derbyshire*.

March 30, 1777.

To COVER this Season,

AT the House of Mr. RICHARD WILD, at Burchill, near Bakewell, at HALF-A-GUINEA a Mare, to be paid at the Time of covering, or at Midsummer next, a noted Black Stallion, the Property of, and bred by, Mr. William Knowles of Nelston, in the County of Leicester, known by the Name of

G A L L I M O R E.

Many Years Experience has proved that he getteth good Stock, and a Number of them.

67. **Derby Mercury** - Friday 4 April 1777

To COVER this Season,

At Ten Shillings and Six-pence a Mare, and 1s, the Servant,
The Well-known BLACK HORSE
C O N Q U E R O R,
The Property of T. MARSDEN, STAMFORD, late the Property of T. ROSE, Tallington.

CONQUEROR is Ten Years old, full of Bone, and reckoned by Judges to be as handsome a Horse as any in England. He was got by Mr. Knowles's noted Black Horse, of Nelson; his Dam, by Mr. Bakewell's Merryman.

88. **Stamford Mercury** - Friday 15 April 1785

STALLION HORSE
TO BE SOLD- A BLACK STALLION
HORSE – of the Cart kind – the property of Widow Morris, of Market Bosworth, well-known to be a certain foal getter.
The Dam of the above horse was got by the old Kirby Horse, the sire was the late Mr William Knowles's Old Derbyshire, who was the sire of Conqueror (and useful horses of note). Old Derbyshire was bred by Mr Knowles, and took the Shew Prize (value £10) at Ashby when 2 years old.
For further particulars, apply to Widow Morris
Market Bosworth Jan. 30 1793

122. **The Leicester and Nottingham Journal** - 1 March 1793

A stallion called *Conqueror* belonging to Mr. Knowles was mentioned again in 1799[140] as the sire of the dam of an eight year old horse called *Sampson*, one of three stallions offered for sale by auction at Chesterton, near Peterborough.

Samuel Knowles [1755 -1814], son of William was a highly regarded breeder, not just of heavy horses but also sheep and cattle, as recorded by Farey [8]. He and other members of the Knowles family probably let their horses, in Derbyshire. It was almost certainly Samuel Knowles who was referred to in the following advertisements.

In 1804[153], *Bald Horse*, rising seven, said to have been got by Mr. 'White's' (Wiles) *Swebstone Horse* was advertised to cover at Mr. Knowles's in Nailstone. The same horse, '*that noted well-bred Bald Horse, late the property of Mr. Knowles of Nailstone, Leicestershire*' in 1806[175], was advertised to cover at Borrowash by Mr. Abbot of Spondon (described by Farey [8] as one of Derbyshire's

To be SOLD by AUCTION,
By EDWARD LEES,
On the Premifes of Mr. George Watts, of FROLESWORTH, in the County of Leicefter, on Tuefday the 28th Day of this inftant February,

SIX Black STALLIONS, of the Draught Kind; the Property of the late THOMAS HADDON, deceafed, and Mr. GEORGE WATTS:—One aged Horfe, got by Mr. Oldacre's Kirby Horfe; three Six-year-olds, one by Mr. Oldacre's Mancetter Horfe, one by Mr. Brown's Derbyfhire, one by the aged Horfe before mentioned; one rifing five Years old, got by Mr. Brown's Derbyfhire; one rifing four Years old, got by the aged Horfe firft mentioned.

The above Horfes are well known in the Neighbourhood to get good Stock,—and are fure Foal-Getters.

The Sale to begin at Half paft Ten in the Forenoon.

most noted stallion letters). He was said to have been got by *Mr. Whiles's Swebstone Horse*, out of a mare by *Tinker*. *Tinker*, in turn was said to have been by *Oldacres' Mansetter*, which was a grandson of *the Packington Blind Horse*. *Old Gallimore* (*Gallimore 903*), got by *Old Mansetter*, and late the property of Mr. John Moore of Winshill was also advertised to cover at the same place. In the same year 1806[178], a colt by *Mr. Knowles noted Bald Horse* was advertised by Charles Radford (page 96).

In 1808[195], *Blaze*, a black horse, said to have been late the property of Samuel Knowles (and identifiable as *Blaze 188*) was advertised to cover at Borrowash. *Blaze* was said to have been got by *the Swebstone old horse*, and out of a mare by *Tinker*. He was also said to have been a full brother to *the Bald Horse* which covered at Borrowash in 1806[175].

Another 1808[194Le] advertisement (opposite) featured the eight-year-old stallion called *Useful*, available to cover at Etwall. He was said to be the property of Mr. Knowles, and a full brother to Knowles' *celebrated Bald Horse*, also advertised, but was to cover at Nailstone. [A similar advertisement for *Useful* was placed in 1809[205].]

Also in 1808[202De] the services of *Nelson*, a black colt rising three years old, got by Mr. Knowles's *Blaze* of Nailstone, were advertised (page 91) by Isaac Bennet of Over Haddon (one mile south-west of Bakewell, Derbyshire).

In 1811[214Le] Mr. Knowles's stallion *Conqueror* was referred to again as the sire of the grandam of a horse called *Sweep*, rising 8 years old, which was being offered for sale (page 54) in Shropshire. Also in 1811[219] Mr. Knowles of Nailstone advertised *Young Ball*, rising six years old to cover for the season. He was said to have been a son of *Old Ball*, and out of a *Mancetter* mare. *Young Ball*, son of Mr. *Knowles's Ball'd Horse* of Nailstone,

CAPITAL CART STALLIONS.

TO COVER THIS SEASON,

AT the Spread Eagle, Etwall, in the county of Derby, at two guineas a mare if in-foal, half-a-guinea barren, and one fhilling the Groom,

USEFUL,
Eight years old, the property of Mr. Knowles, of Nailftone, Leicefterfhire.

Ufeful is full brother to the celebrated Bald Horfe, he has proved himfelf a fure Foal-getter, and his ftock are in the higheft repute.

The BALD HORSE,
Will Cover at Nailftone, at three guineas a mare if in-foal, one guinea barren, and one fhilling the groom.

His Stock are fo highly eftimated by the Public, (having fold for fuch unprecedented prices, fetching at two years and a half old 300 guineas,) that he can require no comment.

Nailftone; 21ft March, 1808.

and out of a mare belonging to Bennett, was advertised to cover at Samuel Bennett's at Ratcliff (Ratcliffe-on-the-Wreake) in 1813[237]. Mr. Bennett's mare was said to have been by *Oldacres's Ball'd horse*, son of *Old Mansetter*. *Blaze* (bred by Mr. Knowles of Nailstone) was advertised again in 1812[229]; this time by William Abbot of Mapperley. Also in 1812[231Le] John Abbot of Spondon advertised (below) a horse called *Swebstone*, bred by Knowles, and got by his *Bald Horse*. (This *Swebstone* was therefore a grandson of *Whiles's Swebstone*).

Also will Cover at Spondon aforesaid,
At Two Guineas if in-foal, and Half-a-Guinea barren, and 1s. the Groom,
A Black Horse of the Cart Kind, called
SWEBSTONE.

He was bred by Mr. Knowles of Nailstone, and got by his Bald Horse. His dam by a grand daughter of Mr. Oldacre's Mansetter, which descended from the Packington Blind Horse. Swebstone has proved himself a sure foal getter.

* The money to be paid at Christmas next.

The Stock of the above Horse needs no comment, as they are such that always find their way to a good market.

Spondon, March 26, 1812.

231. **Derby Mercury** - Thursday 16 April 1812

STALLIONS.
TO BE SOLD BY AUCTION,
On Thursday Morning, 28th March next, at Pitchford Park, near Shrewsbury,
TWO STALLIONS;
SELECTED by the owner, after many years' search, to possess combined most completely these four properties,—Action, Constitution, Temper, and Shape.

The Chesnut Hunter
ACTIVE,
Is 13 years old, 15 hands high; his sire the Stoke Colt, by Collier's Regent, by Eclipse.

His Dam is allowed to have been the floutest and fleetest Mare (in all Paces) ever known.—She carried 17 stone 2 miles on trot in less time than the celebrated Phænomenon was ever known to carry 7 stone. Many proofs can be given of her having worked astonishingly hard and long, but no one that she was ever tired.

Active's stock have proved the stoutest Hunters, Roadsters, and best Fencers in Shropshire.

Three Horse Colts, and two Fillies, of his Stock, (of different ages) to be sold same time.

The Black Cart Horse
SWEEP,
Is rising 8 years old, 16 hands 1 inch high, is well known to be of the best blood of Leicestershire. He was bred by Mr. Haywood, of Osbaston, near Market Bosworth. His sire Young Swebston; his dam own sister to the noted old Gallimore; grandam by Mr. Knowles's Conqueror, out of a Mansettet Mare; great grandam by the Packington Horse, which covered at 5 Guineas. The only brother of Sweep was the famous Colt (Mr. Smith's) bought at 2 years old for 240 guineas (now dead).—Gallimore was sold, when 18 years old, for 300 guineas.

Sweep's Stock are well known in the Neighbourhoods of Wem, Bishop's Castle, and Ludlow, and are remarkably handsome and promising.

214. **Derby Mercury** - 28 February 1811

A four year old horse called *Young Useful* was advertised for sale at Hinckley, Leicestershire, also in 1812[234De] (page 94). He was said to have been got by *Mr. Knowles's Ball Horse, Old Useful*, and out of a mare, *Old Gallimore*.

Another horse called *Young Useful*, rising five years old was advertised for sale in Herefordshire in 1827[277]. He was described as the son of *Warwickshire Lad*, a horse which in turn had been sired by *Knowles's Useful*. *Knowles's Useful* was said to have been sired by *Mr. Wiles's Horse of Caton* (i.e. Coton), near Market Bosworth (and would have been a brother to *Knowles Bald Horse*).

A few years later, a cover advertisement for a two-year-old stallion called *King Charles* in 1832[285], revealed that he was got by Mr. While's *Old Derbyshire*. His dam was by Mr. Oldacre's late *Mansetter*, who in turn was got by Mr. While's *Old Swebstone Horse*. An interesting comment made was that Mr. Knowles's best horses were got by *the old Swebstone horse*.

In 1833[286De], in a cover advertisement (page 87) for the black colt *Derbyshire*, owned by John Sims of Stanton by Bridge, Derbyshire, the lengthy pedigree details included the statement that *Mr. Knowle's Bald Horse* had been sired by *Mr While's Old Swebstone* (i.e. *Wiles's Horse of Coton*), this claim being supported by **Table 2** (page 31).

Oldacres - of Packington, Market Bosworth and Peatling, Leicestershire

Although Thomas Oldacres [1740 -1809] played a leading role as a breeder in the earliest stages of Shire horse development during the eighteenth century, there is no evidence that he made use of newspapers to advertise the availability for cover of any of his horses before 1777. It is however likely that he had been operating in the business before that date. Chivers also recorded that Oldacres, like Bakewell, imported Flemish stallions [6].

Thomas Oldacres, a grazier, lived at Market Bosworth in Leicestershire, but later moved to Peatling Lodge (on the Bruntisthorpe Road, at Peatling Parva, south of Leicester). [At least five of his children were baptised in Market Bosworth between 1766 and 1783]. Thomas Oldakers (Oldacres) placed a notice in the Leicester and Nottingham Journal in April 1785[87] announcing that he had moved to Great Peatling Lodge, but intended keeping and breeding stallions for leaping and for sale, as usual. He also said that he would keep stallions at the Bull's Head Inn in Market Bosworth 'for the accommodation of the neighbourhood', with his best stallion (believed to have been *Mansetter*) leaping there in this year.

Significantly, Thomas Oldacres originated in Packington, being one of several children of Ralph Oldacres (Oldakers) [c1689-1768] and his wife Ann, baptised there from 1725 onwards.

He notably, had stallions called *Kirby* (or *Kerby*), and also *Mansetter*. Mancetter is a village in Warwickshire just south of Atherstone, but within ten miles of Market Bosworth. There may be some Oldacres family connection with Mancetter, as yet undiscovered. Presumably, through his Packington connection he was able to make use of the services of *the Packington Blind Horse* as the sire of his horse '*Kerby*', although we do not whether he bred *Kirby*. *Kirby*, in turn was the sire of *Mansetter*.

The first Stud-book [29] provides confusing and apparently contradictory information. The genealogical table **Table 2** (page 30-31), included with the Stud-book contains information which differs from that in the pedigree details given for individual stallions. In this instance, the genealogical table makes more sense. According to the table Oldacres' *Kirby* was a son of the *Packington Blind Horse*, being foaled in about 1773. He, in turn was the sire of *Mansetter* foaled, it was stated, in about 1780. By contrast, the pedigree details given in the Stud-book for individual stallions suggests that *Mansetter 1476* was sired by *Kirby 1286*, but not until about 1790. *Kirby 1286* is recorded as having been foaled in about 1785, with his sire being Oldacres *Mansetter*!

Old Kirby was recorded as the sire of the dam of a black stallion advertised (page 52) for sale at Market Bosworth in 1793[122Le].

'*Two Black Horses of the Cart Kind*', the property of Mr. Oldacres of Market Bosworth, were advertised to cover at Kerby Muxloe in 1777[68]. This is the first advertisement found which features the Oldacres name. It is tempting to suggest that the name *Kirby* (or *Kerby*), the horse owned by Oldacres, was so named because of some link with Kerby Muxloe, but it can only be speculation.

In 1786[90], Thomas Oldacres advertised that '*BEST HORSE*' would be available to cover at Market Bosworth, as in the previous season. This horse could reasonably be assumed to have been *Mansetter*, since he placed similar advertisements again in 1787[95Le] (below), 1788[99] and 1790[103] when in each case he named the horse *Mansetter*. The cover price was two guineas per mare in each year. These dates are more consistent with a foaling date for *Mansetter* being closer to 1780, rather than 1790 as the Stud-book suggests.

In 1791[106] Mr. 'Oldaker's' (Oldacres') best colt, got by *old Mansetter* was advertised by John Barker to cover near Alfreton, in Derbyshire. *Mancetter* was advertised for cover a few years later (page 56), in 1792[118Le], when he appeared to be no longer in Oldacres' possession. He was advertised by Mr. W. Colman, of Murcott, Northampton. His cover fee was just twelve shillings and sixpence.

To COVER this Seafon, (1787) AT the BULL's-HEAD INN, MARKET-Bosworth, Leicefterfhire, at TWO GUINEAS each Mare, (as ufual)

The noted CART HORSE, call'd

M A N S E T T E R,

The Property of THOMAS OLDAKERS, of Peatling, near Leicefter.

N. B. Good Grafs for Mares.

This advertisement provided the pedigree of *'Mancetter'*, claiming that he was a son of *Oldacres' Kerby*, who in turn was sired by Mr. Wood's (an error - meaning *Hood's*) horse, of Packington. His dam was said to have been sired by Mr. Richard's horse of Ashby-de-la-Zouch, which was sired by *'the Packington Horse'* (suggesting Mr. Hood's horse again). The advertisement also claimed that *'Mancetter'* was rising seven years old, and therefore foaled in 1785. In reality *Mansetter* must have been a little older. Oldacres himself had first advertised *Mansetter* in 1787[95Le] and is unlikely to have been then just a two year old.

Oldacres' 1786[90] advertisement, which featured his *'BEST HORSE'*, would seem not to be for *Mansetter*; that stallion was perhaps instead *Kirby*.

In 1793[125Le] three stallions were advertised to cover at Mr. Hart's at Culloden House (page 61) Two of these horses were said to have been by *Mansetter*. One of them, called *Blaze*, rising seven years old, was said to have been by *'Mr. Oldacres' late horse Mansetter'*. Whether this advertisement really meant that Mancetter was dead, or that he was no longer in Oldacres' possession is uncertain.

Another interesting advertisement, in 1793[129] was for *Waggoner*, a rising eight year old black horse, available to cover near Daventry in Northamptonshire. His grandsire was got by Bakewell's *Old G*, and his dam was said to have been *Mr. Oldacre's Old Bennet*, which in turn had been sired by *the Packington Blind Horse*.

A horse, rising eight years old called *Plow-boy*, the property of Thomas Oldacre (whose address was now given as Peatling Lodge) was advertised to cover in 1794[130]. He was said to have been got by his old horse *Mansetter*, and his dam by *the Kirby Horse*. Assuming this was Oldacres' *Kirby horse*, which was also the sire of *Mansetter,* we have a clear case of inbreeding. *Plow-boy's* parents would have been at least half-siblings, or even full brother and sister!

In 1797[137] John Wagstaff of Atlow (page 88) advertised a horse, rising five years old called *Blaze*, said to have been got by *Mr. Oldacre's Bald Horse*.

A 1799[142] advertisement for a black horse, to cover near Alfreton claimed that both *Mansetter* and a *Mansetter* mare were in his pedigree. *Mansetter* was said to have been got by *Kirby*, and that *Kirby* was a son of *the Old Packington Blind Horse*.

Sons of Oldacres' *Mansetter* seem to have included *Gallimore* (*Gallimore 903*), advertised to cover at Newton Solney in 1803[151], and *Mr. Hart's Bald Horse* advertised as the sire of the dam of *Conqueror* in 1804[156De] (page 93).

An eight year old stallion called *Sampson*, offered for sale by auction at Chesterton near Peterborough, also in 1799[140], was said to have been got by Oldacres' *Mansetter*, with his dam being by Knowles' *Conqueror*. Two other stallions on sale with *Sampson* were *WAG*, seven years old and *Little John*, five years old, both of which were said to have been by Oldacres' *Little John*. There is little information available about the sons of *Kirby*, apart from *Mansetter*.

TO COVER, this Season, 1792, the Property of Mr. W. COLEMAN, of MURCOTT, in the Parish of Long-Buckby, Northamptonshire, at One Guinea each Mare, and One Shilling the Groom,

That Well-bred, Beautiful, Strong, Boney BAY-HORSE,

CHANCE.

Chance is rising five Years old, full 16 Hands high, and is allowed by the best of Judges, to be the compleatest Blood Horse, in this Part of the Kingdom; the two last Seasons he has been very successful in getting Foals; his Stock are very handsome, boney, and active——Those Mares that proved Barren to be Covered at Half Price.

Also, at the same Place, at Twelve Shillings and Six-pence each Mare, and One Shilling the Man,

That very Capital BLACK CART-HORSE,

MANCETTER.

Mancetter is rising seven Years old, 16 Hands high, is a very short legg'd, boney, firm Horse, and his Stock are exceeding good; in short, no Horse has a better character, as a Stock-Getter; he was got by Mr. Oldacre's Kerby Horse, which covered at One Guinea a Mare.—The Kerby Horse was got by Mr. Wood's Horse of Packington, Leicestershire, which covered at Three Guineas a Mare.—Mancetter's Dam was got by a Horse which —— Richards, Esq. of Ashby-de-la Zouch bred; which won the Price of a Foal at Ashby; he was got by the Packington Horse belonging to Mr. Wood. He is a sure Foal-Getter. With my Hand, W. SLINGSBY FOLESHILL.

They will both be at Home during the Season.—— Good Grass for Mares, and proper Care taken of them.

N. B. The Money to be paid at Old Midsummer next.

In 1799[143], a black cart stallion called *Young Kirby* was advertised to cover at Huntington Hall, near Chester. It was claimed that he was got by *Kirby*, but which *Kirby*? The first Stud-book records *Kirby (Kettle's)1287*, foaled in 1800 as a son of *Oldacre's Kirby*, and owned by Kettle of The Marsh, <u>Shropshire</u>, said to have been sold on 25 March 1811 for 525 guineas.

A dispersal sale advertised in 1811 (Cheshire Chronicle, 22 March) on the premises of Samuel Kettle [1744-1820] of the Marsh, Acton, near Nantwich, <u>Cheshire</u>, who was giving up farming, included his brown stallion, *Young Kirby* ('*got by Old Kirby*'), rising 5 years old, due to be auctioned on 25th March. His pedigree details were similar to those given in the Stud-book for *Kirby (Kettle's) 1287*, but he would have been foaled in 1806. **Table 2** (page 30) records *Kettle's Kirby* (a son of *Oldacre's Kirby*) as having been foaled in 1795, a more likely description of the horse which Kettle referred to as *Old Kirby* in the advertisement.

Two advertisements in the Derby Mercury in April 1806[175] confirm that *Mansetter* was a son of *Kirby*, and grandson of *the Packington Blind Horse*. OLD GALLIMORE was advertised, as a son of *Mansetter*. ['*Old Gallimore*' seems to be *Gallimore 903*, as he is described as formerly the property of Mr. John Moore of Winshill, Burton-upon-Trent (page 92)].

Black Legs, formerly the property of Mr. William Slingsby (of Foleshill, Warwickshire) was also advertised (page 100) in 1806[177De], and similarly in 1808[196] and 1809[204]. He was said to have been sired by another of Thomas Oldacres' horses – *Little John*. Inbreeding practice is indicated, both sire and dam of *Oldacres' Little John* being by *Old Mansetter*. **Table 2** records Oldacres' *Little John* as having been sired by *Mansetter*, and foaled in about 1793. The 1799[140] advertisement however indicates that *WAG*, a son of *Little John* was foaled in 1791 or 1792. Consequently, *Little John* himself would have been foaled a few years earlier.

Mr. Oldacres' Bald Horse of Peatling Lodge was described as having been the sire of a black horse called *Young Bald*, advertised to cover in 1807[183]. Similarly, *Mansetter* was said to have sired both the sire and the dam of this Oldacres' horse.

Mr. Oldacres' Muxon Horse was mentioned as the sire of a three year old horse due to cover at Mr. Bulstrode's in 1808[200]. Oldacres also owned *Brown George 301*, foaled in 1802 [29]. Thomas Oldacres died in 1809, and in February 1810[211] nine cart stallions were included in an auction sale, advertised to take place on his premises at Peatling. In the sale details it was stated that Oldacres' horses had been highly esteemed for over forty years.

Bulstrode - of Isley Walton and Worthington, Leicestershire

The Bulstrodes were another family of gentleman farmers. Chivers [6] referred to 'the great Bulstrode of Leicestershire' and 'Mr. Bulstrode' was certainly very influential as a breeder in the early development of the Shire, and over a long period during the 18th century. It now seems likely that two or even three generations of the Bulstrode family were 'Shire' breeders. Confusingly, and frustratingly there are many unspecific references to '*Bulstrode's horse*', and it is difficult to know how many horses were so named, and which horse was which. This sort of problem occurs again and again e.g. with the horses named '*Gallimore*'.

The Bulstrode name was clearly highly regarded so that various horses were probably called Bulstrode as a mark of quality, and not just because a Bulstrode horse was in their pedigree (e.g. in 1806[177De] (page 100), 1807[185],1808[201],1808[202De] (page 91), and in 1812[230]).

The name Bulstrode is notably linked to the tiny Leicestershire village of Isley Walton (a quiet location, despite today being just south of East Midlands airport and the Donington Park motorsport circuit).

The 'Mr. Bulstrode' most associated with 'Shire 'breeding was probably John Mynors Bulstrode [1746 -1804]. He was baptised in Isley Walton (near Breedon-on-the-Hill), the son of John Bulstrode [1716 -1757] and his wife Elizabeth. The following two advertisements however suggest the involvement of John Bulstrode, senior.

In 1762[8Le] Robert Bakewell of Dishley (page 40) advertised a black colt, rising two years whose sire was said to have been the '*late Isley Walton old Horse*'.

In 1763[10Le], Mr. Salisbury (i.e. George Salisbury, Robert Bakewell's companion on his travels) advertised (below) a horse to cover,which was *'got by the famous Easly-Walton Horse'*.
Both of these advertisements referred to a horse of some renown which existed at a very early date, and although in neither case is the Bulstrode name given, the mention of Islay Walton almost certainly indicates that a member of the Bulstrode family was involved.

To Cover this SEASON
At half a guinea a foal, and half
a Crown Barren,
At Barrow, near Loughborough
Mr Salisbury's well-bred Black
HORSE, above 16 HANDS high, which
cover'd there last season.
NB The horse was got by the famous Easly-
Walton Horse, and came out of a fine Flanders
Mare

10. **The Leicester and Nottingham Journal** - Saturday
16 April 1763

To COVER this SEASON, 1770.
AT Mr. GEORGE MALIN's at the King's-Head in *Duffield*, a black Horse, of the Cart Kind, called

PLOUGH-BOY,

at *Ten Shillings* and *Six pence* a Mare ; the Money to be paid at *Midfummer* next.
He is five Years old, ftands feventeen Hands high, and was got by Mr. *Hood's* old Horfe, at *Packington* ; his Dam by Mr. *Boulftridge's* old Horfe, at *Ifley-Walton*, which Horfes got the beft Stock in *Leicefterfhire*. He is a very fure Foal getter.
Alfo the Brown Horfe called, The

FARMER's GLORY,

will be at *Duffield* every *Monday* ; *Uttoxeter*, on *Wednefdays* ; *Burton*, on *Thurfdays* ; *Derby*, on *Fridays* ; and will cover at *Ten Shillings* and *Six-pence* a Mare.
He is allowed to get as good Chapmen's Cattle, and as many of them as any Horfe in England.

28. **Derby Mercury** - 27 April [& 11 May] 1770

Reference has already been made to a Leicestershire-bred black stallion called *Biard*, sired by Mr. *Dunsthorp's* (Donnisthorp's) *old Horse* of Packington which was advertised (page 102) to cover at Wainfleet, near Skegness, Lincolnshire in 1768[18Li]. It was also claimed, in the advertisement that *Dunsthorp's Horse* had, in turn been got by Mr. *Bostridge's* (Bulstrode's) *Black Horse* at 'Easby' Walton (Isley Walton). It was further stated that Mr. *Bostridge's Black Horse* had been got by Mr. *Molliborn's* (Mallaber's) *Black Horse of 'Chilcoat'*. [Chilcote is about four miles south-west of Packington]. Walter Mallaber [-1767] of Chilcote was the probable owner of the horse. He married his first wife in 1741, and married for a second time in 1753. He and his second wife had several children, all baptised at Chilcote between 1754 and 1764]. This advertisement provides further evidence of the importance of Mr. Bulstrode as a 'Shire' breeder at an early date.
A 1770[28Le] cover advertisement (above) by George Malin in Duffield, Derbyshire referred to Mr. 'Boulstridge' (Bulstrode), and featured the five-year-old stallion *Plough-Boy*, where *Boulstridge's old horse* was said have sired his dam at Isley Walton. It seems probable that *Boulstridge's old horse* was owned by John Bulstrode (the father of John Mynors Bulstrode) and he may have bred the dam of *Plough-boy*, although he died in 1757. George Malin placed similar advertisements for *Plough-Boy* again in 1771[37Le] (page 37), 1774[48] and 1775[55].
An advertisement placed by William Redfern of Mickleover (just west of Derby) in 1772[38], (and similarly in 1773[44]) for a *'Strong Black HORSE, rising four years old'*, 'referred to *'Mr. Hood's old horse that went to Mr Bolstridge's, of Islay Walton'* in its pedigree.
Paul Caulton of Shottle advertised a black colt, rising three years old, *got by 'Mr. Donnisthorpe's noted Horse of Packington'* in 1788[96]. Donnisthorpe's horse was said to have been got by *Boulstridge's bald Horse*. Also in 1788[97] a black horse, rising four years old, said to have been got by *Mr. Boulstridge's Horse of Islay Walton*, was advertised by John Wagstaff of Atlow. (Atlow is a somewhat isolated small village about three miles north-east of Ashbourne, Derbyshire.)
In 1789[102], *'Merryman, a black horse of the Cart Kind, rising three years old'* was advertised to cover. *Merryman* was said to have been sired by *Mr. Bullstrode's old horse of Isley-Walton*. Mr. Hart, in advertising (page 61) three stallions which were available to cover in 1793[125Le], claimed

that Mr. Bullstrode's old Horse had sired the dam of his horse *Blaze*, and also the dam of his horse *Merriman*.

Bulstrode horses would have been in service for many years but the Bulstrodes do not seem to have used newspapers to advertise their stallions during this time.

Chivers made the observation that the Bulstrode name appears frequently in old pedigrees, but only one Bulstrode-bred horse appears in the Stud-book [6].

Bulstrode's Bald Horse 93 was said to have been bred by Bulstrode in 1778 [29]. Chivers considered him to be possibly one of the greatest 18th century stallions. Reynolds [29] made reference to this *'bald horse'*, said to have been a grandson of the *Packington Blind Horse*, but clearly a celebrity in his own right. He apparently travelled for fourteen seasons commanding three guineas per service. His sire is recorded as Oldacres' horse *Kirby*, a son of the *Packington Blind Horse*. Bulstrode is thought to have bred his dam, while the Stud-book suggests his dam's sire was *Gallimore 903*. This is impossible, as Chivers [6] pointed out. This dam's sire could however have been an earlier *Gallimore*.

At some stage John Mynors Bulstrode moved to the near-by village of Worthington (two miles south-west of Isley Walton). He did not marry, and in his will in 1804, John Mynors Bulstrode, a gentleman of Worthington, left considerable property, the beneficiaries being principally his two spinster sisters. His nephew, also called John Mynors Bulstrode (son of his brother Augustine) was to have the use of the Worthington farm where he had lately resided. The will makes only a general reference to livestock, and disappointingly no mention of horses [24].

A sale of livestock was advertised in the Derby Mercury dated 29 November 1804 to take place after Mr.Bulstrode's death. In addition to cattle and sheep, five mares, three of them in foal (one of them to Mr. Oldacres' horse), a stallion foal, a gelding and a filley were offered for sale. Either Bulstrode had no stallions at this point, or they were not for sale [5].

An advertisement (page 92) placed in 1804[152De], the year John Bulstrode died, was for another horse called *Blaze*, (in this case owned by the late Mr. Radford of Little Eaton, page 97). He was to have been got by *Mr Bulstrode's noted old Horse of Isley Walton* (presumably *Bulstrode's Bald Horse 93*).

An advertisement in 1805[161Le] *(opposite)*, and again in 1806[176], featured the stallion '*Ball'* (a son of '*Mr Hart's Blaz'd Horse'*), available for cover at Mr. Bulstrode's of Worthington. This suggests continuing involvement in 'Shire' breeding by the nephew John Mynors Bulstrode [1782-1827]. It is this later John and his family, whose finely- carved slate gravestones can be found in the churchyard at Breedon-on the-Hill (near Worthington).

It is however his uncle, John Mynors Bulstrode [1746-1804] who is thought to have been largely responsible for the breeding work with heavy horses.

The Bulstrode reputation was such that many horses were called *Bulstrode* and the name appeared in pedigrees of the developing Shire horse long after his death.

In 1806[177De], a black colt called *Young*

TO COVER THIS SEASON, 1805,

AT Mr. BULSTRODE's, of Worthington, near Breedon, in the county of Leicester, at One Guinea if in-Foal, and 10s. 6d. if Barren, and One Shilling the Groom,

A Black Horse, rising Five Years old,

BALL.

He was got by Mr. Hart's Blaz'd Horse, of Culloden-House, out of a Mare by the late Mr. Bulstrode's Old Horse, of Isley Walton; Grandam by Old Ball.

Also to Cover at the same place,

At One Guinea a Foal and Half-a-Guinea Barren, and One Shilling the Groom,

A Black Horse, Aged,

GENERAL.

He was got by the Old Horse, and out of a Mare by the Dishley G.

161. **Derby Mercury** - Thursday 4 April 1805

Bulstrode was advertised to cover (page 100). His sire was said to have been John Chadwick's famous horse *Marston,* and his dam, appropriately, *Mr. Bulstrode's old bald Horse Massey*. Another horse called *Bulstrode*, a black horse, rising five years old, got by Mr *Massey's Bulstrode* at Birchwood Moor (page 87) was advertised to cover at Winster in

Derbyshire in 1807[185]. *Massey's Bulstrode* was, in turn, said to have been sired by *Mr. Bulstrode's Horse of Isley Walton*.

An advertisement (page 75) by John Chadwick, also in 1807[192St] for his two horses *Young Packington* and *Farmers Glory* supplied pedigree details in which *Bulstrode's Old Horse* and *Bulstrode's Old Ball'd Horse* were both mentioned.

In the same year[188St] John Fallows, of Booth-Hall, Cheadle, Staffordshire advertised his stallion *Lockwood* (page 77). He also gave detailed pedigree information which included a reference to *Bullstrode's old horse of Isley Walton* as the sire of *Ball*, and seemed to imply that the Bulstrode horse had in turn been sired by *Merryman*, a son of *the Packington Blind Horse*.

Willliam Burnet of Grindon, Staffordshire who advertised *Censurer*, also in 1807[189St] referred to a stallion called *Ball* (page 76). In this case he claimed that the dam of *Censurer* was sired by *Ball*, and that *Ball*, in turn was sired by *Bulstrode's old horse*.

In 1808[201] John Chadwick advertised his horse *Bulstrode*, a full brother to *Marston*. He also, in giving pedigree details for this horse, mentioned that *Ball*, in turn, was sired by *Bulstrode's old horse*. Also in 1808[202De] Isaac Bennet of Over Haddon, Derbyshire advertised (page 91) a black colt, rising two years old, to cover. He was called *Bulstrode*! This colt was said to have been got by *Gallimore*, in turn the son of *Old Gallimore* which formerly covered at Winch-hill (i.e. Winshill, near Burton-upon-Trent). An impressive pedigree was claimed which also included *Falkner's Bald Horse*, *Mr Bulstrode's old Horse of Isley Walton*, *Mr. Summerland's Wiltshire Horse* and *the Packington Blind Horse*.

In 1811[222St, 225], a stallion called *Ploughboy* and another one called *Staffordshire Hero* also featured in cover advertisements in which Bulstrode stallions were said to appear in their pedigree (page 66). Similar claims were made for *Little John*, advertised (page 71) by John Chadwick in 1812[233St].

Isaac Bennet advertised his horse Bulstrode to cover again in 1812[230], now rising six years old. Bennet's *Bullstrode* was advertised for sale at Chesterfield in 1813[235].

Also in 1813[239], *The Bald Horse* (son of *Hart's Blazed Horse)* was advertised to cover at the Moira Arms Inn (the property of Mr. Smith), Castle Donington (approximately six miles south-east of Derby). Now in the hands of Mr. Smith, this horse was said to have been bred by Mr. Bulstrode of Worthington, from whom Mr. Smith had purchased the horse.

As late as 1833[286De] the Bulstrode name was being still being included in pedigrees. *Mr. Bulstrode's Old Horse of Isley Walton,* and what seems to have been an earlier horse, *Mr. Bulstrode's old Bald Horse* were both mentioned in the pedigree details claimed for the black colt *Derbyshire*, advertised to cover by John Sims, of Stanton by Bridge, in Derbyshire (page 87).

Hart - of Culloden House, Norton juxta Twycross, Leicestershire

William Hart [c1739-1812], a farmer and grazier of Culloden House (apparently named after the Battle of Culloden in 1746) was named by Chivers as the owner and breeder of *Blaze 183*, the earliest-named Shire in the Stud-book, foaled in about 1770. There is however doubt about this date. Chivers suggested that it was more likely that *Hart's Blaze* was a later *Blaze*, foaled in about 1790, and this view is consistent with current evidence. *Blaze* was also said to be a son of *Oldacres' Mancetter*. There are few references to William Hart within newspaper 'cover' advertisements, and these appear much later than 1770. Farey identified William Hart as a noted Shire breeder, commenting that 'Mr. Hart's stallions had long been in great repute' [8]. No reference to this breeder has been traced to before 1793[125Le] when three black horses were advertised (page 61) to cover at Mr. Hart's at Culloden House. The horse called *Blaze* is perhaps of most significance as he seems to fit the description of *Blaze 183*, although he was said to have been rising seven years old, and would therefore have been foaled in 1786 rather than in 1770. This *Blaze* was described as a son of '*Oldakers' Mansetter*', his dam being by

Mr. Bulstrode's Old Horse, and his grandam by *Mr. Bakewell's Blaze*.
The other two horses included in the same advertisement were a brother to this *Blaze*, rising three year old, and a black horse called *Merryman*, also by *Mansetter*.
In 1803[149De], Charles Radford advertised a black colt, rising two years old, sired by *Mr. Bancroft's Horse of Sinfin* (page 96). Mr. Bancroft's horse was said to have been got by *Mr. Hart's Horse of Culloden*.
A similar advertisement was placed in 1806[178] for what appears to have been the same animal, which was rising five years old.
A reference to *Mr. Hart's bald horse* appeared within the pedigree of a stallion called *Conqueror*, advertised (page 93) in 1804[156De], when Mr. Hart was said to have been of 'Coleoreton'.
In 1805[161Le], and again in 1806[176], a horse

called *Ball* was advertised (page 59) as being available to cover at Mr. Bulstrode's, at Worthington. *Ball* was described as having been got by *Mr. Hart's Blaz'd Horse of Culloden-House.* In another advertisement (page 94) in 1806[171De] for a black horse, rising seven years old, to cover at John Bancroft's of Sinfin, *Mr. Hart's old Horse of Culloden* was said to have been the sire. There may been some confusion between Culloden and Coleorton, also in Leicestershire, about two miles east of Ashby- de-la-Zouch.

Another horse called *Blaze,* rising four years old, was advertised (page 68) to cover at Uttoxeter (in Staffordshire) in 1807[190St]. It was claimed that his sire was by a grandson of *Hart's ball'd Horse*. The *Ball'd Horse*, the property of Mr. Bulstrode of Worthington was advertised in 1811[223]. *Hart's Blaz'd Horse* was said to have been his sire. Also in 1811[225] a horse called *Ploughboy* was advertised to cover. It was claimed that he had been got *the Sinfin Old horse*, he having been was got by *Hart's Blaze of Culloden House*, *Blaze*, in turn, having been by *Mansetter*.
A stallion called *Wonderful,* bred by Mr. Stephenson of Snarston*,* was offered for sale by auction (opposite) at Burton-on-Trent in 1814[247Le]. He was also said to have been got by *Mr. Hart's Blaze of Culloden*. The black horse *Wonderful*, rising six years old,and son of *Wonderful*, had been advertised to cover at Mr. Abbot's in Spondon, Derbyshire in 1813[242].

All the newspaper advertisements refer only to 'Mr. Hart'. John Hart [1771-1838], who succeeded his father at Culloden House could have responsible for some 'Shire' breeding.

William Hart, in his will, dated 1812, named his nephew Joseph Clarke, son of Joseph Clarke of Willesley (page 26) as an executor. There was however another interesting link. In 1796, Joseph Clarke, junior had married Isabella Hood, daughter of William Hood of Packington (page 36)!

Wiles - of Coton, Leicestershire

Chivers referred to him as Joseph Wild; notable as the proprietor of a famous stud for thirty years or more [6]. Joseph Wiles (also Whiles, Whyles or Wilds) [1773 -   ] can be identified as the son of Samuel Wiles [1745 - 1797], a grazier, of Coton, near Market Bosworth, Leicestershire. According to Chivers [6], Joseph Wiles owned *Swebstone 2079* in around 1800 (apparently bred in 1795, a son of *Hart's Blaze 183*). **Table 2** (page 30) also records Wiles' *Swebstone Horse* as having been a son of *Hart's Blaze* (although foaled in 1795).
A horse called the *Swebstone Horse* was advertised (page 97) to cover at John Wagstaff's of Atlow in 1802[145De]. He was said to have been rising nine years old, and would have been foaled in 1793 rather than 1795. However, this *'Swebstone Horse'* was said to have been a full brother of *Radford's Blaze*, and <u>got by *Mr. Bulstrode's old horse*,</u> not by *Hart's Blaze*.
[Swebstone is a village about four miles north-west of Market Bosworth, and only about 2½ miles south of Packington.]
Chivers recorded that eight more of Wiles's stallions are listed in Volume I of the Stud-book [29], foaled from around 1800 to 1830, including *Derbyshire 577*, said to be the earliest example of a Fen x Midland cross [6], and the sire of *Blacklegs 142* which Wiles apparently owned.

Plate 10: The **Old English Black Stallion**, by ***Old Blacklegs,*** from a mare of the Dishley Breed. Bred by Mr Broomes, at Ormiston (probably Mr. Broome of Osmaston), Derby.
Dishley Grange is in the background, although, according to Chivers, the painting dates between 1832 and 1841. Probably artistic licence was used by the artist William Sheils [1785-1857] to draw attention to the horse's Dishley pedigree.

A cover advertisement for *the Bald Horse*, rising seven years old, together with another horse, aged five years, was placed by Knowles of Nailstone in 1804[153]. Both horses were said to have been got by Mr. White's (Wiles) *Swebstone Horse*. The *Bald Horse* was advertised again in 1806[175], now owned by Mr. Abbott of Spondon.

In 1827[277], a black wagon horse called *Young Useful* was advertised for sale in Herefordshire. *Mr. Wiles's Horse at Caton* (meaning Coton) was claimed to be in his pedigree; Wiles' horse (unnamed, but no doubt being his *Swebstone Horse*), was said to have covered at five guineas a mare, and was sold for 700 guineas.

In 1831[283Le] in a cover advertisement (opposite) for a brown cart horse, rising five years old called *Leicester*, customers were informed that *Leicester* was by a stallion called *Leicestershire*. Also *Leicestershire was said to have been 'got by Mr. Wild's (of Cotton, near Market Bosworth) Blacklegs* (presumably *Blacklegs 142, owned by Joseph Wiles). Blacklegs was further described as 'truly descended from the old Swebstone horse, Mansetter, Old Kirby and the noted Packington horse'.*

Interestingly this claim which was made for Swebstone's ancestry, going back to *the Packington Blind Horse*, made no mention of *Hart's Blaze* as his sire.

The first Stud-book [26] records *Leicestershire 1312* as a black horse, foaled in 1827 and *Leicester 1313*, as a brown horse foaled in 1831(a few years later than the dates given in the 1831[283Le] advertisement), both these stallions having apparently been been sired by *Leicestershire 1321*.

Chivers describes *Old Leicestershire 1321*, also known as *Leicestershire Hero*, as a brown stallion, foaled in 1820 [6]. He also states that *Old Leicestershire 1321* was sired by *Blacklegs 142*, and that he was owned by John Beard. These same two points of description were also given in the the 1831[283Le] advertisement (above) for the horse *Leicestershire* - was he the brown stallion *Old Leicestershire 1321*? Or was he the black stallion *Leicestershire 1312*? There are no clear answers to these questions!

In 1833[286De], a black colt, rising six years old called *Derbyshire* was advertised (page 87) by John Sims of Stanton-by-Bridge, in

Also, that well-known Cart Stallion, LEICESTER, at ONE GUINEA each Mare, if in foal,—nothing if barren. (A Groom's Fee, 1s., to be paid at the time of covering.) He is a brown horse, with black legs, possessing immense bone, rising five years old, seventeen hands high, was got by that celebrated horse Leicestershire, (bred by Mr. Gent, of Astin, near Hinckley,) belonging to Mr. John Beard, of Ashover, near Chesterfield, and is considered the best stock-getter in England. Leicestershire was got by Mr. Wild's (of Cotton, near Market Bosworth,) Blacklegs, which horse is truly descended from the old Swebstone horses, Mancetto, Old Kirby, and the noted Packington horse. Leicestershire is now covering at two guineas, and Blacklegs at three guineas each mare. Leicester was bred by Mr. Hardy, of Winshall, Derbyshire, out of a fine brown mare that was got by Mr. J. Smith's (of Coton) Favourite, by Mr. Bulstrode's Brown George, Favourite's dam, by the Isley Warton Horse, grandam by Mr. Walker's General.

LEICESTER has proved himself a sure foal-getter, and his stock is remarkably powerful and very superior in every respect.

The above horses will always be at home except on Mondays, when they will be at the Paddock stables, Hassell's Street, Newcastle, from 25th April to 4th July.

☞ Half-price will be charged for each Mare proving barren, if the parties, through neglect, have them served only once during the season. The money to be paid the first week in February, 1832.

283. **Staffordshire Advertiser** - Saturday 23 March 1831

TO COVER THIS SEASON, 1829,
AT COTON,
A BLACK CART STALLION,
BLACK LEGS.
The Property of Mr. JOSEPH WILES, of Coton, near Market Bosworth, Leicestershire, at Three Sovereigns each mare, if in foal, and One and a Half Sovereign if barren, and Half a Crown the Groom,; all Stallion Horse Keepers to pay Five Guineas each mare.

BLACK LEGS is allowed by competent Judges to be the best black horse in the kingdom, and gets better stock than any other horse in the country.

The Groom's Fee to be paid at the time of covering.

Good Grass for mares, and proper care taken of them.

Black Legs will be at Mr Hollier's, the Ram Inn, Hinckley, every Monday morning at Ten o'clock, and remain there till three o'clock in the afternoon, return home at night, and remain there all the week.

278. **Leicester Journal** - 27 March 1829

Derbyshire as being available for cover. He was said to have been '*got* by *Old Black Legs*', late the property of Mr. 'Whiles' of Coton. This was clearly was not *Derbyshire 577* which Wiles had owned years earlier, but can be identified as *Derbyshire 578*, his sire
'Old Black Legs' having been *Blacklegs 142*. The Stud-book [26] also lists *Derbyshire 579*, foaled in 1826, owned by Joseph Wiles, and also sired by *Blacklegs 142*.
The horse shown in the illustration **Plate 10** (page 62) is also claimed to be of a son of the stallion called *Old Blacklegs*, by a mare of the Dishley Breed. The 'Old English Black Horse' (**Plate 11**) seems to be the same horse.

Plate 11: Old English Black Horse - painted (by William Shiels [1785-1857] of a horse
descended from Bakewell's Black Leicestershire Horses.
Dishley Grange is in the background, as in the picture above.
It appears to be a different view of the same animal shown in **Plate 10**.

Newspaper advertising seems to have been little used by Wiles, but in 1829[278Le], he advertised (page 63) his black cart stallion called *Black Legs,* to cover at Coton for 3 sovereigns a mare. This was presumably the celebrated stallion *Black legs 142* although he would have been rather old by this date if he had really been foaled in 1804, as the first Stud-book records [29].
In January 1830[280], Joseph Wiles was declared insolvent. It appears that he then ceased to farm at Coton and became a publican. In the 1841 Census Wiles was recorded as being an innkeeper at the Royal Oak at Bufton, Ibstock (about four miles north of Market Bosworth).

CHAPTER 7: STAFFORDSHIRE BREEDERS AND OWNERS

Apart from Samuel Gallimore whose contribution is at the heart of this book, early 'Shire' breeders of significance who lived in Staffordshire included those by the name of Hambleton, Summerland, Stych, also with Hinckley, Massey, and perhaps most of all, Chadwick.

Samuel Gallimore lived at Wootton (near Ashbourne, Derbyshire), and most of his customers lived in the northern uplands of Staffordshire, now largely within the Peak District National Park. Nothing is likely to be discovered about the offspring of the stallions he owned in his lifetime. The first *Galymoor (Gallimore)*, which (on evidence presented) was his former stallion, and sold after his death, seems to have left his more immediate descendants principally in Derbyshire and Leicestershire. Amongst the other Staffordshire breeders and owners who made important contributions to the development of the Breed were those who also resided in the north of the county where Gallimore's activities were concentrated. Pitt [26] gave an insight into a horse-breeding tradition in the county when he recorded that '*poorer sort of land in the Moorlands answers well for breeding*'. He also recorded that the '*rich feeding ground on the banks of the Dove, pushes up the young stock surprizingly*'. Pitt also noted the availability of traditional horse fairs, which included Stafford, where some of Samuel Gallimore's horses were sold (page 127), in 1751, Rugeley and Burton-upon-Trent. These fairs provided good markets for local breeders, a number of whom lived in the central part of the county, and around Stafford. Dairying was (and still is) important in these areas of Staffordshire, where horses would have been part of everyday farming practice, but also could be bred to supplement income.

Apart from their use in farming, there would have been a growing demand for horses during the eighteenth century from the developing industrial centres of the Potteries in north Staffordshire, and from the Black Country in the southern part of the county.

Hambleton - of Calton, Staffordshire

According to Chivers [6], in 1778, Mr. Hambleton of Calton Moor sold a horse called *Sweet William* to Mr. Summerland of Ingestre for the considerable sum of 350 guineas. Calton Moor House, stands today at an important road junction on the A52 between Derby and Stoke-on-Trent. At this point, the A523 branches off the A52 in the direction of Leek. In the time of John Hambleton [c1736 -1807], who was the tenant, there was a farm at Calton Moor, and also an inn called the Red Lion [30]. Dealers in livestock such as Mr. Summerland would have been amongst the many travellers he would have accommodated. John Hambleton was also well placed to sell horses which he himself may have bought or bred.

Hambleton does not appear to have used newspapers to advertise his horses, whether they were for sale, or available to cover. Stallions associated with his name include *Staffordshire Hero 2056* (said to have been foaled in 1800), which was owned by Hambleton, and also *Conqueror 524* (foaled 1810), said to have been bred by him.

John Hambleton, innkeeper of Calton Moor died in 1807. *Conqueror* is likely to have been bred by his son, John Hambleton, junior, who is recorded as having been at the Red Lion, Calton Moor, and also having children who were baptised at Calton between 1810 and 1815. In 1811[222St] John Hambleton (junior) advertised (page 66) his stallion called *Staffordshire Hero* to cover at Calton Moor. Rising 5 years old, *Staffordshire Hero* was said to have been brother to *Mr. Styche's Brown Horse* and got by *Mr. Haynes' famous horse*, a son of *Old Bulstrode* (identifiable as *Bulstrode Bald Horse 93*). *Staffordshire Hero* would have been foaled in 1806 which does not quite tally with the date of 1800 given by the first Stud-book [29]. *Hean's Horse* is also given by Chivers as the sire of *Staffordshire Hero*, Hean being a 'mystery man'. Mr. 'Hean's' can be partly identified, as Mr. Haynes. A weathy gentleman of Ashbourne, Thomas Hartshorn [1741 -1822] bred *Staffordshire Hero* [19]. The same advertisement also featured a horse *called Match'em,* rising three years old. He was said to have been got by *Sweet William,* which covered seven seasons at Calton Moor. (This horse was likely to have been *Sweet William 2084*). The breeder of *Match'em,* Joseph Edge [1788 - 1849] lived at an isolated farmstead called the Acre, in Leek parish. **Table 2** (page 31) records Edge's *Conqueror* as a son of *Staffordshire Hero.* The village of Calton only emerges as a separate parish in the late 18th century, and its early parish registers are fragmentary. The baptism of John Hambleton's daughter Sarah was however recorded there in 1776. It seems that John Hambleton, senior was originally from Butterton, a Staffordshire moorland village about five miles north-east of Calton.The Hambleton family were well established in Butterton. John Hambleton married Sarah Cantrel of neighbouring Mayfield in 1766. Sarah Hambleton, thought to be his daughter, was also married at Mayfield. She married Thomas Hodgkinson in 1806. Chivers recorded a link between the names of Hambleton and Hodgkinson through the horse called *Sweet William 2084 (*foaled 1800), which was owned, firstly by Thomas Hodgkinson of Swinscoe (two miles from Calton, and in Mayfield parish), and secondly by Hambleton of Calton. *Sweet William* (Hodgkinson's, late Hambleton's) is recorded in **Table 2** (page 31).

STALLIONS,

The Property of JOHN HAMBLETON, *of Calton Moor*

TO COVER THIS SEASON,

At £1. 6s. if in Foal, 6s. it Barren, and 2s. 6d. the Groom: the 2s. 6d. to be paid at the time of Covering;

A Brown Horse of the Waggon kind, called

STAFFORDSHIRE HERO:

Brother to Mr. Styche's Brown Horse.

HE is rising 5 Years old, 15 hands 2 inches high, uncommonly wide, thort leg'd, full of Bone, and good Action: and is allowed by capital Judges to be one of the first Stallions in the County.—He was bred by Mr. Thomas Harthorn, of Afhborne, out of his noted Brown Mare, and got by Mr. Haynes' famous Horse, which is a fon of Old Bullirode, that covered at Iley Walton at Three Guineas a Mare.—He has covered 2 feafons at Calton Moor, proved himself a fure Foal-getter, and Suckers when 5 months old, have been fold from 20 to 50 Guineas each.

The above Horfe will be at the Tythe Barn near Alton, every Tuefday, ftops all night; Crofs Keys, Uttoxeter, every Wednefday, from thence through Dowridge, Church Broughton, and Rodley to Longford Inn, ftops till Thurfday Morning, returns through Shirley, Ofbafton, Wyafton, Ediafton, Clifton, and Home that Night.

Also to Cover at the same Place,

At £1. 6s. if in Foal, 6s. if Barren, and 2s. 6d. the Groom: the 2s. 6d. to be paid at the time of Covering;

A Brown Colt of the Waggon kind, called

MATCH'EM.

He is rifing 3 years old, 15 hands 3 inches high, uncommonly wide, thort leg'd, full of Bone and good Action.

He was bred by Mr. Jofeph Edge, of the Acre, out of his noted Brown Mare, and got by Sweet William, which covered 7 feafons at Calton Moor; he has covered one feafon, and proved himfelf a fure Foal-getter.

He will be at the Blackmoor's Head, Leek, every Wednefday, and one of the Horfes will be at Farwich every Friday; on Saturday at Mr. Welton's, Ipftones and the remainder of the Week at Calton Moor.

☞ Thofe who pleafe to make ufe of the above Horfes are defired to attend the Horfe Feaft on the 17th of February 1812, or pay 5s. each Mare extra.

222. **Derby Mercury** - Thursday 2 May 1811

Summerland - of Uttoxeter, Staffordshire

The Uttoxeter poet, Mary Howitt [1799-1888], writing in her autobiography, is an unexpected source of information in this context [15]. The three Quaker families of Shipley, Botham and Summerland were linked through her grandmother Rebecca Shipley [1717-1771] who first married John Summerland [1707-1749], and then as a widow, in 1755, married John Botham [1725-1807].

Joseph Summerland [1739-1808] and John Summerland [c1742-1810] were step-brothers of Mary Howitt's father, Samuel Botham [1758-1823]. Mary Howitt makes reference to her two Summerland half-uncles, both of whom were involved in horse breeding.

Joseph Summerland (who also lived in Uttoxeter) advertised stallions at stud for fox hunting and/or racing. He had a sale of stock in 1794 (advertised in the Derby Mercury, dated 13 November 1794) which included horses for fox hunting, hackney and coach horses, but also included some of the waggon, draft and cart type, in addition to cattle and sheep [5]. Joseph Summerland was in partnership with his son William until 1798 (Derby Mercury, 11 January) when they published an agreement to carry on their business separately [5]. A directory entry in 1818 described William Summerland as a butcher, grazier and mule dealer [27]. At the time of his death, in 1808, Joseph Summerland was described as a farmer and grazier.

It was John Summerland (who Mary Howitt said lived next to the Quaker meeting house in Carter Street, Uttoxeter), who gained a reputation as an owner, and perhaps breeder of 'Shires'. Chivers called him the 'Brown-horse Bakewell', although not all his horses were brown! John Summerland appears to have been a very enterprising businessman and trader in livestock. In 1809, a notification was published in the London Gazette which (on 19 July) dissolved the partnership of John Summerland of Uttoxeter and John Whitehurst, for their business as dealers in cattle and horses [5]. That John Summerland was a dealer in a variety of livestock is also revealed by a notice published in the Derby Mercury of 9 September 1784, when he issued a denial (of what may have been viewed at the time to have been unpatriotic activity) that he had purchased sheep in order to export them to France [5].

There is little evidence that John Summerland himself actually bred any horses, but he was clearly an important owner and dealer in heavy horses.

In 1778 Mr. Summerland (probably John) is said to have paid 350 guineas to Mr. Hambleton of Calton Moor (a few miles to the north, near Ashbourne, Derbyshire) for a brown stallion called *Sweet William* [4] [13]. This was a fabulous sum and a bold business venture which he was presumably confident would become profitable.

[Many years later, in 1849[297], in a sale of livestock in Herefordshire, yet another horse called *Gallimore* was advertised for sale. His pedigree was said to include the *'real old Sweet William'* which was sold for 350 guineas when 13 years old.]

Mary Howitt [15] recalled that members of the Quaker community would travel to other Meeting-houses in the area, including those at Stafford and Leek. Perhaps Mr. Summerland met Mr. Hambleton on passing through Calton Moor as he travelled to attend meetings at Leek.

According to Chivers [6], Summerland gained a tremendous reputation as a breeder with his *'Wiltshire Blind Horse'*. Chivers also noted that nothing is known of the pedigree of the *'Wiltshire Blind Horse'* and made the assertion that Summerland sent stallions from Staffordshire to Wiltshire.

A leaping advertisement (opposite) by John Summerland in 1788[100St] featured a black horse to cover at Tutbury, Staffordshire. He informed his potential customers that he had brought the horse to Staffordshire from Wiltshire (on the recommendation of the late Walter Francis, a Wiltshire dealer). In this advertisement another black horse, rising three years old was also said to be available to cover (a brother to the second horse which had stood at the same place (in Tutbury), in the previous year). The horse from Wiltshire cannot however have been the *'Wiltshire Brown Horse'*, which, as its name suggests would have been brown rather than black, but also because Summerland's *Wiltshire Brown Horse'* was apparently the sire of Ploughboy 1719, bred in 1785 at Bollen Hall, (Wilmslow), Cheshire by Occleston (Thomas Occleston) [1759-1826][29].

> *To Cover this Season, 1788,*
>
> AT the DOG and PARTRIDGE, TUTBURY, *A Black Horse, of the Cart Kind,*
> The Property of John Summerland, at One Guinea a Foal, and Five Shillings barren, and One Shilling the Man.
>
> The above Horse was recommended by the late Walter Francis, a Wiltshire Dealer, who was allow'd a competent Judge, and sent to promote a better Breed of true Cart Horses.——In Staffordshire, the above Horse has sufficiently proved himself, in general, to be one of the best Stock-Getters now known of, of the Cart Kind.
>
> Also, WILL COVER AT THE SAME PLACE,
> A THICK BONEY BLACK HORSE,
> Rising three Years old, at 12s. 6d. a Foal, and 5s. if barren, and 1s. the Man.——He is Brother to the second Horse that stood at Tutbury last Year.
>
> N. B. The Money to be collected by the Man who has the Care of the above Horses, and it is expected the same shall be paid within seven Days after the 2nd of February next, or to pay 5s. more each Mare if unpaid after that Time.

100. **Derby Mercury** - Thursday 10 April 1788

Summerland was, according to Chivers, a supplier of stallions to Cheshire from Staffordshire. Summerland's cover advertisements are relatively few. In 1791[108St] he advertised (page 68) his *Brown Horse*. The same advertisement featured his *noted Blind Horse*, and a horse sired by the *Blind Horse*. He also indicated that he had other horses available to cover.

John Summerland had a sale of stock in February 1792[109] which included several stallions. This presumably included his *Brown Horse* which was described as having been late the property of John Summerland when advertised to cover at Burton-on-Trent later in the same year[115]. Chivers recorded that *Blaze 192*, said to have been bred by Summerland in 1795 is his only entry in the Stud-book. This horse (apparently sired by Hart's *Blaze 183*) was black rather than brown. Chivers mentioned that *Blaze 192* had an alias, being also called 'the *Blind Horse.*' This is also confusing as Summerland advertised his noted *Blind Horse* in 1791[108St], clearly foaled well before 1795. Chivers regarded *Blaze 192* as being Summerland's second blind horse. We can conclude that this was the case, the *Wiltshire Blind Horse* being the first.

A stallion called *Brown George*, rising six years old, and got by Mr. Styche's old *Brown George* was advertised to cover in 1807[183]. Mr Styche's horse was, in turn was said to have been got by Mr. Summerland's old *Blind Horse.* Summerland advertised (below) his black horse called *Blaze* to cover at Uttoxeter in 1807[184,190St].

This *Blaze* was however rising 4 years old, and was therefore foaled in 1803, not 1795. According to Summerland, his horse *Blaze* was sired by a grandson of *Hart's Bald Horse* of Culloden House, and his dam by *Old Merryman*. Summerland's six year old *Gayton Brown Horse* was included in the same advertisement. Summerland claimed that his sire was *the Shirleywich horse* which was, in turn, by a son of *Bakewell's old Gee*. His dam belonged to John 'Gratton' (Gretton) of Stowe (Stowe-by-Chartley), described as '*of the Staffordshire old Brown breed of heavy cart horses'*. [Gayton is a small village about four miles north-east of Stafford, and therefore close to both Ingestre, and Marston. Stowe-by-Chartley is one mile south-east of Gayton.]

Brown Shire horses have acquired a particular association with Staffordshire, although how or when this association became established is unknown. Reynolds [29] stated that in Staffordshire the prevailing colour appears to have been brown, with horses being described as descendants of the *old brown Staffordshire breed* as early as 1806. [Evidence for this is in the above paragraph.] However, some of the earliest-known Staffordshire horses were actually black! Pitt [26], in describing horses in Staffordshire recorded that *'the draught horses are generally of the Flemish breed, in colour black or brown, and some valuable stallions are kept of either colour, but mostly black'*.

In 1809[207] Summerland, in partnership with John Whitehurst advertised *Blaze* to cover at Tutbury. Their horse *Drayman* was included in the same advertisement, available to cover at Uttoxeter, together with another '*capital brown horse*', said to be of the '*Staffordshire or Ingestree old brown breed*'.

Chivers [6] recorded that Summerland also had a stallion called *Drayman* which had reached its twenty hundred-weight by the time it was four. This seems to be borne out by John Summerland's cover advertisement (opposite) in 1805[160St] in which he described his horse from Amberley, called *Drayman,* rising 5 years old, as '*one of the thickest horses known'*. An 1814[248] advertisement revealed that *Drayman* had been owned by a fellow Quaker, John Lister [1762 - 1813] of Amberley Farm, near Pentrich, Derbyshire. Another cover advertisement, in 1815[256St] (below) confirmed that *Drayman* weighed one ton when in the hands of John Summerland.

Drayman was also said to have been from the breed of his *old Wiltshire Blind Horse* recommended by the late Walter 'Frances' (probably Walter Francis [1749 -1784] of Ramsbury, Wiltshire).

Chivers also referred to 'the '*Wiltshire Blind Horse*', seemly to imply that this horse and the '*Wiltshire Brown Horse*' were one and the same. However, Summerland's advertisement (page 68) in 1791[108St] indicates that his *Brown Horse* and his *Blind Horse* were different horses. The advertisements also imply that *the Wiltshire Blind Horse* was black! It would appear that Summerland obtained more than one horse from Wiltshire. *Summerland's Wiltshire Horse* also featured in the pedigree of a black colt called *Bulstrode* advertised (page 91) to cover in 1808[202De] at Over Haddon in Derbyshire, and again similarly in 1812[230].

John Summerland may have traded widely, but why Wiltshire? There was perhaps a connection through his uncle Thomas Shipley [1733-1794], a farmer originally from Uttoxeter who later lived, and died in Zeals, Wiltshire.

A final comment on (John) Summerland concerns the apparent link with the village of Ingestre (about four miles east of Stafford). Chivers [6] referred to '*Mr. Summerland of Ingestre*' as having bought *Sweet William* from Mr. Hambleton in 1778, and also '*Summerland's Brown Horse of the Ingestre Breed'*. There seems to be no

160. **Derby Mercury** - Thursday 14 March 1805

http://www.britishnewspaperarchive.co.uk/viewer/bl/000005 2/18050314/002/0001

256. **Derby Mercury** - Thursday 11 May 1815

http://www.britishnewspaperarchive.co.uk/viewer/bl/000005 2/18150511/003/0001

evidence of a direct link between the Summerland family and Ingestre; in 1778 they were living in Uttoxeter. Samuel Botham, who was Mary Howitt's father, and half-brother to John and Joseph Summerland was a surveyor of some reputation and is said to have been, 'constantly employed' by Earl Talbot of Ingestre Hall, but this was at a later date [15].

Information contained within an advertisement in 1798[141St] (page 80) for a sale of horses at Shirleywich, near Stafford does provide some link, not with Ingestre, but with a place close by. The horses belonged to Mr. Preston Moore of Shirleywich which is a village within one mile of Ingestre.

Lot 1 in the sale was a stallion, rising 8 years old 'out of a famous mare, own sister to Mr Summerland's late best brown horse, which was sold for three hundred and fifty guineas, bred at Shirleywich, and got by Mr. Webb's old brown horse at Marston'.

Summerland may not have been of Ingestre, but could this explain why Summerland's 'best brown horse' (bred at Shirleywich) was described as having been 'of the Ingestre Breed'? The question also arises - was this also a reference to Sweet William, the horse which Summerland purchased for 350 guineas ? A further implication would be that Sweet William was sired by a horse belonging to Webb of Marston (page 76)!

Stych - of Bellamore (Great Haywood), Barton-under-Needwood, Staffordshire [and Stenson, Derbyshire]

The name of Stych (or Styche) was linked with Stenson (a small township about five miles south of Derby) by Chivers [6], but the family were originally from Staffordshire, with strong connections to a place called Bellamour or Bellamore, Great Haywood which is about four miles east of the county town of Stafford, and perhaps more significantly, within two miles of Ingestre. William Stych [c1766-1853], who at his death was living at Stenson was born at Bellamore, the son of John Stych. Bellamore Hall was owned by Sir Walter Blount, and inherited by his wife Mary from her father Lord Aston of nearby Tixall. Walter Blount lived in Shropshire. John Stych took over from his father as tenant at Bellamore Hall, then used as a farm, in 1770. A document in the Blount papers [28], dated 1772 makes reference to (John) Stych vacating a farm in his holding at 'Caulton' i.e. Colton, a village about two miles east of Bellamore. The run-down condition of Bellamore Hall was indicated by a number of letters written in the 1770s by Sir Walter to his attorney in which he complained about the cost of proposed improvements [28]. It seems the Stychs, like the Aston family of Tixall were Catholics, as the attached Bellamore chapel was a Roman Catholic chapel. John Stych's children, including his two sons William and John were all born at Bellamore, his last child being born there in about 1783.

Chivers [6] made reference to 'Stych's Brown Horse', foaled in 1790 or earlier as being 'descended from the Ingestre Stud'. Another reference occurs in an 1812[233St] cover advertisement (page 71) placed by John Chadwick for his stallion Little John, formerly owned by Styche. 'Stych's Old Brown Horse of the Ingestrie Breed' was described as being the sire of the dam of Little John, and also of the dam of the six year old stallion Merryman adverted by Chadwick (page 73) to cover at the same place. Merryman was said to have been got by Mr. Massey's noted old horse Merryman.

The first Stud-book records Stych of Stenson as being the owner of Merryman 1552, foaled in 1805, although his sire is given as Bakewell's G 890. Possible Ingestre connections have been discussed above, but the Stych family could also have had links to Ingestre. While no record has been found of any Ingestre Stud, Stych's Brown Horse could have originated or had descent from within the Ingestre area. John Stych [1737-1822] or his sons William [c1768 - 1853] or John [c1770 -   ], or other members of the Stych family may have been owners and/or breeders of this horse.

There seems little to connect Stych with Summerland until a cover advertisement in 1807[183] for a brown horse called Brown George, rising six years old. He was said to have been got by

Mr. Styche's old Brown George, which horse was, in turn, got by *Mr. Summerland's old Blind Horse.*

The Stych family involvement in 'Shire' breeding occurred over a long period, from 1790 or earlier, and into the 1850s, and as Chivers pointed out, more than one generation must have been involved. William Stych was married at Mayfield (near Ashbourne) in 1793. At some stage he moved to Barton-under-Needwood (near Burton-upon-Trent), his daughter, Ann having being baptised there in 1797. He married again in 1805 and three sons were baptised at Barton-under-Needwood between 1807 and 1815. In the 1818 Directory of Staffordshire Willam Stych was described as a maltster and cattle dealer, living at Barton-under-Needwood [27]. It is not known when he moved to Stenson but his son, William Stych [1807-1839] was resident in Stenson at the time of his marriage in 1829, when William Stych, senior was recorded as still living at Barton. Both of them were however living at Stenson by 1835, the year in which the Register of Electors for Twyford and Stenson listed William Stych and William Stych, junior [7]. William Stych, senior was recorded in the censuses of 1841 and 1851 living at Stenson a substantial farm of over 300 acres. He died in 1853, but his son John Stych [1815-1868] was listed in the 1857 Directory of Derbyshire as living at Stenson [32].

Chivers [6] commented on the considerable contribution made to 'Shire' breeding by the Stych family. However, any links to Ingestre must link to a period well before 1800, and remain a mystery.

'*Stych's Brown Horse*' is recorded as the sire of the dam of *Derbyshire 577*, in turn the son of the celebrated Lincolnshire stallion, *Honest Tom 1062* [29].

TO COVER THIS SEASON,
At JOHN CHADWICK's, of GRINDON,
In the county of Stafford,
A Dark Brown Horse, of the Cart Kind, called
LITTLE JOHN,
At Two Guineas each Mare if in Foal, Half-a-Guinea Barren, and One Shilling the Groom.
(Late the Property of Mr. Styche, in whose hands he has covered Six Seasons,)

HE was out of a capital Brown Mare belonging to Mr. Hartshorn of Ashborne, which was got by Mr. Styche's noted old Brown Horse, of the Old Ingestrie breed; he was got by Mr. Shaw's Old noted Horse, called Farmer's Glory, which was got by Mr. Bulstrode's Old Horse, that covered 14 Seasons at Three Guineas a Mare.—He is warranted a sure Foal-getter, and is allowed by competent Judges, to be one of most superior shortest leg'd, and fullest of Bone and Hair, of any Horse that is known of his kind; & is allowed to have gotten the most valuable Stock of any Horse in these parts of the Kingdom.

Little John will be at Mr. Downes', the Bell Inn, in Ashborne, on Friday Night and Saturday during the Season, and the rest of the Week at Home.

Also at the same Place,
PACKINGTON,
At £1. 11s. 6d. each Mare, if in Foal, and 10s. 6d. Barren.
(Late the Property of Mr. Clarkson, of Breedon, in the county of Leicester.)

He was got by Mr. Radford's Blaze, Blaze by Bulstrode's Old Horse; his Dam by a Mare of Mr. Donnisthorpe's of Packington, by his Old Horse, which was got by Mr. Bulstrode's Old Ball'd Horse; the Dam of Mr. Donnisthorpe's Old Horse by the Packington Blind Horse.

Also to Cover at the same Place,
A Black Horse, of the Cart Kind, called
MERRYMAN,
At £1. 5s. each Mare if in Foal, 5s. Barren, & 1s. the Groom.

He is 6 years old, and is 16 hands and a half high, full of bone, and his action will speak for itself.—His Dam was got by Mr. Styche's Old Brown Horse, of the Ingestrie breed; he was got by Mr. Massey's noted Old Horse, Merryman; has proved himself a sure Foal-getter, and his Stock will always find their road to a good Market.

Merryman, will be at Longnor, on Tuesdays; at John Smith's, Blackshaw-Moor, every Tuesday Night; at Mr. Lowndes', the Buck and Plough, in Leek; on Wednesdays; and the rest of the Week at Home, during the Season.

☞ Those who please to make use of the above Horses, are desired to attend the Horse Feast on the 14th Day of February, 1813, or they will be charged 5s. each Mare, extra.

N. B. Good Grass for Mares at 6s. per Week, and proper care taken of them.

The Groom's Fee to be paid at the time of Covering.

233. **Derby Mercury** - Thursday 23 April 1812

Chivers also mentioned *Dumpling 679* (foaled 1810), bred and owned by Stych, and *Invincible 1138* (foaled 1816), his dam having bred by Chadwick by '*Stych's Old Chestnut Horse*'. Much later Stud-book records [29] are for *Bang-Up 94* (foaled 1834), bred and owned by Stych of Stenson, and *Bang-Up 95* (foaled 1844) and owned by Stych. The sire of *Bang-Up 94* was recorded as having been a stallion called *Sancho 1993*, said by Chivers to have been a grey horse but whose pedigree was muddled. However, an advertisement (page 95) in 1832[284De] featuring *Sancho* described him as a rich bay, and a cart horse of the '*Flemish Breed*', rising

8 years old (also foaled in 1824, not 1829). Also in 1832[284De], Mr. Bancroft owned *Sancho*. Stych of Stenson is recorded in the first Stud-book [29] as the owner of the brown stallion *Derbyshire Hero 588*, foaled in 1846, and sired by *Bang-Up 94*. The executors of the late William Styche held a sale of farm stock at Stenson in 1847[294]. A number of heavy horses were included in the sale, including two sired by *Sancho*. [Why this sale took place in 1847 is unexplained. William Styche, junior had died in 1839.]

An 1849[295St] cover advertisement (below) for a horse called *Barton*, rising 5 years old claimed that he was got by *Mr. Hinckley's Brown horse, Invincible*, and that *Invincible* was got by the noted horse of Mr. Styche's of Stenson called *Bang-Up*. This was clearly another horse called *Invincible*.

William Stych, senior [c1768 -1853] seems likely to have been the main 'Shire' breeder. The involvement of his son John Stych [1815-1868] is implied by a bankruptcy notice in the London Gazette of June 12 1866 which described John Stych of Stenson as a dealer in cattle and horses, and a cattle and sheep salesman [5]. William Stych, senior's brother John Stych [c1770 -   ] did not live at Stenson or Barton-under-Needwood, and is thought to have lived at Colwich, near to the old family home at Bellamore. He is therefore not likely to have contributed to 'Shire' breeding, unless it was in an earlier period, before 1800.

Hinckley - of Colton, Staffordshire

Chivers [6] made reference to an important partnership between Thomas Hinckley of Colton, near Rugeley and his brother-in-law 'Styche'. Thomas Hinckley [1783 -1861] married Teresa Stych at Gayton, near Stafford in 1809. Teresa Hinckley [c1786 -1859] is believed to have been the sister of William Stych, senior and his brother John. This information reinforces the view that it was William Stych, senior who was the major contributor to 'Shire' breeding activity, as he would have been the brother-in-law of Thomas Hinckley. Interestingly, Thomas and Teresa's children were also baptised at the Bellamore chapel. The 1841 census reveals that the Hinckley family were living at Lount House, Colton, which is about two miles east of Bellamore. Chivers [6] noted the practice of Thomas Hinckley and his brother-in-law (probably William Stych) of exchanging horses, and also changing their names. He gave the example of the stallion which was called *Derbyshire Hero* (*Derbyshire Hero 588*) when travelling for, or when let by, Stych of Stenson.

When in Thomas Hinckley's hands this stallion was called *Staffordshire Hero* (*Staffordshire Hero 2057*).

Chivers stated that by the 1840s and 1850s Hinckley had found fame, and had taken over from Chadwick as the best-known 'Shire' man in Staffordshire.

Mr. Hinckley's Brown horse, *Invincible* was described as the sire of a stallion called *Barton*, advertised (opposite) to cover at Derby in 1849[295St].

The Stud-book [29] records Hinckley as

DERBY.

VALUABLE BROWN STALLION CALLED BARTON,

The Property of Mr. ARTHUR SKEVINGTON, Barton-house,

TO BE SOLD BY AUCTION,

By ROWLAND BREAREY,

IN THE MORLEDGE, DERBY,

On FRIDAY, March 2nd, 1849, at 12 o'clock.

BARTON is a Dark Brown Horse of the Cart kind, with superior action, rising 5 years old, stands 16 hands 3 inches high, and is warranted sound and a sure foal getter.

He was got by Mr. Hinckley's Brown Horse, Invincible. Invincible was got by that noted Horse of Mr. Styche's, of Stenson, called Bang-Up, out of a favourite Brown Mare of Mr. Henshaw's, of Aston.

Barton and his dam took the premium for the best Mare with a Foal at her foot at the South Derbyshire Agricultural Show, held at Ashbourn in 1844.

Derby, February 9th, 1849.

295. **Derby Mercury** - Wednesday 14 February 1849

having been the owner and breeder of *Honest Ben 1049*, foaled in 1853. The stallion *Champion 419*, otherwise known as *Stych's Champion* seems to have been the crowning glory of the Stych-Hinckley partnership [6]. He sired the mare *Flower*, the dam of that most celebrated stallion, *Harold*, and of sons who in turn became leading sires in Derbyshire in the 1860s (although, by this date William Stych was dead, and it was probably his son John who selected this stallion). *Styche's Champion* is recorded as having been foaled in 1855 [29], but in a report in the Derby Mercury, dated 8 October 1851, giving the results of the North Staffordshire Agricultural Society exhibition of stock, Thomas Hinckley's grey horse *Champion*, aged 3 years and 4 months was placed second in the class for best stallion. Assuming this was the same horse, he would therefore have been foaled in 1848!

Chadwick - of Grindon, Staffordshire

John Chadwick [1755 -1832] of the upland village of Grindon in North Staffordshire, was regarded by Chivers as the greatest name in the history of Shire horse breeding prior to 1880. This was based on the fact that 24 of his stallions were recorded in Volume I of the Stud-book [29].

Chivers [6] reported that John Chadwick inherited the stallion business from his father, and was of the opinion that the business had been in the family for many generations. John Chadwick was a son of George and Elizabeth Chadwick, from within a very extensive wider Chadwick family. A notice in the Derby Mercury of 10 July 1772 recorded that George Chadwick was living at the Bull's Head, in Grindon [5].

George Chadwick [1729-1801] placed a cover advertisement (opposite) in 1786[89St] featuring a black horse of the cart kind called *Young Bumper*, said to have been got by *Mr. Harrison's Old Bumper*.

Chivers referred to a horse called *Bumper* (of unknown origin) as the sire of *Ruler 1905*, said to have been bred by Joseph Webb of Marston in 1773. Chivers suggested that the first of the stallions listed in the Stud-book under the Chadwick name, *Drayman 603*, (foaled 1790) was probably owned by John Chadwick's father.

The earliest newspaper advertisement in which John Chadwick's name appears seems to be that (opposite) in 1803[148St], featuring a horse called *Regulator*, which he had formerly owned. *Regulator* was said to have been got by *Tom*. His dam was said to have been by *Bumper*, presumably the same *Bumper* mentioned above.

Chadwick advertised (page 74) his black stallion *Marston* and brown colt *Bulstrode* (a full brother to *Marston*) in 1804[155St]. *Marston* was described as rising 5 years old, indicating he was foaled in 1799 (which is at odds with

To **COVER** this **SEASON,** 1786, AT George Chadwick's, in Grindon, Staffordshire, at 15s. a Foal, and 5s. barren;

Young **BUMPER;**

A remarkable boney black Horse, of the Cart Kind, got by Mr. Harrison's Old Bumper, out of his best Mare, that bred so many famous Stallions. He has got several fine Stallions, and gets excellent Stock, many of which may be seen in the Neighbourhood of Stafford, as well as in and about Grindon.

Likewise, A BLACK COLT, rising two Years old, to Cover at the same Place; he was got by Young Bumper, allowed by good Judges to be a very capital Colt; at One Guinea a Foal, and 5s. barren.

N. B. Those who please to make use of the above Horses, are desired to attend the Horse Feast the 14th February, 1787, or they will be charged One Guinea a Foal each Horse.

89. **Derby Mercury** - Thursday 23 March 1786
http://www.britishnewspaperarchive.co.uk/viewer/bl/0000189/17860323/006/0001

STALLIONS.

TO COVER THIS SEASON, 1803, AT GEORGE WALL's, Barton Fields, near Long-ford, in the County of Derby, at One Guinea and a Half a Mare; and 2s. 6d. the Groom,

THE OLD BLACK HORSE CALLED

REGULATOR,

Late the Property of John Chadwick, of Grindon, Staffordshire,

He was got by Tom, his Dam by Bumper; stands 16 Hands high, uncommonly Wide, short Leg'd, full of Bone, and very Active.— His Stock need no Comment, as they are such as will always find the way to a good Market.

He has Covered Eight Seasons at Grindon.

ALSO, AT THE SAME PLACE,

A BROWN COLT,

At One Guinea a Mare, and 2s. 6d. the Groom.

N. B. The Money to be paid at the time of Covering, or at Midsummer next.

148. **Derby Mercury** - Thursday 7 April 1803
http://www.britishnewspaperarchive.co.uk/viewer/bl/0000052/18030407/005/0002

the Stud-book date of 1791 given for *Marston 1486*). Chadwick claimed that *Marston* was bred by Webb of Marston, and got by *the Pave-Lane Horse* called *King Tom.* He also gave details of the dam's pedigree, going back to *the Packington old horse.* 'Marson' (meaning *Marston*) was advertised to cover again in 1805[169]. Chadwick gave similar detail to that provided in the previous year. Chadwick's stallion *Marston* was mentioned as the sire of a black horse called *King Tom* in an 1805[162] cover advertisement (and similarly in 1806[174St] (below) and 1809[206]). The same advertisement referred to *Chadwick's Old Tom* as the sire of the grandam of *King Tom.* [*Old Tom* was presumably the horse owned by Chadwick which was said to be the sire of *Regulator*, adverted (page 73) in 1803[148].] A similar advertisement for *Marston* appeared in the Chester Chronicle of 14 February 1806, the stallion then being in the ownership of Samuel Jones of Poulton, near Chester who advertised *Marston* to cover for the 1806 season in Cheshire [5]. [Samuel Jones of Poulton is recorded in the first Stud-book [29] as the breeder of *Derbyshire Hero 587*, foaled in 1813 and sired by *Marston 1486*.]

Marston (*Marston 1486*) was said to have been sold by, or bought by Chadwick for 500 guineas. *Bulstrode 348*, also owned by Chadwick was said to have been let, in 1806 for 100 guineas, and for 150 guineas in the following year. These last two horses alone, both bred by Webb (page 76) were it seems very profitable for John Chadwick [6].

Chadwick also advertised his stallion *Farmers's Glory* in 1805[170]. He was said to have been rising 4 years old, and like *Marston*, bred by Webb of Marston. It was also claimed that he been got by *Old Gallimore* (*Gallimore* 903), with *Old Gallimore,* in turn, having been sired by *Mansetter. Farmer's Glory's* dam was by *Old Tom* and his grandam by *Bakewell's Old G.* From his pedigree details *Farmer's Glory* can be identified as *Farmer's Glory 808.*

Table 2 (page 31) similarly recorded Chadwick's *Farmer Glory* as having been sired by Moore's *Old Gallimore* (*Gallimore 903*). However, *Farmer's Glory 808* is recorded in the first Stud-book as a son of *Gallimore 904* [29].

John Chadwick advertised (page 75) his stallion Farmer's *Glory* again in 1807[192S] together with

155. **Derby Mercury** - Friday 12 April 1804

174. **Derby Mercury** - Thursday 3 April 1806

Young Packington, which was formerly owned by Clarkson of Breedon, Leicestershire. (*Young) Packington* was given an impressive pedigree with well-known earlier breeders including Donisthorpe and Bulstrode being mentioned, and inevitably *the Packington Blind Horse* being claimed as his earliest ancestor. Usefully in this advertisement, Mr. Webb, the breeder of *Farmer's Glory* was said to be of Marston, near Stafford.

Young Packington was advertised again in 1808[201], this time together with *Bulstrode*, described as a full brother to *Marston*. *Bulstrode* can be identified as Chadwick's horse *Bulstrode 348*.

In 1811[221] John Chadwick advertised *Packington* (formerly *Young Packington*), identifiable as *Packington 1703*, together with his black horse *Regulator*, but he was rising five years old (and clearly not the same *Regulator* advertised in 1803[148St], page 73). *Regulator* was said to have been by *Marston*. In this advertisement Chadwick said that at different times he had been offered 500 guineas for *Marston*. With *Packington*, in 1812[233St], Chadwick also advertised (page 71) *Little John* (a brown horse) and a six year old black horse called *Merryman*.

Mr. 'Styche' was named as the former owner of *Little John*. The dam of *Little John* was said to have been got by Mr. Stych's *'noted Old Brown Horse, of the Old Ingestrie breed'*, whilst his sire was claimed to have been *Mr. Shaw's old horse*, called *Farmer's Glory*. Two horses called *Little John* are listed in the Stud-book [29] under John Chadwick's name. The one advertised in 1812[233St] fits the description of *Little John 1401*, except that a foaling date of 1818 is recorded. According to the advertisement, *Little John* had covered six seasons when in the hands of his former owner, Mr. Styche, suggesting that he cannot have been foaled later than about 1803. Chadwick advertised *Little John* again in 1814[250], together with his son, the rising two year old brown colt *Robin Hood* (*Robin Hood 1863*); as recorded in **Table 2** (page 31).

'Marston*'*, advertised at the same time, was said to have been got by *Chadwick's Old 'Marstone'*, and out of a dam by *Shaw's Old Horse*, and was presumably *Marston 1488*, although his dam is recorded by Chivers as having been got by *Farmer's Glory 807* [6].

The dam of *Merryman* was also said to have been got by *Mr. Stych's old Brown horse*, his sire being in this case *Mr. Massey's old Horse Merryman*. *Massey's Merryman* may have been *Merryman 1548*, bred and owned in 1800 by William Massey of '*Birchall Moor*' [29].

Little John was advertised by Chadwick again in 1815[257], this time with *Young Packington* (*Packington 1704*), a son of his horse *Packington* (*Packington 1703*).

John Chadwick was very successful over a long period of time. Nineteen of the 24 stallions which belonged to him are recorded as having foaled between 1790 and 1820 [6].

The suggestion that John Chadwick owned *Honest Ben 1046* (foaled 1833), and that he bred and owned *Ben 120* (foaled 1840), cannot be true, as he had died in 1832 [29]. It would, however, have been surprising if some other member of the extensive Chadwick family had not continued in the business. In 1791, at Leek, John Chadwick married Ann Edge, a cousin of Joseph Edge of the Acre (page 66), John and Ann Chadwick had two daughters, Elizabeth and Mary, and one son William, all baptised at Grindon.

TO COVER THIS SEASON,

AT John Chadwick's, of Grindon, in the County of Stafford, a Black Horse of the Cart Kind, called YOUNG PACKINGTON, At One Guinea and a Half a Foal, and 10s. 6d. Barren, late the property of Mr. Clarkson, of Breedon, in the County of Leicester.

He was got by Mr. Radford's Blaze, Blaze by Bulstrode's Old Horse, his dam by a Mare of Mr. Donisthorpe, of Packington, by his Old Horse, which was got by Mr. Bulstrode's Old bald Horse, the dam of Mr. Donisthorpe's Old Horse by the Packington Blind Horse.

He has covered eight Seasons at Breedon, and his Stock is no ways inferior to any Horse of the kind in this kingdom.

Also to Cover at the same place, A Black Horse of the Cart Kind, called FARMERS GLORY, At 11. 6s. a Foal, and 6s. Barren.

He is rising 6 years old, 16 hands 1 inch high, he was bred by Mr. Webb, of Marston, near Stafford, got by Old Gallimoor, Gallimoor by Manfetter, his dam by Tom, his grandam by Bulstrode's Old Horse of Isley Walton, Leicestershire, which covered 13 Seasons at 3l. 3s. a Mare, and his great grandam by Bakewell's Old G. of Dishley, which covered at 5l. 5s. a Mare; he is an uncommon sure foal-getter, and his stock always finds the first Markets.

Farmers Glory will be at the Black's Head, Leek, every Wednesday, and the remainder of the Week at Home.

☞ Those who please to make use of the above Horses are desired to attend the Horse Feast the 15th February, 1808, or they will be charged 5s. each Mare extra.

192. **Derby Mercury** - Thursday 14 May 1807

John Chadwick's son, William inherited land at Grindon, and continued in the family business as a 'Shire' owner [19]. William Chadwick [1794 - 1844] lived at Grindon, but also also Totmonslow (near Draycott in the Moors, Staffordshire) [19]. He is recorded in the Stud-book [29] as being the owner of the grey Shire stallion called *Britain's Hero*, foaled in 1824, and also *Little David 1397*, foaled in 1828. William Chadwick married Ann Ginders in 1820. She was the daughter of Joseph Ginders [1730 - 1809], a gentleman farmer of Lockwood Hall, Kingsley, recorded (page 77), in 1807[188St], as the breeder of the stallion called *Lockwood*! William and Ann Chadwick had at least ten children, some of whom may have continued in the Shire-breeding tradition. Chivers [6] recorded that the last horse owned by one of the Chadwick family was *Lord Byron* (foaled in 1870).

Just how long the Chadwick family had been in the 'Shire business' cannot be known but there is evidence of this activity even before the involvement of celebrated John Chadwick and his father George. An earlier John Chadwick [1704-1771] is also buried in Grindon churchyard. His gravestone records that's he was of Braden Brook, an apparent corruption or variation of Black Brook, a small habitation near Mixon, about 2½ miles north-west of Grindon. He and his wife Sarah had a number of children, baptised at Grindon between 1727 and 1738.

This John Chadwick was distantly related to the more famous one. The later John Chadwick's grandfather, William Chadwick was first cousin to this earlier John Chadwick.

John Chadwick of Blackbrook is recorded (pages 124,125) as owing 'leaping money' to Samuel Gallimore of Wootton following the death of the latter in 1750 [19].

Webb - of Marston, Stafford, Staffordshire

Webb was said to have been the most noted breeder in the county of Derbyshire.

This view relied upon the memories of long past events, but it seems that compilers of the first Stud-book were convinced that this was true [29].

Chivers [6] noted that they confidently recorded a stallion called *Ruler* had been bred by Webb of Marston in 1773, and that *Ruler* had been sired by a horse called *Bumper*. Chivers particularly noted the lack of information about *Bumper*, although in 1786[89St] George Chadwick advertised (page 73) a horse called *Young Bumper*, got by *Mr. Harrison's Old Bumper*.

This, at least indicates that *Bumper* was bred and/or owned by a Mr. Harrison.

An advertisement (opposite) placed in 1807[189St] by William Burnett [1756 -1832], brother-in-law of the above John Chadwick, was for a horse called *Censurer*.

It confirmed that Mr. Webb of Marston had bred *(Old) Ruler*, and that *(Old) Ruler* was got by *Bumper*. [*Ruler* was also recorded as the sire of a horse called *Honest John*, advertised to cover in 1806[179] by a noted breeder, Richard Gibbs [1758 -1841] of of Tissington, Derbyshire. Richard Gibbs bred and owned *Little John 1398*, his sire having been *Ruler 1906* [6].

Webb is also recorded [29] as having bred *King Tom 1260* (foaled in 1786), a horse owned later by Mr. Handley of Pave Lane. (page 83).

Webb is also credited with having bred two famous horses, *Marston 1486* and *Bulstrode 348*, both sons of *King Tom 1260*, who was

THIS SEASON,

AT Mr. Wm. Burnett's, Grindon, Staffordshire, at 17s. 6d. a Foal, and 5s. Barren, a Black Horse of the waggon kind, called CENSURER.—He is rising 4 years old, 15 hands 3 inches high, uncommonly wide, short legg'd, full of bone and hair, and is a capital Horse of his age. He has covered one Season, is a sure Foal-getter, and his Stock is much approved of as suckers. He was bred by Mr. Hodgkinson, of Kniveton, Derbyshire, got by that capital horse Little John, the property of Mr. Gibbs, of Tissington, his dam was got by a famous horse called Ball, which covered at Cobley, Derbyshire. Little John was got by Mr. Wagstaff's old horse called Ruler, Ruler's dam by Ball, which was got by Bullstrode's old horse of Isley Walton, Leicestershire. Little John's dam by a Son of the Old Packington horse. Ruler was bred by Mr. Chatterton, of Ashburn Lodge, and was got by Old Ruler, which was bred by Mr. Webb, of Marston; Old Ruler was got by Bumper.

Those who please to make use of the above Horse, are desired to attend the Horse Feast the 6th of April, 1808, or they will be charged five shillings each Mare extra.

189. **Staffordshire Advertiser** - Saturday 25 April 1807

also called *the Pave Lane horse*. He is also said to have bred *Farmer's Glory 808*. All three of these horses, perhaps significantly, were owned by John Chadwick.

Mr. Webb's old brown horse of Marston was referred to as the sire of *Mr. Summerland's 'best brown horse'* within descriptions of one of the horses which were advertised (page 80) to be sold by auction in 1798[141St]. [This, as discussed (page 70), may have been a reference suggesting that the horse sired by Webb's horse was Summerland's *Sweet William*.]

The horses had belonged to Mr Preston Moore of Shirleywich and were for sale following his death. Preston Moore had advertised the same horse as being available to cover, in similar advertisements placed in the Staffordshire Advertiser for 18 April 1795 and 22 April 1797 [5].

No further newspaper advertisements mentioning either Webb or Handley have been found before 1804[155St], when John Chadwick advertised *Marston* and *Bulstrode* (page 74).

Marston was said to have been bred by Mr. Webb of Marston, and got by the *Pave-Lane Horse* called *King Tom*. In 1805[169, 170], John Chadwick advertised both '*Marson*' and *Farmer's Glory*, both having been bred by Webb of Marston. '*Marson*' (presumably *Marston*) was described as having been got by *the noted Pave-Lane Horse,* called *King Tom* while *Farmer's Glory* was said to have been got by *Old Gallimore*, with his dam being by *King Tom*. Another advertisement (page 75) for *Farmer's Glory*, in 1807[192St], claims that he was bred by Mr. Webb of Marston, near Stafford.

Chivers was unsure about where Mr Webb lived. Because, on occasion Webb is recorded 'of Staffordshire', Chivers suggested that Webb lived at either Marston Montgomery or Marston on Dove, as both Derbyshire villages are near the border with Staffordshire. The true Marston lies about two miles north of Stafford.

Also in 1807[188St], a cover advertisement (below) by John Fallows [1743 -1811], a wealthy yeoman, for a horse, rising four years old called *Lockwood* (identifiable as *Lockwood G 1418*), got by Chadwick's *Marson* of Grindon, provides confirmation that *Marson* was got by the *Pave-Lane horse, King Tom*. It was also stated that the dam of *King Tom* was Webb's own '*noted brown horse'*. Similar information was supplied by John Chadwick when he advertised *Bulstrode* in 1808[201]. [The Stud-book [29] records a foaling date of 1799 for *Lockwood G 1418*. It is however clear from the advertisement in 1807[188St] that *Lockwood* was foaled in 1803.]

The eight year old *Young Marston*, son of *Marston* was advertised to cover in 1812[226]. Once again it was stated that *Marston* was sired by the noted *Pave Lane horse*.

So who was Mr Webb? It is now clear that he lived at Marston, near Stafford (and doubtless the horse *Marston* which he bred was named after that place).

Webb's horse-breeding activities indicate close connections with the Chadwick family of Grindon. Supporting evidence is provided in the will, dated 1801, of George Chadwick (father of John Chadwick), in which he described William Webb of Marston as his friend, and appointed him as an executor, jointly with his wife Elizabeth Chadwick [19].

'Mr. Webb of Marston' can be identified as Joseph Webb [1730 – 1802], who had sons, William Webb [1762 -1845] and Joseph Webb, junior [1766 - 1839]. Joseph Webb was born in Lapley, Staffordshire, the Webb family being well-to-do gentlemen farmers who lived around Lapley and Church Eaton, villages which are

STALLIONS.

THIS SEASON,

A Black Horse, of the Waggon Kind, called
LOCKWOOD,

THE property of JOHN FALLOWS, of Booth-Hall, near Cheadle, at One Pound Five Shillings a Foal, and Six Shillings Barren, rising four years old, sixteen hands one inch high, uncommonly wide, short legg'd, full of bone, and hair, and is allowed by competent judges to be one of the most compleat and active waggon horses of his age in the kingdom. He has covered two Seasons at Booth-Hall, and is an uncommon sure foal getter, and his stock very promising. He was bred by Mr. Ginders, of Lockwood, and got by Mr. Chadwick's Marson, of Grindon, which was got by that noted Pave-lane Horse, called King Tom, which was got by Mr. Webb's noted brown horse, his dam by Mr. Rushton's old horse, which was got by Massey's g- his great grandam by Ball, which was got by Bulstrode's old horse, of Isley Walton, Leicestershire; his great, great grandam by old Merryman, and his great great great granriam by the Packington old horse.

He will be at the Black Swan, in Leek, every Wednesday; and all other days at Booth-Hall, during the Season.

close to the Shropshire county boundary. Joseph Webb's nephew, Humphrey Webb lived at Orslow, in the parish of Church Eaton. It is likely that the Webb family of Orslow would have been acquainted with the Handley family (page 83), who lived less than three miles away at Pave Lane, near Newport. Joseph Webb was living at Fole, in Leigh parish, near Uttoxeter when his sons were born, but later moved to the Stafford area where he had a (half-) brother, John Webb [19]. The Staffordshire Advertiser, 5 September 1795 listed Joseph Webb, William Webb, and Joseph Webb, junior as having been issued with game certificates in Staffordshire during that year. All three were described as being gentlemen of Marston [5].

'Mr. Webb, an eminent farmer' was recorded in the Staffordshire Advertiser, dated 2 October 1802, as having died at Marston, at the age of 72 [5]. A burial record for 30 September, at Seighford (2½ miles south-west of Marston) shows that it was Joseph Webb who had died [5]. William Webb later moved to Clownholme, in the parish of Doveridge, near Uttoxeter, having married Lydia Orme in 1796, only child of Thomas Wharton Orme (page 120) [19].

Perkin - of Whitgreave, Stafford, Staffordshire

The small township of Whitgreave lies about one mile to the west of Marston, Stafford where the Webb family lived. Joseph Webb, junior, formerly of Marston was also, at the time of his death, living at Whitgreave [19]. They were near neighbours, but there is no known evidence of any horse-breeding activities which directly linked the Webb and Perkin families.

Chivers [6] made just one reference to Perkin of Whitgreave, believed to be the breeder and owner of *Gallimore 904* (said to have foaled in 1790, although perhaps a few years later). An auction sale of farming stock near Trentham, Staffordshire in 1808[193] included two draught mares which were in foal by *Mr. Perkin's horse Gallimore*. This is the earliest known reference to Perkin's *Gallimore* (*Gallimore* 904), (**Table 1**, page 22), a stallion which the first Stud-book, and **Table 2** (page 30) both record as having been sired by *Moore's Gallimore* (*Gallimore 903*)[29].

In 1814[245, 246St] a black horse called *Young Gallimore* was advertised (below) to cover in Cheshire. He was said to have been got by *Mr. Perkin's Gallimore* of 'White Grave' (Whitgreave), near Stafford. His dam was said to have been by *Old Kirby*.

TO COVER THIS SEASON, 1814,

At Halton, near Warrington, at one Guinea each Mare, and two Shillings and Sixpence the Groom: (the money to be paid at Midsummer next), that beautiful black horse.

YOUNG GALLIMORE.

HE is a strong black horse, of the waggon kind, stands 16 hands 3 inches high. He was got by Mr. Perkin's Gallimore, of White Grave, near Stafford; his dam was got by the noted horse, Old Kirby, which horse covered at five guineas each mare.

He will attend during the season, at Warrington, every Wednesday; Northwich, every Friday; at Chester, every Saturday; and the rest of the week at his own stable, at Halton.

246. **Chester Courant** - Tuesday 26 April 1814

TO COVER THIS SEASON, 1815,

THE FOLLOWING HORSE,

The Property of RICHARD HILL, of East Langton,

At One Guinea and a Half, If foaled; and Sixteen Shillings, if Barren; and One Shilling the Men.

YOUNG GALLIMORE,—he is a beautiful brown Horse, of the Cart kind, six years old, 16 hands and a half high, and full of bone.— He was got by Mr. Perkins's Horse, of Witgreve, near Stafford, called Bold Will, which was got by Old Gallimore; allowed to be the best Cart Stallion in England.

Young Gallimore was out of a Mare the property of Mr. Ward, of Church Langton, which was also got by Old Gallimore.

Young Gallimore has proved himself a sure foal-getter, and his stock rises remarkably good.

The above Horse to be Sold by Private Contract. Apply as above.

255. **Leicester Journal** - 7 April [& 14 April] 1815

In the following year, 1815[255St] a horse called *Young Gallimore*, six years old, was advertised (opposite) to cover in Leicestershire.

He was said to have been got by Mr. Perkin's horse of 'Witgrave' (Whitgreave), near Stafford. This was, however, clearly a different horse, firstly because his sire was called *Bold Will* (although *Bold Will* was said to have been sired by *Old Gallimore*). Secondly, his dam was said to have been also by *Old Gallimore*, not *Old Kirby*, and thirdly because he was brown, not black! Perkin's *Bold Will* is recorded in the first Stud-book as the sire of the dam of the Shire stallion *Bold Will 236*, foaled in 1823, and owned by Anthony Wright (page 99) of Wheston Hall, Tideswell, Derbyshire. Anthony Wright is also recorded as the owner of *Gallimore 905*, claimed to have been a son of *Perkin's Gallimore* (*Gallimore 904*) [29].

Some years later, an advertisement in the Staffordshire Advertiser of 7 March 1835 made reference to *Perkin's brown horse of Whitgreave* within the pedigree details of a stallion called *Royal George*, advertised for sale by auction at Eccleshall, Staffordshire [5].

William Perkin [1796-1854] of Longdon (near Penkridge, Staffordshire), and formerly of Whitgreave was buried with his wife Mary, and two of their infant children within an ornate chest tomb in the church yard of Whitgreave. [The small church was not built until 1844, and the churchyard therefore lacks earlier graves of the family.]

William and Mary Perkin, and their family were recorded within the 1841 census as living at Whitgreave, with William's widowed mother as head of the neighbouring household. William Perkin was the son of James and Elizabeth Perkin (and baptised at St Mary's, Stafford in 1796). James Perkin of Whitgreave [1761 -1833], buried at Seighford, also in an elaborate tomb, was William Perkin's father, and he is most likely to have been the horse breeder referred to above. It is interesting that *Young Gallimore* should be advertised (page 78), to cover in 1814[246St] in Cheshire. The will of James Perkin, dated 1833 reveals that he had family connections with Cheshire; he had another son, James who lived in Northwich, Cheshire and two married daughters who lived in the same county [19].

The earlier generation of the Perkin family resided at Ingestre. James Perkin was baptised at Ingestre, the son of William and Margaret Perkin. James Perkin had an elder brother, William, also baptised at Ingestre, who later farmed at New Buildings Farm, Hopton, near Stafford, which is only about ½ mile south of Marston [19].

No advertisements or notices featuring heavy horses have been found which refer to James Perkin by name. In 1796, a horse called *Young Dragon* was advertised (in the Staffordshire Advertiser, dated 16 April) to cover at Penkridge. He was said to have been in the possession of James Perkin. This stallion was however a hunter, not of the cart kind [5].

Harrison - of Combridge, Staffordshire

John Harrison of Combridge, a hamlet about two miles north of Uttoxeter, but in the parish of Rocester, was the owner of *Bumper*.

Chivers [6], it would appear, in frustration, as he was unable to trace this stallion, referred to him as 'that mysterious, breederless, ownerless, placeless and timeless *Bumper*.

As already recorded, *Bumper* is said to have sired a stallion called *Ruler, Ruler* apparently having been bred by Webb of Marston (page 76) in 1773.

In 1786[89St], George Chadwick of Grindon advertised (page 73) a horse called *Young Bumper*. He was said to have been got by Mr. *Harrison's Old Bumper*. This cover advertisement, reveals that *Bumper* was owned by a Mr. Harrison, identified here as John Harrison. A notice (page 80) published in 1781[79St] advertised the sale by auction of '*that well-known black Stoned Horse, call'd OLD BUMPER, late the property of Mr. John Harrison of Combridge, in the County of Stafford*'. The advertisement also indicated that Mr. Harrison was bankrupt. It is disappointing however, that *Old Bumper's* pedigree was not given; such were the fine qualities of this stallion it was considered unnecessary to give details of his pedigree!

Further notices were placed in the Derby Mercury during the 1780s which were associated with the bankruptcy of John Harrison, describing him as a brickmaker, dealer and chapman [5]. His farm and land were advertised for sale in August 1784 [5].

A cover advertisement featuring a black colt, rising four years old was placed (page 81) in 1778[73St] by William Cantrell. He was said to have been got by Mr. *Harrison's old horse of Combridge*. Harrison's old horse was presumably *Bumper* which also means that *Ruler* could have realistically been sired by *Bumper,* and foaled in 1773.

Another black colt, said to have been sired by *Old Bumper* was advertised to cover in 1787[93].

To be SOLD by AUCTION,
At the House of Mr. Holland, known by the Sign of the Saracen's-Head in Burrowfash, in the County of Derby, between the Hours of Three and Six in the Afternoon, on Thursday the 19th Day of July, 1781.

THAT well-known black Stoned Horse, call'd OLD BUMPER, late the Property of Mr. John Harrison of Combridge, in the County of Stafford, now a Bankrupt.——The great Character the above Horse has acquired and maintained for many Years by the great Strength, fine Proportion, and Health of his very numerous Stock, makes it unneffary to trace his Pedigree, or infert a Catalogue of his many good Qualities.

And the Proprietors of such Mares as have been covered by the faid Horse this or former Seasons, and not yet paid for, are hereby required to take Notice, that the Money must be paid into the Hands of Mr. THOMAS BLURTON, Bailiff at Afhborne, in the County of Derby, who is authorifed to receive the fame by the Affignees of the faid Bankrupt's Eftate.

79. **Derby Mercury** - Thursday 5 July 1781

The owner of the original *Bumper* cannot be identified with certainty.

John Harrison [1677 -1772] of Combridge, was a substantial yeoman who held several farms [19]. He was originally from Ellastone parish (the same parish in which Samuel Gallimore of Wootton lived), where he, and later his sons John and George were all baptised.

John Harrison, junior [1715 -1781], his younger son, was an apothecary living in Uttoxeter.

George Harrison [1706 - 1804], the elder son, inherited his father's property at Combridge.

He in turn had a son, John Harrison [1741 - 1811], also of Combridge. It was this John Harrison who became bankrupt and had owned *Old Bumper* before the stallion was advertised for sale in 1781. Although John Harrison had been the owner of *Old Bumper*, the old horse mayhave previously been owned by his then aged father George Harrison, or by his similarly aged grandfather John Harrison, who had died in 1772.

Moore - of Shirleywich, Staffordshire

Preston Moore [1743-1798] had a salt works at Shirleywich [22]. [Shirleywich is a village in the parish of Weston-on-Trent, but also within one mile of Ingestre].

The salt works were alongside the Trent and Mersey Canal and a regular supply of horses would have been needed to pull barges conveying salt and coal etc. along this important route [26].

Following the death of Preston Moore, an auction sale of his horses was advertised (opposite) to take place at Shirleywich in April 1798[141St].

The most significant lot was a brown stallion, rising 8 years old, got by Mr. Massey's old horse of Birchwood Moor, and *'out of a famous mare, own sister to Mr. Summerland's late best brown horse, which was sold for three hundred and fifty guineas, bred at Shirleywich, and got by Mr. Webb's old brown horse at Marston.'*

Capital Stallions, &c.
TO BE SOLD BY AUCTION,
AT SHIRLEYWICH,
By Mr. Henfhaw,

On THURSDAY the 26th of APRIL, 1798, at 11 o'Clock in the forenoon :

THE undermentioned Valuable Stallions and Fillies, the property of the late Mr. PRESTON MOORE, of Shirleywich aforefaid, near Stafford, in the faid County.

LOT I. That well known brown Stallion, of the Waggon Kind, rifing 8 years old, 17 Hands high, was got by Mr. Maffey's old Horfe of Birchwood Moor, out of a famous Mare, own fister to Mr. Summerland's late beft brown Horfe, which was fold for Three Hundred and Fifty Guineas, bred at Shirleywich, and was got by Mr. Webb's old brown Horfe of Marfton.

LOT II. An excellent Stallion of the Waggon Kind, rifing four years old, fixteen Hands and a Half high, got by the above Horfe, out of a famous Waggon Mare, which may be feen at the place of fale.

LOT III. A famous ftrong Filly, rifing three years old, got by the above aged Horfe, and out of a capital Mare.

LOT IV. A capital Filly, rifing two years old, got by Mr. Boulftridge's noted Horfe, of Ilfley Walton, that covered at Three Guineas a Mare, and out of Mr. Moore's beft Waggon Mare, which may be feen at Shirleywich.

N. B. The above Horfes are truly useful, the Fillies of great fize & full of bone, and handfome, and allowed by the beft Judges to be nearly as good a fort as this Kingdom produces.

141. **Staffordshire Advertiser** - Saturday 21 April 1798

Preston Moore had advertised the same horse as being available to cover, in similar advertisements placed in the Staffordshire Advertiser for 18 April 1795 and 22 April 1797 [5]. With stallions owned or bred by Bulstrode, Webb, Summerland and Massey in their pedigree the horses which had belonged to Preston Moore were clearly of quality. Another reference to Shirleywich appeared in a cover advertisement (page 68) in 1807[190St] for the *Geaton* (meaning Gayton) *Brown Horse*, six years old, and the property of Mr. Summerland of Uttoxeter. The *Shirleywich horse* was named as the sire of this horse, and he, in turn, was claimed to be by a son of *Bakewell's old G*.

Massey - of Ilam, Staffordshire

In his book, Chivers [6] warned of the complex nature of the several generations and branches of the Massey family. This family, who made a very important contribution to 'Shire' breeding was primarily from Derbyshire (page 86).

In reference to William Massey of '*Birchall Moor*' Chivers noted that he and other members of his family had a strain of horses which had their origins in Leicestershire (although he did not explain his point here). He also hinted that the Massey family had considerable breeding activities which were not represented by entries in the Stud-book. This statement is more true than he could have known, as discussed under the Massey family of Derbyshire, to which William Massey was related.

William Massey [1750-1827] was a son of Bartholomew Massey of Alstonfield [1717-1771], Staffordshire. [Bartholomew Massey was a brother of Thomas Massey of Little Ireton, Derbyshire who first advertised (pages 18,86) the stallion *Galymoor* (*Gallimore*) in 1757[1De].] Chivers pointed out the proximity of the small village of Ilam, just about one mile north-east of John Hambleton's at Calton Moor, and also within three miles of John Chadwick at Grindon. '*Birchall Moor*' is difficult to locate with certainty, but can probably be identified as Beechenhill Farm, about ½ mile north of Ilam village. Massey of Ilam and Massey of Birchall Moor are likely to have been the same individual, or at least members of the same family.

William Massey and his wife Rebecca had children who were baptised at Ilam between 1778 and 1794. Their gravestone at Alstonfield records that at the time of their death they were living at Damsgate. [Damsgate, Alstonfield is a small habitation, only about ½ mile to the north of Beechenhill Farm, and between the centres of the villages of Ilam and Alstonfield.] Their eldest son William [1781-   ] and his wife Sarah had children between 1810 and 1824 who were also baptised at Ilam.

A cover advertisement (opposite) placed by William Cantrell in 1778[73St] for a black colt rising three years old, claimed that he was got by *Mr. Massey's Horse of Birchall-Moor*, which was got by Mr Bakewell's noted horse *G*.

William Massey's entries in the Stud-book [29] are however for later stallions and include *Mansetter 1479*, bred (in 1813) and owned by him. He also bred his sire *Mansetter 1477* in 1807. Additionally, Massey bred the dam of *Mansetter 1479* (by *Summerland's Blaze 192*), and the grandam (by *Farmer's Glory 807*); the great-grandam being his own mare. *Mansetter 1477* was a son of *Merryman 1548* also owned and bred (in 1800) by Massey of Birchall Moor.

To COVER this Season, 1778,
At WILLIAM CANTRELL's, at Stanlow, near Ashborne, Derbyshire,

A Strong Black COLT, of the Cart Kind, rising four Years old; near 17 Hands high, and very full of Bone.—He was got by Mr. Harrison's old Horse, of Combridge.

To Cover at Half-a-Guinea a Mare, if with Foal; if barren, Four Shillings.

Likewise to COVER at the same Place,

A Black COLT, of the Cart Kind, rising three Years old, 16 Hands high: He was got by Mr. Massey's Horse, of Birchall-Moor, which was got by Mr. Bakewell's noted Horse G.

He Covers at Fifteen Shillings a Mare if with Foal; if barren Five Shillings.

N. B. He will be at Ashborne on Saturday the 9th of May.

73. **Derby Mercury** - Friday 24 April 1778

The Leicestershire origin of these horses becomes clear. According to the Stud-book [29] the sire of *Merryman 1548* was Oldacres' celebrated *Mansetter 1476*, and the dam's sire Bulstrode's *Bald 93*, the dam's breeder being Capp of Loughborough (page 48).
Whether it was William Massey, senior, his son William Massey, junior, or both of them who were involved in the breeding of all of these horses cannot be determined, but it can be seen as continuing a tradition established by earlier generations of the Massey family in Derbyshire.

Plate 12: *Harold* [1881-1901] was a highly successful stallion; and the ancestor of most 20th century Shires. He belonged to A.C. Duncombe at his famous Calwich Abbey stud, in Staffordshire.

Plate 13: *Premier* [1880-1892] was another highly successful Shire stallion belonging to A.C. Duncombe at his Calwich Abbey stud, in Staffordshire.

CHAPTER 8: SHROPSHIRE BREEDERS AND OWNERS

This is a very short chapter as only one breeder of note has been discovered.
Mr Handley's *Pave Lane horse* seems to have been an important stallion.

Handley - of Pave Lane, near Newport, Shropshire

Pave Lane is a cluster of a few houses at Chetwynd Aston, but in the parish of Church Aston, about one mile south of Newport.
Handley of Pave Lane is credited with having owned *King Tom 1260*, bred by Webb in 1786 [29].
King Tom 1260 is recorded as the sire of two celebrated stallions, *Marston 1486* and *Bulstrode 348*, both also bred by Webb. These two stallions, which were full brothers, were later owned by John Chadwick of Grindon, who apparently used them to his considerable financial benefit.
The first reference which has been found to Mr. Handley (in the Chester Chronicle for 29 March 1793) is within an advertisement for the sale of farming stock at High Offley, near Eccleshall, Staffordshire. Included in the sale was a mare in foal by '*Mr. Handley's noted black stallion of Pave-lane*' in the county of Salop [5].

In 1795[133Sh] the sale, by auction in Nantwich, Cheshire of a four-year-old black stallion called *Merryman* was advertised (opposite). He was said to have been got by *Mr. Handley's old Star horse* of Pave-lane, near Newport, Shropshire. It was also claimed that *Merryman's* dam had been sired by *Bakewell's Gee*.
Mr. Henley's old Star horse was mentioned a few years later, as the sire of a three year old draught filly, included in a sale of farming stock, advertised (Staffordshire Advertiser 17 March 1804) to take place at Beffcote, near Gnosall, Staffordshire [5].
The *Pave-Lane Horse* called *King Tom* was described (page 74) as the sire of *Marston* in a cover advertisement in 1804[155St] by John Chadwick which also featured *Marston's* full brother *Bulstrode*.
'*Marson*' [meaning *Marston*] was advertised to cover again in 1805[169]. Chadwick gave similar detail to that provided in the previous year. Similar references to the *Pave-lane horse* were made in a cover advertisement (page 77) for *Lockwood*, a son of *Marston* in 1807[188St],

TO BE SOLD BY AUCTION,

BY MR. JOHN COWAP,

At Mr. Davenport's, the Pigeons, in Nantwich, at three o'clock on Saturday the 10th of January, 1795;

A Fine young black STALLION, of the waggon kind, four-years old, known by the name of MERRYMAN; the property of Adam Preston, of Bradfield-green, late of Stonyford, near Drayton, Shropshire.

He is sixteen hands high, was got by Mr. Handley's Old Star horse, of Pave-lane, near Newport, Shropshire, and came out of a beautiful black mare belonging to Mr. Heley, of Tyrley-castle, near Drayton aforesaid; she was got by Mr. Bakewell's waggon horse, GEE; which covered at five guineas a mare.

N. B. The above horse is in fine condition, is allowed to have every good property, and his flock is very promising. He covered at Drayton, Whitchurch, and Nantwich, the two last years.

133. **Chester Courant** - Tuesday 6 January 1795

and to *Bulstrode* in 1808[201]. *Bulstrode* was said to have been got by *Mr. Hanley's* (Handley's) *brown horse of Pave Lane*, which would have been *King Tom*. This was not the same horse which had featured in the 1793 and 1795[133Sh] advertisements, which was black. That black stallion seems likely to have been *Old Star*.
Church Aston parish registers reveal that the Handley (variously also Hanley or Henley) family were well established in the area. Several newspaper advertisements indicate that the stallion owner was Lionel Handley [1737- 1812]. Lionel Handley (or Henley) of Pave Lane was a gentleman of considerable means and in his will he left the bulk of his property to his

niece and her son. Lionel Handley bequeathed to his great-nephew 'all my blood waggon and other horses' [19].

A cover advertisement in 1805 (Staffordshire Advertiser, 23 February) featured a stallion called *George*, the property of Lionel 'Henley', of Pave-Lane, near Newport [5]. Lionel Handley also owned a stallion called *Lignum Vitae* which was similarly advertised (Staffordshire Advertiser, dated 21st March) to cover, in 1807 [5]. Both *George* and *Lignum Vitae* were however racehorses!

Of greater interest, is a cover advertisement, (opposite) dated 1807[181Sh] for a black waggon horse, rising seven years old called *Conqueror*, formerly owned by Lionel 'Henley'. *Conqueror* was said to have been got by *Old Star*, and his dam also got by '*Old Star, which covered twenty-four seasons at Pave-Lane*'.

Some years later, in 1836 (Staffordshire Advertiser, 12 March), a dark brown horse, rising eight years old called *Valiant* was offered for sale at Loggerheads, near Market Drayton. His dam was said to have been by Mr. Till's horse of Whitgreave, but his grandam was said to have been by *North Star* of Pave Lane - suggesting another Handley connection [5].

> **TO COVER THIS SEASON,**
> At One Guinea and Half each Mare, at Sheppenhall, near Nantwich, Cheshire, the property of Mr. John Downs,
>
> THE famous black horse, CONQUEROR, late the property of Lionel Henley, near Newport, Shropshire. Conqueror was bred by Mr. Yates, of Bingmill, got by Old Star, and dam by Old Star, who covered twenty-four seasons at Pave-Lane. Conqueror is a black horse, rising seven years old, stands seventeen hands high, with as much bone and power as any waggon-horse in the kingdom.
>
> *Sheppenhall, March 2d, 1807.*

181. **Chester Chronicle** - Friday 6 March 1807

Fig. 14: A ploughman at work during a ploughing match at Brockton, Newport, Shropshire, in 1913.

CHAPTER 9: DERBYSHIRE BREEDERS AND OWNERS

The earliest-known Derbyshire breeders resided mainly around Derby. Those who lived south of Derby were in close proximity to breeders living in northern parts of Leicestershire, and in the south-east of Staffordshire. Other breeders lived to the north-west near Duffield and Belper, and north of Derby, in an area which extended towards Chesterfield.

Horses such as the Shire may have been bred here primarily for agricultural purposes and much of Derbyshire today is still very rural. However, parts of the county, including the area around Derby saw major change during the second half of the 18th century.

The Industrial Revolution gave rise to the rapid growth in manufacturing, particularly in this part of Derbyshire. The mills and mines and other places of industrial activity were served by new roads but also assisted in their development by a new means of transport. Raw materials and end products could now be much more efficiently transported by a system of canals.

The seven canals of Derbyshire included the Chesterfield Canal (opened in 1776), the Erewash Canal (opened in 1779), and the Trent and Mersey Canal (opened in 1771) which ran south of Derby, with a link to Derby from Swarkestone provided via the Derby Canal (opened in 1793). Breeders in these areas may have been meeting a growing demand for working horses suited to the various tasks associated with these industries, such as hauling heavy wagons and drays along the roads, and pulling barges along the canals.

Tateham - of Tupton Hall and Aldercar, Derbyshire

Samuel Tateham [1726 - 1803] of Tupton (a township in the parish of North Wingfield) provides a direct early link between horse-breeding activity in Leicestershire and that in the developing industrial area north of Derby. A newspaper report in 1765[13Le] recorded that a two year old colt bred by John Knowles of Odstone (page 51) had been sold to Samuel Tateham at Ashby-de-la-Zouch Fair. In 1765[15De] Samuel Tateham advertised (below) the same horse to cover at Tupton Hall, and in 1769[22De], John Wagstaff of Atlow advertised (page 89) a colt which had been got by Mr. Tateham's horse of Tupton.

In 1770[29] the *famous heavy stallion horse*, rising seven years old (presumably the same colt which once belonged to John Knowles) was advertised to cover at Tupton Hall, and then later in the year at Aldercar (near Heanor).

A black horse, late the property of Mr. Tatam (Tateham), having covered the last two seasons at Mr. Wagstaff's of Atlow was advertised to cover by John Porter at Sandiacre in 1774[46].

THE HORSE that won the Second PREMIUM at *Ashby-de-la-Zouch*, the 10th of this Instant *April*, is to be kept for a STALLION at Mr. SAMUEL TATEHAM's, at *Tupton Hall*, in the Parish of *Northwingfield* and County of *Derby*, and will cover this Season at *Ten Shillings* and *Six-pence* a Fole, and *Four Shillings* and *Six-pence*, if barren. ——This Colt was thought to be the best in *Ashby*: He is sixteen Hands high, and well Whited; he was bred by Mr. KNOWLS, of *Nelson* in the County of *Leicester*, who is noted for a good Breed of Horses; the said Mr. *Knowls* refused One Hundred Guineas for the Dam of this Colt. The Horse that got him is in Possession of the said Mr. *Knowls*, and hath got some of the best Horses in the Country.

15. **Derby Mercury** - 12 April 1765

Also in 1774[47], Gilbert Walker at Kirk Hallam adverted the noted black horse called *SNIP*, commonly known as the *Tupton Horse*. This horse was said to have been bred by Mr. Knowles of Nelson (Nailstone) and had covered the last six seasons at Kirk Hallam. The 'facts' do not quite tally, but the *Tupton Horse* was probably the horse Samuel Tateham had owned. In his will, Samuel Tateham described himself as a maltster. In his later life he may have recognised the benefits of horse power in relation to the evolving canal system locally. He purchased shares in both the Erewash and Cromford canals which be bequeathed to his children [19].

Massey - of Norbury, Swarkestone, Muggington and Hilton, Derbyshire

John Massey [c1671 -1740] of Norbury, and later of Swarkestone had several sons, including Bartholomew Massey of Alstonfield (page 81), John Massey [1709 -1799] of Birchwood Moor, Norbury, Thomas Massey [1721 -   ] of Little Ireton, Muggington and Sampson Massey [1723 - 1764] of Swarkestone.

The Harpur (later Harpur-Crewe) family owned Swarkestone, their ancient family seat being at Swarkestone Hall before Calke Abbey was built and became their principal residence. Swarkestone Hall was largely demolished in around 1750, and it seems likely that the Massey family lived at Old Hall Farm, close by. The Harpur family also owned a large estate in and around Alstonfield. As the Masseys were tenants of the Harpur family at Swarkestone, Bartholomew Massey may have moved to Alstonfield to take up a tenancy on land belonging to the Harpurs there [28].

The important contributions of the Massey family to the early development of the Shire breed are revealed by cover advertisements and notices placed in the Derby Mercury, beginning in the 1750s, for a stallion they owned, called variously *Galymoor*, or *Gallymoor*, (or properly *Gallimore*). Thomas Massey's first known advertisement (below) for his horse '*Galymoor*' to leap at Little Ireton was in 1757[1De]. Also advertised, but to leap a Swarkeston Hall, was a colt by 'Galymoor'. Thomas Massey placed a similar advertisement in 1758[3], but additionally advertised another horse (which he also owned), sired by 'Gallymoor', to leap at 'Cowlyshire's' (or Cowlishaw's) of Tupton, near Chesterfield. Thomas Massey placed similar advertisements for 'Gallymoor' to cover again in 1759[De] (below), 1761[7] and 1762[9] when he also advertised another horse to leap at Little Ireton *gotten by Mr. Hacket's Horse, of Nelson'* (i.e. Nailstone), Leicestershire.

[Little Ireton was in the parish of Muggington but actually just on the northern boundary of Kedleston Park, 3½ miles north-west of Derby]. Muggington is where Thomas Massey and his wife Hannah baptised several children between 1742 and 1759.]

The Leicestershire connection is worthy of note. Thomas Massey's brother Sampson Massey (of Swarkestone) married Ann Hackett of Nailstone in 1755 (as already recorded, page 50). In relation to 'Shire' breeding, a connection with 'Mr. Hackett' is of interest, but any links made between the Massey family and the Knowles family of Nailstone (page 50) would have been of greater significance.

The Famous Black HORSE, call'd

GALYMOOR,

IS in the Hands of THOMAS MASSEY, at *Little Ireton* near DERBY, and will Leap this next Seafon, at *Twelve Shillings and Sixpence* a Mare; if Barren *Five Shillings and Sixpence, &c.*

N. B. His Colt got by the above Horfe, will Leap this next Seafon at *Swarkefton Hall* near DERBY: To be there the 20th Day of *April*, and will Leap at *Half a Guinea* a Mare; if Barren, *Five Shillings* and *Sixpence, &c.*

1. **Derby Mercury** - 25 March & 1 April 1757

In 1771[36De] (page 87), and again in 1772[41], John Massey [1744 - 1814], Thomas Massey's son advertised a horse called *Fair*

The Famous HORSE, Call'd

GALLYMOOR,

IS now in the Hands of THOMAS MASSEY, at *Little-Ireton* near DERBY, and will Leap at 12s. 6d. a Mare, if with Foal, and if barren, but 5s. 6d.

Likewife a COLT, gotten by Mr. HACKET's Horfe of *Nelfon* in *Leicefterfhire*; will Leap with him at Home, at 8s. 6d. a Mare, if with Foal, and if barren, but 2s. 6d.

Likewife a HORSE gotten by GALLYMOOR, will Leap at Mr. WILLIAM COOLY's of *Alvafton*, at 10s. 6d. a Mare, if with Foal, and if barren, but 2s. 6d.

Alfo another HORSE, gotten by GALLYMOOR, will Leap at *Cowlyfhire's* of *Tupton*, near *Chefterfield*, at 7s. 6d. a Mare, if with Foal, and if barren but 2s. 6d. and you may change from one Horfe to another, as you pleafe. And all the above Horfes the Property of the faid THOMAS MASSEY.

The HORSES are at the Places above-mentioned, ready for Covering.

N. B. The Six-pences to be paid down at the Stable Door.

6. **Derby Mercury** - 20 April 1759

Leaper to cover at Cockshuthill, (also in Muggington parish, and less than a mile from Little Ireton). Two years later, in 1774[53, 54], he announced that he was leaving the farm, and that he was having a sale of stock, implements and produce. The stock for sale included *'well bred mares got by very good horses such as old Gallimore, the noted Packingon blind Horse* etc'. One mare was said to be in foal by Mr. Massey's colt of Birchwood Moor. [His father's brother, John Massey [1709 -1799], and cousin Bartholomew Massey [1739 -1803] lived at Birchwood Moor, in the parish of Norbury with Roston, and about four miles south-east of Ashbourne].

To Cover this Seaſon,

AT John Maſſey's, of *Cockſhutbill*, at his old Price, Half-a-Guinea each Mare, a famous Black Horſe, of the Cart Kind, call'd

FAIR LEAPER,

the Property of Mr. Timothy Clarkſon, of Aſhby-de-la-Zouch in Leiceſterſhire; lett to John Maſſey, for two Years.

He was bred by the above Mr. Timothy Clarkſon, and got by Mr. Hood's famous old Horſe, of Packington, commonly call'd The Blind Horſe.

N. B. He is as ſure a Foal-getter as any in England, for the laſt Seaſon there is not more than one barren Mare out of Six or Seven, which is very Remarkable.

36. **Derby Mercury** - Friday 19 April 1771

In 1772[43De] The Blind Horse was advertised (above) to cover at John Massey's of Birchwood Moor. This stallion was said to have been bred by Mr. Hood of Packington, and got by *Mr. Boulstridge's Old Horse*. This horse was said to have covered for the last four years, but would seem to have been too young to be Mr. Hood's famous *Packington Blind Horse*.

In 1798[141St] *'Mr. Massey's old horse of Birchwood Moor'* was also mentioned as the sire of a brown stallion offered for sale by auction at Shirleywich, near Stafford (page 80). The elder John Massey continued to live at Birchwood Moor until his death, whereas John Massey of Muggington moved to the village of Hilton in the parish of Marston on Dove, seven miles south-west of Derby.

Mr. Massey's G was mentioned in a cover advertisement in 1797[136] as the sire of the dam of a horse belonging to William Harrison of Little Eaton. The Stud-book [29] records Massey of Birchwood Moor as the breeder and owner of *G 891* (a son of *Bakewell's G 890*), apparently having been foaled in 1805. Clearly *Massey's G* must have been foaled much earlier.

To Cover this Seaſon, 1772.

AT JOHN MASSEY's of Birchwood-Moor, in the County of Derby, at Eight Shillings and Sixpence if with Foal, and Four Shillings if barren;

The Blind HORSE,

which has covered out four of the laſt Years; he was bred by Mr. Hood of Packington, Leiceſteſhire, got by Mr. Boulſtridge's old Horſe; his Stock is very well known to be good.

43. **Derby Mercury** - Friday 8 May [& 15 May] 1772

TO COVER THIS SEASON,

THE PROPERTY OF MR. JOHN SIMS, OF STANTON BY BRIDGE, IN THE COUNTY OF DERBY, At Two Sovereigns a Mare, if in-foal, and 7s. if barren, and One Shilling the Man.

THAT Capital BLACK COLT, of the pure Old Black Breed, called

DERBYSHIRE;

Rising six years old. He has proved himself a sure Foal-getter, and is allowed to be one of the truest bred, as well as one of the best Horses in the country.

He was got by Old Black Legs, late the property of Mr. Whiles, of Coton, his dam by Mr. Elson's old Horse, which was by Mr. Knowle's Bald Horse, the Bald Horse by Mr. While's Old Swebstone, grandam by Mr. Edge's Old Horse, of Quorn, which was by the Old Swebstone Horse, grandam by Mr. Bulstrode's Old Horse, of Isley Walton, great great grandam by Mr. Falkner's Old Horse, of Bradby, great great great grandam by Mr. Bulstrode's old Bald Horse, great great great great grandam by the Packington Blind Horse, great great great great great grandam by Mr. Massey's Gallimore Horse of Swarkstone, which was the sire of the Packington Blind Horse, &c.

Several first-rate Colts, by the above Horse, are now keeping for Stallions, on account of their superiority. Derbyshire will not travel.

ALSO TO COVER THIS SEASON,

That Capital GREY HORSE of the Cart kind, rising eight years old, called

FARMERS' GLORY,

At £1. 11s. 6d. if in-foal; 7s. if barren; and 2s. 6d. the Groom.

N.B. Farmers' Glory will travel, the particulars of which will be stated in hand Bills.

286. **Derby Mercury** - Wednesday 17 April 1833

A cover advertisement placed (page 81) by William Cantrell in 1778[73St] for a black colt rising three years old, claimed that he was got by *Mr. Massey's Horse of Birchall-Moor*, which was got by Mr. Bakewell's noted horse *G*. This tends to suggest that this horse belonging to Mr. Massey may have later been called Mr. Massey's *G*. It also suggests some confusion between Birchwood Moor and the address of the Massey family's relative of 'Birchall-Moor', near Ilam, Staffordshire.

No more cover advertisements seem to have been placed by the Masseys, although those placed by other owners and breeders frequently link back to this family, particularly through the descendants of the first advertised horse 'Galymoor'. In 1833[286De], a cover advertisement (page 87) by John Sims of Stanton by Bridge, Derbyshire featured a black colt of the '*pure Old Black Breed*' called *Derbyshire*. A detailed pedigree was supplied going back many generations leading ultimately to '*Mr. Massey's Gallimore of Swarkestone*'. This advertisement traces a path all the way back to the cover advertisements placed in the 1750s by Thomas Massey. Even after this time the Derbyshire branch of the Massey family made further contributions to Shire breeding. Stud-book records [29] reveal that Sampson Massey [1780-1860] of Swarkstone Hall was the breeder and owner of *Royal Albert 1882*, foaled in 1858. The Masseys of Swarkestone also bred *Derbyshire Hero 589* in 1848, *King Charles 1206* in 1851, and *Prince Charles 1799* in 1862 [29].

Coxon - of Atlow, Derbyshire

The stallion *Galymoor*, advertised by Thomas Massey in the 1750s is not the only named horse in this early period. In 1757[2Le], John Coxon of the small village of Atlow (three miles north-east of Ashbourne) advertised (page 48) a black horse called the *Grinn Horse*. He was said to have been got by another named stallion called the *old Shottle Horse* and bred by John Chadwick. Possible links with the Chadwick family of Grindon (page 73) come to mind but this was probably a coincidence. Parish records for Duffield, which included Shottle (about 4½ miles east of Atlow) indicate that another (probably unrelated) Chadwick family was living there at this period. John Coxon's links to Leicestershire are revealed through his young black horse which he advertised at the same time, in 1757[2Le], this horse having been bred by John Donnisthorpe of Packington. Chivers [6] made no reference to John Coxon, and no more is known of either the *Grinn Horse* or the *Shottle horse.*

John Coxon [1717-1781] of Atlow was formerly of the parish of Norbury with Roston where his elder brother, Thomas Coxon resided at Birchwood Park, a substantial farmstead [19]. Thomas Coxon's neighbour was John Massey [1709 -1799] of Birchwood Moor, the adjoining farm. In Snelston, the next village, John and Thomas Coxon had an uncle, Nicholas Coxon, and cousins John and Thomas Coxon, who had all used the leaping services of Samuel Gallimore's stallions before 1750 (pages 122,125,126).

Wagstaff - of Atlow, Derbyshire

Also in the small village of Atlow lived a 'Shire' owner and breeder by the name of Wagstaff. The earliest reference to John Wagstaff seems to be in 1769[22De], in an advertisement (page 89) which informed his customers that '*his Old HORSE will cover as usual*'. The same advertisement referred to a two year old black colt bred by John Wagstaff and seemed to suggest (in correcting an earlier advertisement) that the sire of the colt was Mr. Tateham's Horse of Tupton (page 85), which had been bred by Mr. 'Knowls' (presumably Knowles of Nailstone, or Odstone, Leicestershire).

A 1774[51De] advertisement (below) by Thomas Marsden of Hilton, Derbyshire for his brown horse *Merryman* (got by the *Packington Old Horse*, and out of a *Stanhope brown mare*) claimed that this horse was formerly the property of Mr. Wagstaff of Atlow.

This is to inform the Public,

THAT the Old HORSE, belonging to JOHN WAGSTAFF of *Atlow* near *Ashburn*, will cover this Season as usual.

Likewise a Black Colt, rising two Years old, upwards of sixteen Hands high, and very full of Bone, which was bred by *John Wagstaff*, and not by Mr. *Tateham of Tupton*, as was mentioned in the last Week's Paper, but was got by Mr. *Tateham's* Horse of *Tupton*, which Horse was bred by Mr. *Knowls*. He will cover this Season at 12s. 6d. a Foal, if barren 5s. 6d.

Also a Brown Colt, with a beautiful Forehand, and a remarkable good Trotter. He was bred by Mr. *Frost of Stanfop*, and got by Mr. *Hood's* Old Horse. He will cover this Season at 10s. 6d. a Foal, if barren 5s. 6d.

☞ Good Grass for Mares, and proper Care taken of them.

22. **Derby Mercury** - Friday 7 April 1769
http://www.britishnewspaperarchive.co.uk/viewer/bl/000018 9/17690407/004/0004

To COVER this Season, 1774.

AT Thomas Marsden's at Hilton, in Derbyshire, the famous brown Horse, called **MERRYMAN**; late the Property of Mr. Wagstaff of Atlow. He was got by the Packington Old Horse, and out of the Stanhope brown Mare.

He will attend at the Black Greyhound at Hopton, every Monday; at Wirksworth on Tuesday; at Brailsford on Wednesday; at Hilton on Thursday; at Clifton on Friday; at Ashborne on Saturday; and on Saturday Night at Atlow.

To Cover, also, at the same Place, the bay Horse, called **CHAMPION**, seven Years old, and free from all Blemishes. He was got by the Son of Blaze, and out of the Daughter of Fearnought; his Dam was got by Royal, well known to Lord Granby's Hunt, and out of a thorough bred Mare.—The above Horse will attend at the Crown, in Stone, every Tuesday; on Wednesday at the Green Man in Uttoxeter; on Thursday at the Crown in Burton; on Friday at the Ship, in the Full-Street, Derby; at Ashborne on Saturday; and at Hilton every Sunday.

The above Horses will Cover at Half-a-Guinea a Mare each, and One Shilling the Man; the Money to be paid at the Time of Covering, or at Midsummer next. The said Horses are well known for the good Stock they get, and being very sure in Foal-getting.

N. B. Any Mares that are covered with either of the said Horses, and prove barren, shall be covered at Half Price next Season.

51. **Derby Mercury** - 8 April 1774
http://www.britishnewspaperarchive.co.uk/viewer/bl/0000 189/17740408/005/0004

A similar advertisement in 1775[56] further claimed that *Merryman* was now six years old, his dam having been a brown mare belonging to Mr. Frost of Stanhope. [Stanhope is one mile south of Alstonfield, Staffordshire.]

Mr. *Frott* (Frost) of Stanhope, probably John Frost [1733 -] had presented a horse foal to be judged at the Annual Show of Foals held at Ashby-de-la-Zouch in 1765[14Le] (page 40). There seem to have been many horses called *Merryman*, including a son of the *Packington Blind Horse* which was said by Chivers [6] to be unidentifiable. Wagstaff's stallion *Merryman,* could have been this horse, recorded as as a son of the *Packington Blind horse* in the genealogical table (**Table 2**, page 30). In 1784[84De] John Wagstaff advertised (opposite) a *'Black HORSE of the Cart Kind, called E, rising five years old, bred by Bakewell, and got by old G'.* His dam was said have been Mr. Bakewell's mare, and got by *K*. A black colt bred by Wagstaff himself by his own horse out of a daughter of *Blaize* (*Blaze*) was featured in the same advertisement. John Wagstaff, senior of Atlow died in 1774 [19]. His son, John Wagstaff of Atlow [1740 - 1796] may have been responsible for the above advertisements as well as that placed in 1786[91] for a black (unnamed) horse of the cart kind, which he had bred himself by his own horse, out of a dam sired by a horse called *Blaze*. *Blaze* was said to have covered many seasons at (the more costly than usual) five guineas a mare. [The owner of *Blaze* is not identified but thoughts are immediately of Robert

To COVER this Season,

AT JOHN WAGSTAFF's, of Atlow, at FIFTEEN SHILLINGS a Mare, if in Foal; if barren, SEVEN SHILLINGS and SIX-PENCE.

A Black HORSE,

Of the Cart Kind, called E. rising Five Years old, a remarkable sure Foal Getter, and the Stock very promising; he was bred by Mr. Bakewell of Dishley, and got by old G. which Horse covered many Seasons at Five Guineas a Mare; his Dam is the best Mare Mr. Bakewell has; she was got by K. which covers this Season at Dishley, at Five Guineas a Mare.

N. B. He will be at Duffield every Wednesday, and the rest of the Week at Atlow.

Also to Cover at the same Place,

A Beautiful Black COLT,

Of the Cart Kind, rising two Years old; he is very full of Bone, and was bred by John Wagstaff; he was got by his old Horse, and out of a Daughter of Blaize.

He will cover at Twelve Shillings and Six-pence a Mare, if in Foal; if barren, Five Shillings and Six-pence.

84. **Derby Mercury** - Thursday 15 April 1784
http://www.britishnewspaperarchive.co.uk/viewer/bl/00 00189/17840415/005/0004

Bakewell, whose usual fee seems to have been five guineas.] This horse appears to be the same animal advertised as a colt in 1784[84De]. The same advertisement, in 1786[91], featured a colt, got by Mr. Oldacres' Horse, of Market Bosworth. The inclusion of the Oldacres name is a clear indicator of the quality of his stock.

In 1788[97] John Wagstaff advertised two horses and a colt. One of the horses was *Merryman*, bred by Mr. Capp of Loughborough (page 48). The colt advertised was said to have been by *Ruler*. Chivers [6] referred to Wagstaff of Atlow as the owner of *Ruler 1906*, foaled in 1783, a son of *Ruler 1905*.

Wagstaff advertised three horses in a cover advertisement in 1797[137]. *Blaze*, five years old, was said to have been by *Mr. Oldacre's Bald Horse*. The other horses advertised to cover were *Ruler* and *Ball*. Mr. Wagstaff's old horse *Ruler* was mentioned in the pedigree of a horse called *Censurer*, advertised (page 76) to cover in 1807[189St]. *Ruler* was said to have been sired by *old Ruler* and bred by Webb of Marston.

Chivers also referred to a stallion of some significance called *Nelson 1609*, foaled in 1803, and owned by Wagstaff of Atlow (page 88), probably John Wagstaff, junior [1767-1836].

Faulkner - of Bretby, Derbyshire

Mr. *'Falkner of Bratby'* (Faulkner of Bretby), together with Francis Bond of 'Bratby', and *'a man from Bratby Hall'*, were all customers, recorded in 1750, as having used the cover services of the stallions of Samuel Gallimore, the Staffordshire yeoman (page 121)[19].

It is likely that it was the same Mr. *'Falconer'* of Bretby who bred the horse advertised (below) to cover in 1758[4De] at Duffield, near Derby. This stallion was described as a *'Black Horse of the Heavy Breed'*, and *'bred by him out of his best Black Mare'*. [Mr. 'Falconer's' horse was to leap at the same place as a racing thoroughbred called *Silver-Leg*, formerly owned by Nathaniel Curzon of nearby Kedleston Hall.]

In 1765[14Le], at the Annual Show of Foals at Ashby-de-la-Zouch, a horse foal of Mr. 'Falkner's of Bratby', Derbyshire was one of those judged by the committee awarding premiums (page 40). Mr. Faulkner was in competition with Robert Bakewell.

Mr. Faulkner's presence and involvement in the Show is an indication of his standing amongst the 'Shire' breeders of the time. It also demonstrates his links with Leicestershire breeders at an early date.

Bretby (sometimes referred to as Bratby or Bradby) is a small village in Derbyshire, but only about three miles east of the Staffordshire town of Burton-upon-Trent. The Earls of Chesterfield owned the Bretby estate up to the 19th century, and the possible significance of the importation of Frisian mares by the 4th Earl has already been discussed (page 13).

'Mr. Falkner of Bratby' was probably Thomas Faulkner, whose will, dated 1781 reveals that he had a leasehold estate which he rented from the then, 5th Earl of Chesterfield [19]. Thomas Faulkner and his first wife Elizabeth, both of Bretby were married at Derby in 1730.

The FAMOUS RUNNING HORSE, call'd

SILVER - LEG,

Late the PROPERTY of

NATHANIEL CURZON, Esq;

And since of Captain SHAFTO, and the Marquis of ROCKINGHAM:

Is NOW in the HANDS of

ROBERT FELL, at the King's-Head in DUFFIELD, near DERBY,

Who has purchas'd him in order to propagate his SPECIES, and to preserve the BREED of so fine and beautiful a CREATURE.

Note. He has been very successful in getting FOALS the last Season; and will LEAP this Season, at ONE GUINEA a MARE, and Half a Crown the Maid; the Money to be paid down at the Stable Door.

There will be good Grass for Mares, and proper Care taken of them.

P. S. No bred Horse in Britain ever got finer Foals

Also at the same Place there is kept for a STALLION, a Black Horse of the Heavy Breed. He was bred by Mr. Falconer, of Bretby in Derbyshire, out of his best Black Mare; and will Leap this Season at Half a Guinea a Mare, if a Foal, and Five

4. **Derby Mercury** - 7 April 1758

He married his second wife, Sarah at Hartshorne, the neighbouring village (about two miles from Bretby) in 1733. Thomas Faulkner [-1780], a yeoman of Bretby, in his will, expressed the wish that his son John should take his estate at Bretby.

John Faulkner [c1740-1824] clearly continued to live at Bretby where he and his wife Mary had several children baptised there between 1771 and 1791.

Thomas Faulkner also had a son William, but William Faulkner [c1746-1832] and his wife seem to have lived at Newton Solney (about 1½ miles north-west of Bretby), where most of their children were baptised.

John Faulkner's son Thomas [1771-1845] was a farmer, recorded as residing at Bretby Farm in 1829. He, in turn had a son John, and this last John Faulkner [1814-1874] is of interest in a number of ways. At the time of the 1841 census John Faulkner was living at the Hall, Bretby. In 1851 he was a farmer of 390 acres, living at Bretby Farm. By 1861 his holding had grown to 571 acres; at which time he was also land agent to the 6th Earl of Chesterfield. In his obituary in the Derby Mercury in 1874 John Faulkner was described as an eminent agriculturalist. It seems he was a breeder, exhibitor and judge of cattle, sheep and poultry; although there was no mention of horses [5]! The Faulkner family, however certainly owned and bred horses, and as we have seen in other families, more than one generation was involved.

Chivers [6] made only one reference to the Faulkner family, the dam of *Sim's Horse 2019* (foaled in 1795, and bred by John Sims of Stanton by Bridge, about five miles from Bretby) being recorded as having been by *Faulkner's Old Horse*. Cover advertisements in newspapers reveal much more.

In 1772[38De], '*a Strong Black Horse, rising four years old*', bred by Mr. Bull of Newton Solney was advertised (below) as available to cover. He was said to have been '*got by Mr Falkner's Old Horse of Bratby*'. The unnamed horse's pedigree included notable references to Mr. Hood, *the Packington blind Horse* and Mr. 'Bolstridge' (Bulstrode) of Isley Walton.

In this instance the breeder of '*Mr. Falkner's old Horse*' is likely to have been Thomas Faulkner [-1780], or his son John Faulkner [c1740-1824].

To Cover this Season,

AT WILLIAM REDFERN's, of Mickleover, Derbyshire, at 12s. a Foal, if barren 5s. 6d.

A Strong Black HORSE,

Of the Cart Kind, rising four Years old, standing upwards of sixteen Hands; was bred by Mr. Bull, of Newton Solney, and got by Mr. Falkner's old Horse of Bratby; his Dam by Mr. Hood's old Horse that went to Mr. Bolstridge's, of Isley Walton; his Grandam by the Packington blind Horse.

The Faulkner family do not then feature in newspaper advertisements until about thirty years later when in 1803[150], Mr. Abbott of Borrowash, Derbyshire advertised a horse called *Young Gallimore*, '*bred by Mr. Falkner of Bretby, out of his famous Mare*'.

TO COVER THIS SEASON.

AT Mr. ISAAC BENNET's of Over Haddon, in the county of Derby, at One Guinea a Mare, and Half-a-Guinea Barren, a Black Colt, of the cart kind, rising three years old, called

NELSON.

Nelson was got by Mr. Knowle's Blaze, of Nailstone, in Leicestershire, out of a capital Mare, near Burton-upon-Trent.

Also will Cover this Season,

At the same place, a Black Colt, of the cart kind, rising two years old, at One Guinea a Mare, and Half-a-Guinea Barren,

BULLSTRODE.

Bullstrode was got by Gallimore, and Gallimore was got by Old Gallimore, that formerly Covered at Winchhill. He was bred by Mr. Falkner, of Bretby, his Dam by Mr. Falkner's Bald Horse, and his Grandam by the Packington Blind Horse.—The Colt's Dam was got by Mr. Harp's Bullstrode, of Birchwood Moor; Bullstrode was got by Mr. Boulstridge's Old Horse, of Isley Walton; his Grandam by Mr. Summerland's Wiltshire Horse.

In a similar advertisement (page 93) in 1804[156De], *Young Gallimore* was said to have been rising eight years old, *'got by Old Gallimore, and bred by Mr. Faulkner, of Bradby; his dam by Mr. Faulkner's bald Horse, and his Grandam by the Packington Blind Horse'*.

It is interesting to see the Gallimore name linked once more with that of Faulkner, a connection, as noted above, known to have existed much earlier, at a time before 1750. Further cover advertisements in 1808[202De] (page 91), in 1812[230], and again in 1813[235] featured a colt called *Bulstrode*, bred by Mr. 'Falkner' of Bretby out of the horse *Young Gallimore* he had bred (Mr. Faulkner's own *Bald Horse* having apparently sired the dam of *Young Gallimore*). In this case the colt's dam was said to have had another famous horse in her pedigree, *Mr. Summerland's Wiltshire Horse*. At these later dates John Faulkner [c1740-1824] was probably the breeder of *Young Gallimore*. Alternatively, his son Thomas [1771-1845] is most likely to have bred this stallion.

Following the death of John Faulkner, a farm dispersal sale was advertised (Derby Mercury, 9 March 1825). His stock included cattle, sheep, pigs, and amongst other horses, three draught mares in foal to a stallion called *North Star* [5].

Reference has already been made to a cover advertisement (page 87) in 1833[286De] by John Sims of Stanton by Bridge, Derbyshire which featured a black colt of the *'pure Old Black Breed'* called *Derbyshire*. The detailed pedigree which was supplied, going back many generations, and leading ultimately to *Massey's Gallimore of Swarkestone*, also included a reference to *Mr. Falkner's Old Horse* as the sire of the great great grandam of *Derbyshire*.

Moore - of Winshill, Derbyshire

Mr. Moore of Winshill was named by Chivers as the owner and breeder of the earliest of a series of stallions called *Gallemore* (*Gallimore*) which were listed in the first volume of the Stud-book [6]. [Winshill was formerly a village in Derbyshire, only about 1½ miles west of Bretby, but is now a suburb of Burton-upon-Trent].

This particular stallion, *Gallimore 903,* is said to have been foaled in about 1780, by a sire which the editors of the Stud-book could not determine.

Several references to Mr. Moore and his horse *Gallimore* do however occur in cover advertisements already mentioned, and these generally also feature his near neighbour, Mr. Faulkner of Bretby. In 1803[149De], Charles Radford (page 96) placed a cover advertisement for a black colt, rising two years old. The colt was said to be out of a mare got by Mr. Moore's *Gallimore*.

Paul Holmes [1765-1849], a yeoman of Newton Solney, in a cover advertisement dated 1803[151], for '*a Black Horse of the Cart Kind called Gallimore*', similarly claimed that the stallion was '*late the property of Mr. Moore of Winshill*' (and presumably identifiable as *Gallemore 903*). This advertisement also tells us what the editors of the Stud-book did not know,

TO COVER THIS SEASON,
AT Mr. ABBOTT's, Borrowash, in the county of Derby, that Noted Horse
BLAZE,
At One Guinea and a Half a Foal, and Half-a-Guinea Barren.

Blaze was the property of the late Mr. Radford, of Little Eaton; he was bred by Mr. Ashby of Eggington, and got by Mr. Bulstrode's noted Old Horse, of Ifley Walton.

Also at the same place, that Favorite Horse
OLD GALLIMORE,
At Two Guineas a Foal, and Half-a-Guinea Barren.

Gallimore was late the property of Mr. Moore of Winshill, and is allowed to be the best Horse of his kind in the kingdom. He was got by that noted and well known Horse Old Mansetter.

His Stock need no comment, as they are such as always find the way to a good market.

Borrowash, March 23d, 1804.

152. **Derby Mercury** - 29 March 1804

that *'he was got by Old Mansetter'*.
A similar advertisement (page 92) by
Mr. Abbott of 'Borrowash' appeared in
1804[152De], this horse now being called
Old Gallimore, whilst in the same year[156De],
Daniel Moore of Winshill advertised (opposite),
together with a horse called *Conqueror*, the
rising eight year old *Young Gallimore*, the
son of *(Old) Gallimore*. Mr. Faulkner of
Bradby was said to have bred *Young Gallimore*.
Gallimore 904 was considered to have been
a son of *Gallemore 903*, and the horse *Young
Gallimore*, (who like *Old Gallimore*, was
owned by the Moore family), seems to fit
the description. The first Stud-book [29]
records that Perkins of Whitgreave (page 78)
owned and bred *Gallemore 904*. Assuming,
however that the above *'Young Gallimore'*
was *Gallimore 904*, he was bred by Faulkner
and not by Perkins!
[The importance of Daniel Moore's
advertisement in providing a pedigree which
links back to *Mansetter* and the original
Old Gallimore has already been discussed.]
Mr. Abbott of Borrowash placed a similar
advertisement for *Old Gallimore* in 1805[164],
and in 1806[175]. In 1806[175] he identified the
former owner as Mr. John Moore of Winshill.
In 1808[202De] Isaac Bennet [c1748 - 1825] of
Over Haddon, Derbyshire (but later of
Bramshall, near Uttoxeter, Staffordshire)
advertised (page 91) the cover services of
the black colt, rising two years old, called
Bulstrode, together with another black colt,
rising three years old called *Nelson*.
Bulstrode was said to have been got by
Gallimore, and *Gallimore* was got by *Old
Gallimore* (*Gallimore 903*), that formerly
covered at 'Winchhill' (Winshill). He was bred
by Mr. 'Falkner', his dam by Mr. *'Falkner's'
Bald Horse*. The *Packington Blind Horse*,
Mr. *Boulstridge's (Bulstrode's) Old Horse* and
Summerland's *Wiltshire Horse* also featured
in his pedigree.
Isaac Bennet placed a similar advertisement
for *Bulstrode* in 1812[230]. This advertisement
indicated that *Bulstrode's* sire, *Gallimore*,

STALLIONS.

TO COVER THIS SEASON, at DANIEL MOORE'S, WINSHILL, near Burton-upon-Trent, a Black Horse of the Waggon kind, called,

CONQUEROR,

At ONE GUINEA and a CROWN a Foal, 7s. 6d. Barren, and 1s. the Man.

He is rising six years old,—sixteen hands one inch high,—uncommonly wide,—short-legged,—full of Bone and Hair,—and his Action will speak for itself. Conqueror was bred by Mr. Oakey, of Doveridge, out of his well-known blind Mare, which Mare was allowed by competent judges, to be one of the best Waggon Mares in these parts; the blind Mare was got by Mr. Hart's bald Horse, of Coleoreton; the bald Horse, by Old Mansetter:—Conqueror's Grandam was got by the original Old Gallimore, that covered at Wotton, which Horse was supposed to be the Sire of the Packington blind Horse:—Conqueror was got by Mr. Massey's Horse, called Bulstrode, his Dam by Old Mansetter.

☞ The above Horse is an uncommon sure foal-getter, and his Stock very capital; there has been two-year-olds of his getting, sold for 100gs. each.

Also, to COVER at the same Place, That well-known Stock-getter,

YOUNG GALLIMORE,

At ONE GUINEA and a CROWN a Foal, 7s. 6d. Barren, and 1s. the Man.

He is rising eight years old,—stands sixteen hands one inch high:—was got by Old Gallimore, and bred by Mr. Faulkner, of Bradley; his Dam by Mr. Faulkner's bald Horse, and his Grandam by the Packington Blind Horse.

He will be at the Coach and Horses, in Egginton, Monday noon; from thence he will go to the Talbot, in Hilton, and stop all night; on Tuesday morning he will be at the Greyhound, in Scropton, and at night, at the Anchor, in Doveridge; on Wednesday he will be at the Buck, in Draycott, at night at the Wheel, in Tutbury; at Winshill on Thursday, until Friday morning; Friday noon, at the Bull's Head, in Hartshorn, at night at the Dog and Duck, in Stanton; returns home on Saturday, and stops there till Monday morning.

⁎ The above Horses are allowed, by competent judges, to be the best pair of Horses in these parts:—the Money to be paid at the Horse Feast, of which, timely Notice will be given.

was the stallion which Daniel Moore had advertised in 1804[156De] as *Young Gallimore*.
In another cover advertisement (page 94) in 1812[234De] there was the interesting example
of a named mare , owned by Mr. Moore of Winshill. It was stated that a stallion called *Young*

Useful was out of a mare called *Old Gallimore,* and that *'Old Gallimore was sold for Two Hundred Guineas when 13 years old by, Mr. Moor of Winsall'.*

Farey, in his *'General View of the Agriculture of Derbyshire',* published in 1817 gave a list of the most noted Derbyshire *'Stallion letters'* of the improved cart-horse [8]. Daniel and John Moore, of Winshill, near Burton-on-Trent were both included in this list (page 26), together with John Abbott of Spondon (probably the same John Abbott sometimes described as being of Borrowash, who advertised stallions for cover in 1803[150], 1804[152De] (page 92), and 1806[175]).

John Moore [1767 - 1838] and Daniel Moore [1770- 1849], baptised at Burton-upon-Trent, were both sons of Daniel and Elizabeth Moore, farmers of Winshill, where the family was long established.

The death of John Moore, farmer of Winshill, aged 71, was announced in a newspaper report, in October 1838. The 1841 Census records that his brother, Daniel Moore was then still living at Winshill.

A Capital Cart Stallion.

TO BE SOLD BY AUCTION,

By Mr. EDWARD LEES,

At the house of Mr. Richard Nutt, known by the sign of the Game Chicken, in Hinckley, in the county of Leicester, on Wednesday the 26th of August, 1812, at twelve o'clock,

THAT capital well-bred Cart Horse, Young Useful, four years old, remarkably full of bone, sixteen hands one inch high.

Young Useful was got by Mr. Knowles's Ball Horse, Old Useful for the five last seasons covered at Four Guineas each mare, and this season he covered at 5 Guineas each mare. He is allowed by judges to be the best Horse ever shewn in Leicester-shire. Young Useful was got out of a mare, Old Gallimore, bred by Thomas Manford, of Winsal, Old Gallimore was sold for Two Hundred Guineas when 13 years old, by Mr. Moor, of Winsal. Young Useful covered last season, and proved himself a sure foal getter.

N. B. Young Useful may be seen at Mr. Thomas Radburn's, of Bourton upon Dunsmore, in the county of Warwick, until the 24th of this instant, and on the 25th instant, at the house of Mr. Richard Nutt, at Hinckley.

234. **Leicester Journal** - 21 August 1812

Bancroft – of Sinfin, Derbyshire

The *Sinfin Old horse* was another of those horses whose origins seem to be a mystery. He is said to have been the sire of the dam of *Blaze 185* (foaled 1786), bred by Mr. Ashby of Eckington (about five miles north of Chesterfield), Derbyshire [6]. Chivers [6] did not mention the Bancroft family of Sinfin. Sinfin is now a southern suburb of the city of Derby; it adjoins Stenson where the Stych family resided. [Sinfin is better known for its association with horses of a different kind, the large expanse of Sinfin Moor, which extended to about 350 acres was also the location of Derby Races for many years during the 18th century.]

The *Sinfin Old Horse* was probably owned and/or bred by a member of the Bancroft family. Parish registers of Swarkestone and Barrow-on-Trent indicate that the Bancrofts had been resident in this area near Derby for centuries.

A cover advertisement (page 96) by Charles Radford in 1803[149De] for a black colt, rising two years old, gave his sire as by *Mr. Bancroft's Horse of Sinfin,* which was in turn said to have been got by *Mr. Hart's Horse of Culloden,* Leicestershire.

TO COVER THIS SEASON,

At John Bancroft's, of Sinfin, near Derby, at a Guinea and a Half a Foal and 10s. 6d. Barren;

A BLACK HORSE,

Of the Cart Kind, seven years old.

HE was got by Mr. Hart's old Horse of Culloden, which was got by Old Manletter, his dam by Mr. Donnisthorpe's Bald Horse, his grandam was sister to the Kirby Old Horse, which was got by the Packington Blind Horse, and he has proved himself a good stock getter.

Also to Cover at the Same Place,

At Fifteen Shillings a Foal and 5s. if Barren,

A BLACK COLT,

Of the Cart Kind, three years old.

He was got by the Sinfin Horse, and out of a well bred Mare, and he has proved himself a sure foal getter.

171. **Derby Mercury** - Thursday 25 April 1805

In 1805[171De] John Bancroft of Sinfin advertised (page 95) the cover services of an unnamed seven year old black horse, said to have been by *Mr. Hart's old Horse at Culloden*, which in turn was by Old *Mansetter*. His dam was said to have been by *Mr. Donnisthorpe's Bald Horse*. John Bancroft gave a detailed pedigree of this stallion which included Oldacres' horses *Mansetter* and *Kirby*, and, inevitably, *the Packington Blind Horse*, but he gave no clue as to the identify of the *Sinfin old Horse*, named as the sire of a three year old colt in the same advertisement .

In an advertisement in March 1811[216], for a rising six years old unnamed black horse, to cover at Brailsford (a village halfway between Ashbourne and Derby), it was claimed that his sire was the *Sinfin Old Horse*. A later cover advertisement, in May 1811[225], for the rising six year old stallion called *Ploughboy,* also got by *the Sinfin Old Horse,* seems to describe the same horse. Both advertisements also stated that the *Sinfin Old Horse* was got by *Hart's Blaze* of Culloden House, and that *Blaze,* in turn had been got by *Mansetter*.

Indications are that the *Sinfin Old Horse* was the seven year old black horse which John Bancroft advertised in 1805[171De]. He would have been foaled in 1797 or 1798. This is however at odds with the view that he was the sire of *Blaze 185*, foaled in 1786, bred by Mr. Ashby of Eckington, and owned by Radford of Little Eaton. If there was an earlier *Sinfin Old Horse*, no evidence has been found. Two cover advertisements, in 1803[150], and again (page 92) in 1804[152De] for a horse called *Blaze*, bred by Mr. Ashby of Eggington, and formerly owned by Radford of Little Eaton fit the description, where *Blaze* would have have been sired in about 1800, rather than 1785. There is evidence however that Francis Radford of Little Eaton (page 97) owned an earlier *Blaze*. [Eggington is just north of Burton-upon-Trent and only about three miles south-west of Sinfin, where the Bancroft family lived. The Stud-book reference to Eckington must be an error]. Farey [8], as mentioned earlier, described Luke Ashby [1757-1818], a farmer of Eggington as a breeder of work horses; he was, almost certainly the 'Mr. Ashby' of these advertisements.]

The Bancroft family was extensive and it is difficult to identify any specific individual who may have been a breeder of 'Shires' except to say that one of them was called John. 'John Bancroft' was listed (page 26) by Farey as one of the most noted Derbyshire *'Stallion letters.'* Fary also noted that John Bancroft of Synfin kept eight breeding cart mares; hired or used the stallions of Mr. Samuel Knowles (of Nailstone), and kept a stallion for his own and his neighbours' use. This John Bancroft was probably John Bancroft [1743 - 1826], senior, a farmer of Sinfin, and a son of Gervase Bancroft, a prosperous yeoman of Sinfin [19]. Alternatively, John Bancroft [1771 -   ], a younger son of the above John could have been the John Bancroft referred to by Farey. William Bancroft [1767-1847] was the elder son of John Bancroft, senior and took over the farm at Sinfin from his father. William Bancroft is likely to have been the tup breeder also mentioned by Farey [8]. William Bancroft's widow, Elizabeth Bancroft [1778 - 1867] continued to run the farm, and was recorded in the 1851 Census as living at Synfin House, a substantial farm of over 200 acres.

TO COVER THIS SEASON,

AT MR. BANCROFT's, Sinfin, near Derby, at One Sovereign and a half each Mare if in-foal, Five Shillings if barren, and One Shilling the Man,

TOMMY,

A Brown Cart Stallion, rising 6 years old, and has proved himself a sure Foal-getter.

ALSO, AT THE SAME PLACE,

A BROWN COLT,

Rising 4 years old, at One Sovereign and a half each Mare if in-foal, Five Shillings if barren, and One Shilling the Man.

Also, at the same Place,

SANCHO,

(Late the Property of Sir Geo. Crewe, Bart. now belonging to Mr. Bancroft,)

A Cart Horse, of the Flemish breed, Will serve Mares at one Pound Ten Shillings each Mare, and One Shilling the Groom.

Sancho is a sure Foal-getter, stands 16 hands high, rising 8 years old, colour a rich bay, in point of substance, bone, shortness of legs, he is seldom equalled, his stock has proved him a horse of the first value, many, both colts and fillies at one year and a half old, -have been sold from Thirty to Fifty Pounds each.

, A specimen of his Stock may be seen at Mr. Webb's, of Barton, or Mr. Smith's, of Swarkestone Lowes.

Sinfin is 2 miles from Swarkestone Bridge, 3 miles from Derby, and 8 miles from Burton-upon-Trent.

284. **Derby Mercury** - Wednesday 25 March 1832
http://www.britishnewspaperarchive.co.uk/viewer/bl/0000052/18320425/007/0002

John Bancroft [1801 - 1848], the son of William could have had a role in further Shire horse breeding, the later involvement of the Bancroft family as owners and breeders of Shires being indicated by an advertisement (page 95) in 1832[284De], for a stallion called *Tommy*, available to cover at Mr. Bancroft's at Sinfin. The same advertisement also featured *Sancho*, then owned by Bancroft.

Also, in 1835[288De], the six years old cart stallion *Ben* (by *Big Ben* possibly, *Big Ben 130*), the property of Mr. Bancroft was advertised (opposite) to be sold by auction in Derby.

TO BE SOLD BY AUCTION,
BY MR. BREAREY,
In the Corn Market, Derby,
On Friday, 24th April, 1835, precisely at 12 o'clock;
THAT CELEBRATED CART STALLION
BEN,

The property of Mr. Bancroft, six years old, he has proved himself a sure foal getter, and was got by Big Ben, dam by Mr. Edge's Brown Horse, grandam by Gallimore, great grandam by Mr. Bulstrode's Old Horse which covered at three guineas a mare, great great grandam by Mr. Summerland's Brown Horse.

Also to be Sold at the same time,
A handsome Phaeton, a Broad and Narrow wheel'd Cart and Waggon, Straw Cutter, Winnowing Machine, &c. &c.

288. **Derby Mercury** - Wednesday 22 April 1835

Stych - of Stenson, Derbyshire
[See **Stych - of Bellamore (Great Haywood), Barton-under-Needwood, Staffordshire**]

Radford - of Denby, Derbyshire

Two (apparently unrelated) families by the name of Radford have contributed significantly to the breeding of Shire horses. In this case it is a farming family of Denby (a village about eight miles north of Derby).

In 1770[26] John Radford [1737 -1798] advertised his '*coming two years old black colt'* to cover at Denby, said to be by *Mr. Hurd's (Hood's?) blind Horse* and bred from a mare of Mr. Garner's of Packington. Two years later, in 1772[39De] John Radford of Denby advertised (below) what seems to have been the same horse, now a rising four year old called *Fair Leaper* (being out of a mare of Mr. Garner's of Packington and got by *the Packington old horse*). He also advertised a stallion called *Old Blaze*.

To Cover this Seafon, 1772.
AT JOHN RADFORD's of Denby, a black Horfe, of the Cart Kind, rifing four Years old, known by the Name of
FAIR LEAPER.
He was out of a Mare of Mr. Garner's of Packington, and was got by the Packington old Horfe. He will cover at Half a Guinea a Foal; if barren 5s. He is as fure a Foal-getter as any in England.
LIKEWISE
OLD BLAZE
Will cover this Seafon at the fame Place, at Half a Guinea a Foal; if barren 5s. They may change from one to the other as they think proper.
*** Grafs for Mares and proper Care taken.

39. **Derby Mercury** - 17 April 1772

To Cover this Season,
AT CHARLES RADFORD's, of Denby, in the County of Derby, at One Guinea and a Half a Foal, and Half a Guinea if Barren;
A BLACK COLT,
Rifing Two years old, out of a Mare got by Mr. Moore's GALLIMORE, which was a Son of Mr. Oldacre's MANSETTER, then the property of the late Mr. Leicefter, of Harthorn; his Sire by Mr. Bancroft's Horfe, of Sinfin, which was got by Mr. Hart's Horfe, of Culloden, in Leicefterfhire.
Derby, April 7, 1803.

149. **Derby Mercury** - Thursday 14 April 1803

In 1785[86] John Radford of Denby advertised two black colts which were available to cover, the first, rising two years old he said was got by his old horse which was covering in Nottinghamshire. The other colt, rising three years old, he claimed was bred by Thomas Winson of Shottle, and got by John *Wagstaff's Horse of Atlow.*

In 1803[149De], Charles Radford [1766-1853] of Denby, son of John, advertised (below) a black colt, rising two years old, said to have been sired by Mr. *Bancroft's horse of Sinfin,* and out of a mare got by *Mr. Moore's Gallimore* (in turn a son of Mr. *Oldacre's Mansetter*). A few years later, in 1806[178] Charles Radford advertised a black colt got by Mr. Knowles's noted *Bald Horse* of Nailstone, his dam by the *Derbyshire Horse* owned by Mr. Brown of Stretton (under Fosse), Warwickshire. He also advertised his 'noted BLACK HORSE', rising five years old, which was got by Mr. *Bancroft's horse of Sinfin,* which in turn was got by Mr. *Hart's Blaze* horse, his dam being by *Old Gallimore*. This seems to have been the black colt he advertised in 1803[149De].

[Mr. Z. Brown and his horse *Derbyshire* also featured in advertisements in 1792[111Le], 1792[119], 1797[135] and 1802[146]. He can be identified as Zephaniah Brown [-1801] of Warwickshire, although his origins seem to have been in the Duffield area of Derbyshire.]

Radford - of Little Eaton, Derbyshire

According to Chivers [6], the stallion *Blaze 185* (foaled in 1786) was owned by Radford of Little Eaton.

In 1802[145De], John Wagstaff of Atlow advertised (opposite) a black horse, said to have been got by a son of *Blaze*, and formerly the property of the late Mr. Radford of Little Eaton. Interestingly, a black horse, rising nine years old, known as the *Swebstone Horse* (page 62) featured in the same advertisement. He was said to have been a full brother of *Radford's Blaze*, also having been got by Mr. *Bulstrode's old horse.*

In 1803[150], and again in 1804[152De], Mr. Abbot of Borrowash advertised (page 92) a horse called *Blaze* to cover, said to

To Cover this Season,

AT John Wagstaff's of Atlow, at ONE GUINEA a Mare, if in Foal; and SEVEN SHILLINGS and SIXPENCE barren;

A BLACK HORSE,

Of the Cart kind, rising three Years old.——He was bred by Mr. Soresby, of Brailsford; and got by a Son of Blaze, the property of the late Mr. Radford, of Little Eaton.

Likewise to Cover at the same place,

At ONE GUINEA a Foal, and SEVEN SHILLINGS and SIX-PENCE barren,

A BLACK HORSE,

Of the Cart kind, rising nine years old. He is known by the name of the Swepstone Horse. He is full Brother to the late Mr. Radford's Blaze; and was got by Mr. Bulstrode's old Horse, which covered at Three Guineas a Mare.

145. **Derby Mercury** - Thursday 29 April 1802

have been the property of the late Mr. Radford of Little Eaton. *Blaze* (*Blaze* 185) was advertised as having been bred by Mr. Ashby of Eggington, and got by *Mr. Bulstrode's noted old Horse*, of Isley Walton.

In 1812[232] *Blaze* was advertised to cover at William Mason's at Woolscote, near Hartington in Derbyshire. It was stated that he had covered nine seasons at Mr. Hudson's, of Rowland, near Bakewell. *Blaze* was said to have been got by Mr. *Radford's Blaze* of Little Eaton, and out of a mare belonging to Mr. Soresby, of the Bakewell breed. *Radford's Blaze* was sired by Mr. *Bulstrode's Horse of Islay Walton* which covered for 14 seasons. Interestingly, this pedigree is supported by the genealogical table (**Table 2**, page 30-31) which records that *Bulstrode's Bald Horse* (*Bald Horse 93*) sired *Radford's Blaze* (*Blaze 185*) who, in turn, sired *Hudson's Blaze* (*Blaze* 184 - apparently bred by Robert Bakewell, but owned by Thomas Hudson). [Thomas Hudson [1746 - 1838] of Rowland was said by Chivers [6] to have been a great man in his day with seven horses linked to his name in the first Stud-book, but of whom nothing more was known.]

John Chadwick advertised (page 75) his black horse called *Young Packington* in 1807[192St], and again in 1808[201]. He claimed that his horse had been got by *Mr. Radford's Blaze*. He also stated that *Blaze* had been sired by *Bulstrode's Old Horse*.

Chadwick advertised the same horse, now simply called *Packington* in 1811[221], and again (page 71) in 1812[233St]. *Packington* was said to have been got by *Mr. Radford's Blaze*. Also in 1811[224], in a cover advertisement for a Black Horse, rising five years old, his dam was said to have been by the late *Mr. Radford's old Blaze* of Little Eaton.

Radford can be identified as Francis Radford [1745-1801] of Horsley, Breadsall and Elms Farm, Little Eaton, a prosperous gentleman farmer.

Chivers noted that Radford was a member of the Dishley Society which seems to have been formed to ensure high prices were maintained from the sale of, and services of rams [6].

Francis Radford also bred New Leicester sheep [8].

Glossop - of Upper Haddon and Stonegravels, Chesterfield, Derbyshire

Joseph Glossop at Stonegravels, near Chesterfield advertised (below) the noted horse *GALLIMORE* in 1777[64De] which was said to have been formerly the property of Francis Glossop of Upper Haddon where he covered for ten seasons. Glossop stated that that he was *'got by that noted Horse OLD GALLIMORE*, otherwise *MASSEY'*.

March 25, 1777.

To COVER this SEASON,
AT JOSEPH GLOSSOP's at Stonegravels, near Chesterfield, the noted black Horse
GALLIMORE,
late the Property of Francis Gloſſop of Upper Haddon, where he has covered ten Seaſons ſucceſſively; his Stock is his Recommendation. He was got by that noted Horſe OLD GALLIMORE, otherwiſe MASSEY. He will attend at the abovementioned Place, and no where elſe this Seaſon. The Price is 12s. 6d. the Foal, and 5s. the barren Mare.— Good Care will be taken of Mares, &c.
JOSEPH GLOSSOP.

To COVER this SEASON,
AT the Houſe of Mr. JOSEPH GLOSSOP, at Stonegravels, near Cheſterfield, at 12s. 6d. the Foal, and 4s. the barren Mare;
Young **GALLIMOORE,**
A Black Horſe, of the Waggon Kind; he was got by Gloſſop's old Horſe Gallymoore, and out of a Mare that was bred by Mr. Knowles of Nelſon, Leiceſterſhire; ſhe was got by his Horſe Conqueror, and out of his noted Mare Mettle; he is very full of Bone, and a great Size.

This interesting advertisement indicates that this horse was a son of the horse 'Galymoor' or 'Gallymoor' (Gallimore) which Thomas Massey had advertised between 1757[1De] and 1762[9] (page 86).

In 1783[81De] Joseph Glossop advertised (above) *Young GALLIMOORE, 'got by Glossop's old Horse Gallymoore'*, and out of a mare bred by Mr. Knowles of Nelson (Nailstone), which in turn was got by his horse *Conqueror*. This advertisement suggests that *Young GALLIMOORE* was a son of *the old horse Gallimore* he had advertised in 1777[64De] (a son of *Glossop's old Horse Gallymoore*). A pedigree naming Mr. Knowles's mare as his dam attests to his quality.

Bakewell parish registers indicate that Joseph Glossop [1748-1824] and Francis Glossop [1743-1835] were brothers. Francis Glossop was probably a yeoman farmer, but Joseph Glossop of Stonegravels described himself as a coalmaster (i.e. in overall charge of managing a coalmine). Joseph Glossop's occupation and property interests were in fact more varied. He did have farming concerns, and his will reveals that he had real estate which included farms, but he also had lead, coal and other mines, and these would seem to have been his primary interest. He also had shares in such mines, in particularly the Mandale lead mine (near Over Haddon) [19].

This information serves as a reminder that the demand for heavy horses did not come solely from agriculture but also from developing industries. Draught horses were needed for road work, hauling carts and waggons which carried e.g. coal, metal ore and quarried stone, or manufactured goods.

Caulton – of Shottle, Derbyshire

A number of individuals, who owned heavy horses, or had horses let to them, operated in an area of Derbyshire between Derby and Chesterfield.
Paul Caulton [1750-1822] was a yeoman in possession of a number of farms and a breeder producing a ready supply of horses in this area, but we can see from the pedigree information supplied in the following advertisements he placed in newspapers, that he was in contact with some of the best-known breeders from further afield.

In 1783[82De] he advertised (opposite) a black horse, rising five years old, out of one of his best mares which was got by *Mr. Avarne's horse of Breedon*, whose horse in turn was said to have been sired by the noted *Packington Horse* (presumably *the Packington Blind horse*). The same advertisement featured a black colt, rising three years old, got by *Mr. Wagstaff's Horse of Atlow*.

In 1785[85] Paul Caulton advertised what seem to have been the same animals which he advertised in 1783, together with a black colt, rising three years old, by *Mr. Radford's old Horse of Denby*.

In 1788[96] he advertised a black colt rising three years old, got by *Mr. Donnisthorpe's noted horse of Packington* which in turn had been got by *Boulstridge's Bald Horse*. Caulton also had three old horses available to provide cover.

> To COVER this Season, 1783,
> AT PAUL CALTON's in Shottle, in the County of Derby, at Ten Shillings and Six-pence a Foal, and Two Shillings and Six-pence if barren; that beautiful
>
> **Black HORSE,**
>
> Of the Cart Kind, riſing five Years old, ſtands ſixteen Hands high, full of Bone, goes well on his Legs; is remarkably gay on the Fore-Hand, and allowed by the greateſt Judges, to be the moſt beautiful Horſe in this Part of the Kingdom.
> He was got by Mr. Avarne's Horſe of Bredon, Leiceſter-ſhire, which was got by the noted Packington Horſe, and out of one of Paul Calton's beſt Mares.——His Stock is very promiſing.
>
> A L S O
> To COVER at the ſame Place and on the ſame Terms, a
> *Black COLT,*
>
> Of the Cart Kind, riſing three Years old, full ſixteen Hands high, full of Bone, goes well on his Legs, and is allowed by good Judges, to be one of the beſt Colts in theſe Parts.
> He was got by Mr. Wagſtaff's Horſe of Atlow, and out of the ſame Mare with the above Horſe.
> ** The above Horſes are ſure Foal-getters.
> ‡§‡ Good Graſs for Mares, with proper Care.

82. **Derby Mercury** - Thursday 8 May 1783

In 1794[131], a black horse, rising five years old, got by *'Mr. Donesthorpe's best horse of Packington, out of his own* mare' was advertised by Paul Caulton. He claimed that his mare had bred '*several capital mares and six covering stallions, one of them having won a £20 premium in South Wales in 1790, and again in 1791'*. In the same advertisement Caulton included a black colt which was available to cover, said to have been got by *Bulstrode's best horse of 'Risley'* (Isley) Walton.
Paul Caulton advertised 'his aged horse', rising 14 years old, as being available to cover in 1807[191]. This stallion was said to have been by Mr. Bulstrode's favourite horse, and out of a sister to the horse sold into South Wales which won the £20 premium in 1790.

Wright - of Wheston Hall, near Tideswell, Derbyshire

Chivers [6] noted that the Wright family of Wheston Hall (about one mile north-west of Tideswell) had made a very special contribution to Shire horse history, beginning with Joseph Wright [1758-1838], who was followed by his son Anthony Wright [1777-1852]. Anthony's son William Wright [1822-1893] is said to have continued the family business. The Wright family are said to be notable because they owned a very large number of stallions (at least sixteen of which are listed in the first Stud-book [29]), and because of their widespread trading links with noted breeders and owners in Derbyshire, Leicestershire, Staffordshire and beyond.

There is little evidence, however that the Wrights made use of newspaper advertising, on which basis the importance of this family's contribution may be underestimated. They are also not mentioned within advertisements and notices placed in newspapers by other 'Shire men'; this being perhaps because the Wright family were owners rather than breeders.

Interestingly, the surname Wright, presumably referring to this family, appears frequently within the genealogical table **Table 2** (page 30-31), which was produced with the first Stud-book. Almost all the entries for stallions listed in the Stud-book [29] in which the Wright name is mentioned refer to them as owners, but not breeders, exceptions being *Blacklegs 141*, foaled in 1798, owned and bred by Joseph Wright, and *Gallimore 905*, foaled in 1815, and owned and bred by Anthony Wright. The only newspaper advertisements found which feature the Wright name were from 1806[177De] (opposite), 1808[196] and similarly in 1809[204] when *Blacklegs* (identifiable as *Blacklegs 141*) was available to cover. *Blacklegs* was said to have been got by Oldacres' *Little John* (as also indicated by the genealogical table, **Table 2**), his sire and dam by old *Mansetter* and his grandam by Oldacres' *Kirby* horse. These advertisements were however placed by <u>William</u> Wright of Matlock Bridge (a hamlet just outside Matlock).

The Stud-book entry [29] for *Blacklegs 141* contains similar details but names Joseph (not William) Wright of Matlock Bridge as the owner and breeder. Joseph Wright of Wheston did have an elder brother, William (baptised in 1754 at nearby Wormhill (two miles south-west of Tideswell.

Whether William Wright of Matlock Bridge was Joseph Wright's brother has not been determined, but the advertisement (opposite) suggests that William Wright rather than Joseph Wright should have been named as the owner of *Blacklegs 141*.

> **CART STALLIONS.**
> TO COVER THIS SEASON,
> AT WILLIAM WRIGHT's, Matlock Bridge, Derbyshire, at One Guinea and Half a Foal, and Half a Guinea Barren; and Half a Crown the Groom,
> That Well Known Stallion
> **BLACKLEGS,**
> Late the property of Mr. Wm. Slingsby, of Foleshill, near Coventry.
> He was got by Mr. Oldacre's Little John, of Peatling-Lodge, near Leicester: his sire and dam by Old Mansetter, his grandam by his Kirby Horse, which was got by Mr. Hood's Horse, of Packington, near Ashby-de-la-Zouch.
> A sample of the above Horse's Stock may be seen at Mr. Higgott's Rolleston.
> The above Horse will be at the Red Lion, Wirksworth, on Monday night and stop till Tuesday night; from thence to Weston Inn, and stop till Wednesday night; he will then return to Wirksworth, and home on the Thursday morning, where he will be the remainder of the Week.
> Also to COVER at the same Place,
> At one Guinea a Foal, and Ten Shillings and Six-pence Barren, and two Shillings and Six-pence the Groom,
> A Black Colt, call'd
> **YOUNG BULSTRODE,**
> He is uncommonly wide, short legg'd, full of bone & hair,
> He was got by Mr. Chadwick's noted Horse, Marston, and out of a capital Mare, by Mr. Bulstrode's old bald Horse Massey.

177. **Derby Mercury** - Thursday 17 April 1806

CHAPTER 10: LINCOLNSHIRE BREEDERS AND OWNERS

Lincolnshire is a county of contrasts, having deep clay soils in river valleys, higher ground consisting of limestone hills and undulating chalk wolds, together with extensive, low-lying marsh and fen. Cattle, and especially sheep once grazed in large numbers. Here the medieval wool trade was of great economic importance; very different from today where arable crops dominate.

The Lincolnshire Wolds produced sheep and barley, with horses being used for ploughing. Here farmers also bred horses which could be sold at Horncastle, the town at the gateway to the Wolds which for centuries had a fair where all kinds of horses were sold. By the early nineteenth century Horncastle Fair had become the biggest horse fair in the country [2].

Farmers living in the Lincolnshire Fens before the Agricultural Revolution had to battle with poorly-drained soils and resurgent flooding, but it was not all watery wasteland. They had some land which supported arable crops, but also good grazing land on which they could raise cattle, sheep and horses. These horses are presumed to have included descendants of those imported in the early seventeenth century by the Dutch engineer Vermuyden, used to assist him in his attempts to drain the Fens [2].

For these horses, their heyday was yet to come. The 'Fen Blacks' or 'Lincolnshire Blacks' were considered to be slow, coarse, lumbering creatures by Marshall [21] who described them as 'elephants or slugs', compared with the more refined Leicestershire type, but they must have included some with good qualities who were later to make such an important contribution to the development of the Shire horse.

The Agricultural Revolution came late to Lincolnshire. Drainage of fenland was essential to improvement but real progress was not made until after 1750, and often not until the early nineteenth century. Enclosure has been considered the most important factor, resulting in more-manageable blocks of land which had higher value, and which in turn, justified investment in drainage schemes. By the 1760s, wheat prices were on the rise and there was growing confidence in arable farming. In Lincolnshire, *as once powerful graziers with their huge flocks of sheep declined, sheep still had a place, but now the plough and ploughman were supreme'* [2]. Enclosure, accompanied by success in draining of the Fens opened up large areas of land to cultivation, and consequently more heavy horses would have been required to do the work.

The price for wheat was maintained during the 1790s, followed by high prices during the period of the Napoleonic Wars. In Lincolnshire, with profit to be gained by putting more land under the plough, these circumstances may have provided the stimulus which led to a sudden large-scale breeding of Shire horses [2].

The increase in the number of 'cover' advertisements placed in newspapers by Lincolnshire owners and breeders at this time reflects this change.

The main Shire-breeding areas of Lincolnshire appear to have been in the extreme west of the county, between Newark (in Nottinghamshire) and Lincoln, and far to the east in the Fens around Spalding. Most of the best-known owners and breeders lived in the Fens where they farmed on land reclaimed through drainage schemes.

The area around Spalding seems to have developed as a centre of 'Shire' breeding from about the year 1800. This is also the area which apparently produced William Wiseman's horse *Honest Tom 1060*, acknowledged to be the ancestor of the modern Shire.

Whilst there was much 'Shire' breeding activity, in Leicestershire and Derbyshire, in particular during the second half of the 18th century, with owners and stallion letters using extensive newspaper advertising to promote their businesses, there is little evidence of the equivalent practice in Lincolnshire.

A lack of advertising by Lincolnshire breeders and owners during this earlier period is difficult to explain. It is also frustrating because whilst there are general indications that breeding, buying and selling of heavy horses was well established in Lincolnshire, little detailed information has come to light from before 1800. Reasons for this lack of evidence are open to speculation. There was certainly no lack of opportunity to advertise through the use of newspapers. The Stamford Mercury, which claims to be Britain's oldest newspaper with a circulation which covered Lincolnshire and beyond, dates from 1695. [A complete set of copies of the newspaper exist from the middle of the 18th century onwards.] Perhaps owners and breeders chose instead to buy and sell their horses, or advertise them (e.g. by stud-cards), at markets or horse fairs at e.g. Horncastle or Swineshead (near Boston), therefore leaving no written record. Perhaps there was simply not as much demand for horses before 1800, although evidence from Young [34], in his book, dated 1799, suggests that while in some parts of Lincolnshire oxen were still much in favour at this time, he reported that *'Around Grantham many oxen have been worked, but all let off, once they were seen all the way from Grantham to Lincoln, now scarcely any; a pair of mares, and one man, will do as much work as four oxen, and two men.'* Revolutionary change in agriculture did not take place in Lincolnshire until the early nineteenth century, particularly as there were no large industrial centres developing close by which would have provided a market for horses. It is also possible that Lincolnshire farmers were loyal to their local breed which served them well, and saw no need to seek improvement.

In an early reference to heavy horses in Lincolnshire, in 1758[5], Nicholas Rose [1726-1784] of Denton (just west of Grantham, and close to the Leicestershire border) placed a notice in the Derby Mercury newspaper offering a reward for the return of *'Three Black MARES of the Cart Kind'* which had strayed or been stolen near Grantham.

Interestingly, although Lincolnshire breeders and owners are almost absent from earlier newspaper advertisements, there are indications that the heavy horse did not develop in the county in isolation. A number of newspaper advertisements provide evidence that Robert Bakewell, and other breeders from outside Lincolnshire were at work. There is also evidence that the *Packington Blind Horse* may have left descendants in the area.

A particularly interesting early 'cover' advertisement (opposite), placed in the Stamford Mercury in 1768[18Li] has already been mentioned, as horses bred by the noted Leicestershire breeders, Donnisthorpe and Bulstrode were recorded in the pedigree of a Leicestershire-bred black stallion called *Biard*. This horse was however advertised as being available to cover in Lincolnshire, at Wainfleet, near Skegness!

[A legendary blind horse by the name of *Biard* or *Byard* has a connection in Lincolnshire folklore. He is said to have made a gigantic leap (in another sense) when attacked by a local witch who stuck her long nails into his flank. The horseman then killed the witch with his sword. The event is said to have occurred in Lincolnshire at a place called, appropriately, Byard's Leap, which is a hamlet about five miles north-west of Sleaford.]

To COVER this Seafon,
At the Green Man in Wainfleet, Lincolnshire, the Property of John Bellamy and John Younger, at Twelve Shillings and Sixpence a Mare, the Money to be paid at Midsummer next,

A Fine Black Horse called BIARD, well marked, with a Blaze and Snip, and a white Heel behind. BIARD was bred by Mr. Ward of Adstone Hill in Leicestershire, and got by Mr. Dunsthorp's old Horse at Packington. Mr. Dunsthorp's Black Horse got by Mr. Bostridge's Black Horse at Easby Walton. Mr. Bostridge's Black Horse, got by Mr. Mollikout's Black Horse at Chilceat, which was thought the best Horse in those Parts. His Dam was bred by Mr. Ward, his Great Grandam by Mr. Harley's favourite Mare. The faid Mr. Harley was thought to have the best Breed of Black Mares in England. BIARD is Seventeen Hands high, and has been very fuccefsful in getting Foals.
Witness my Hand,
Thomas Ward.

Advertisements featuring horses of the cart kind which were bred in Lincolnshire appeared infrequently before 1800. Those which were placed also often provided evidence of influences from outside the county, as demonstrated by some of the following:

Pycroft - of Donington, Lincolnshire
Trimnell - of Bicker, Lincolnshire

A black stallion of the cart kind, rising four years old was advertised for sale by auction in 1791[105] in Spalding. He was said to have been got by *Young Gee*, a famous horse belonging to Mr. Pycroft of Donington. *Young Gee*, described as a black stallion, rising eight years old was advertised (opposite) in 1793[123Li] to be sold together, with another black stallion, rising four years old called *Young Gallimore. Young Gallimore* was said to have been by Mr. *Pycroft's old black horse.* Both horses were advertised as being the property of the late Mr. Johnson of Culverthorpe (a hamlet, five miles south-west of Sleaford).

Mr. Pycroft can be identified as William Pycroft [1761-1812], and Mr. Johnson as Richard Johnson [1752-1792]. The name *Gee* or *G* brings to mind Robert Bakewell's noted stallion *G*, and the name *Gallimore*

123. **Stamford Mercury** - 8 March 1793
Image © THE BRITISH LIBRARY BOARD. ALL RIGHTS RESERVED
http://www.britishnewspaperarchive.co.uk/viewer/bl/000023 7/17930308/013/0002

certainly suggests these two horses may have had an ancestry which linked back to Leicestershire and Derbyshire. [An advertisement (page 42) of 1778[70Le] provides evidence that Bakewell used a *Gallimore* mare in breeding a colt which was available to cover for the season. The sire of the colt was also Bakewell's famous stallion *G*.]

An advertisement (opposite) in 1812[227Li] for the sale in Grantham of a black stallion, 5 years old, called *Useful* claimed that he was got by Mr. Trimland's black horse of Bicker Fen. Mr. Trimland's horse, in turn, was said to have been got by Mr. 'Bycraft's' *old noted black stallion of Donington.* [Bicker and Donington are neighbouring villages about eight miles south-west of Boston, and a similar distance north-west of Spalding.] In 1815[252] a similar advertisement featured an unnamed black stallion (possibly *Useful*), rising 8 years old, got by the late Mr. Trimnell's Black horse of Bicker Fen, son of the noted old horse of the late Mr. Pycroft of Donington. Mr. Trimnell can be identified as Charles Trimnell [1789-1814], incorrectly called 'Trimland' in the 1812[227Li] advertisement. His grandfather, also called Charles Trimnell was vicar of Bicker for thirty

227. **Stamford Mercury** - Friday 27 January 1812
Image © THE BRITISH LIBRARY BOARD. ALL RIGHTS RESERVED
http://www.britishnewspaperarchive.co.uk/viewer/bl/0000 237/18120327/017/0002

years. Additionally, in 1812, Mr. Pycroft was incorrectly called 'Bycraft'.

The above advertisements provide a link to a stud card of 1820, referred to by Chivers [4] in giving examples of some of Lincolnshire 'forgotten' horse breeders of the past. The stud card was used by John Savidge of Carlton Scroop (a village about six miles north of Grantham). John Savidge [1772-1835] was, interestingly, born at Bassingham (the supposed place of origin of the mysterious *Milton and Colley's brown horse of Bassingham*, the sire of that most celebrated of all ancestral Shire stallions, *Honest Tom 1060*).The stud card advertised a horse to cover for the season – this was *Useful*, which Savidge then owned. However, his repeated incorrect references to *Useful* as being by 'Mr. Trimland's' (rather than Trimnell's) horse, and he, in turn being a son of Mr. 'Bycroft's' or 'Bycraft' (rather that Pycroft's) horse can only have contributed to them, in time, becoming 'forgotten men'!

Buck - of Billingborough, Lincolnshire

A 1797[139Li] advertisement (opposite), which was repeated in a similar form in 1800[144], 1805[166] and 1808[198], was for a horse called *Young Farmers Glory*. Although advertised for Wellingborough in Northamptonshire, it was claimed that *Young Farmers Glory* was by a stallion called *R.T.* belonging to Mr. John Patrick of Thorney Fen (actually east of Peterborough in the Cambridgeshire Fens, but only just outside Lincolnshire). Chivers [6] made an early reference to this place. [*Odam's (or Odham's) Horse of Thorney Fen* was another important ancestral stallion about which nothing is known. This horse is recorded in the first Stud-book [29] as the sire of the dam of the celebrated stallion *England's Glory 705*]. *R.T.* was said to have been got by *Mr. Hood's horse of Packington* (actually written as Wood in earlier advertisements, but corrected as Hood in 1808[198]). *Farmers Glory*'s dam was said to have been by *Mr. Buck's Horse of Billingborough*. Mr. Buck's horse was also said to have been sold in 1792, aged thirteen years old for 130 guineas. This early reference is interesting, but Mr. Buck is unfortunately untraceable in Billingborough (about five miles west of Donington).

Chivers [6] made a reference to a later *'Buck's Horse of Deeping'* of around 1825 (presumably *Buck's Horse 347*, foaled in 1829 [29]), and certainly a family by the name of Buck was well established in Deeping St James. Unfortunately, no individual by the name of Buck can be identified as having had a role as a horse owner, breeder or stallion letter. [Deeping St James is about 15 miles south of Billingborough, and close to Lincolnshire's southern county boundary, but only about eight miles from Thorney.]

> **YOUNG FARMER's GLORY.**
>
> Rising seven Years old, fixteen Hands and one Inch high, remarkably full of Bone, and short Legs. He was got by that capital Stallion, R. T. of Mr. John Patrick's, of Thorney-Fen. R. T. was got by Mr. Wood's Horfe, of Packington, which was well known by all Judges to be one of the firft Stallions in England; his Dam was got by Mr. Buck's Horfe, of Billingborough, Lincolnfhire, which was fold in March, 1792, thirteen Years old, for 130 Guineas.
>
> He will be at the Swan, at Wellingborough, on Wednefdays, and ftays all Night; at the Saracen's-Head, Kettering, on Thurfdays, ftays there till Two o'Clock on Friday; at the Swan, at Thrapfton, on Friday Night; and at Home the remainder Part of the Week.
>
> He proved a very fure Foal-Getter laft Year.
>
> *** Grafs for Mares at 3s. per Week, and good Care taken of them.
>
> ☞ The Money to be paid at Midfummer or November next.

139. **Northampton Mercury** - 6 May 1797

Rockcliffe - of West Ashby, Lincolnshire

Also in 1797[138De], John Bradder of Syston, Leicestershire advertised (opposite) the services of a horse called *'Young King'*, bred by Mr. Rockcliffe of West Ashby, near Horncastle, Lincolnshire. His sire was named as *Old King of the Levels*. Bakewell's horse *'Little David'*, and also *Bakewell's 'G'* were claimed to be part of his pedigree. [The 'Levels' is a reference to the three areas of the Great Levels or Bedford Levels, parts of the drainage scheme for the Fens (not including the Lincolnshire Fens) carried out in the 17th century. The North Level, closest to Lincolnshire, contained Thorney Fen.]

> To Cover this Season 1797
> At One guinea a mare, and one shilling the man.
>
> Young King
> The most noted Stallion in Leicestershire,
> the Property of John Bradder of Syston,
> was bred by Mr Rockcliffe,
> of West Ashby, near Horncastle in Lincolnshire.
> He was got by Old King of the Levels: his Dam
> by Mr Bakewell's Little David: Old King was got
> by the Wainfleet G, and the latter by Mr
> Bakewell's G, which covered at five guineas a Mare.
>
> Will be shown at Leicester the 15th April 1797.
>
> 138. **The Leicester and Nottingham Journal** - 7 April 1797

Mr. Rockcliffe was probably Rev. Francis Rockcliffe [1760-1824], rector of West Ashby, or perhaps his brother Thomas Rockcliffe [1762-1833].

Carter - of Dunsby, Lincolnshire

'That noted horse Robin Hood', belonging to Mr. Carter of Dunsby was claimed to be the sire of a black cart stallion called *Young Little John*, advertised for sale in 1809[209] by Robert Palmer of Toft, near Bourne.

According to Chivers [6] 'Mr. Carter of Dunsby' (a small village about four miles north of Bourne) was a well known stallion breeder. He was probably John Carter [1776-1861].

Old Robin Hood, late the property of Mr. Carter of Dunsby (and formerly owned by Mr. Reynolds of Dunsby) was said to have been the sire of a black stallion called *Robin Hood*, advertised to cover at Sleaford in 1810[212]. *(Old) Robin Hood* had been advertised to cover at Melton Mowbray (in Leicestershire) in 1803[147].

In 1814[249], the dam of a stallion called *Robin Hood*, rising 8 years old, and advertised to cover in Derbyshire, was described as being *'allowed by Judges to be the heaviest best mare in Lincolnshire'*. *Robin Hood's* dam was the property of Mr. Castle of Dousby (Dowsby, a small village is only about two miles north of Dunsby). This *Robin Hood*, the property of Mr. John Coy of Billinghay (7½ miles north-east of Sleaford), being chestnut rather than black, cannot have been the stallion advertised to cover at Sleaford. He may however, be of interest in other respects. Chivers [6] stated that the sire of the dam of *Honest Tom 1062* had been *Cox's Robin Hood*, but was unable to identify Mr Cox. Perhaps he was *Coy's Robin Hood*?

In 1810 two black stallion colts of the cart kind were advertised (Stamford Mercury, 23 March 1810) to be sold by auction, one of which had been got by Mr. Cox's horse of Pinchbeck. Years later, the sale by auction, was advertised to take place at Folkingham, in 1821[271] of a cart stallion, rising 4 years old, belonging to Thomas Jacques of Rippingale (a village between Dunsby and Dowsby). This stallion, was said to have been *'got by that famous brown horse Honest Tom, late the property of Mr. Seward of Quadring'*, and *'out of a mare by Robin Hood, and late the property of Mr. Cox of Pinchbeck, which was sold to Mr. Butler of Ruskington for 300 guineas'*. These two advertisements suggest that *Robin Hood*, owned (not by Coy) but by Mr. Cox of Pinchbeck may have sired *Honest Tom 1062*. The stallion advertised for sale in 1821[271] would however have been inbred if both its parents were sired by Cox's *Robin Hood*!

In an advertisement (below) of 1814[251Li], a black stallion called *Wax-work*, due to be sold in auction in Melton Mowbray was said to have been got by Mr. Carter of Dunsby's horse, *Old Wax-work*. *Old Tom of Lincoln* was mentioned as the sire of the dam of *Wax-work*. *Dixon's Waxwork*, a stallion of unknown origin, said to be the sire of the dam of a stallion advertised (below) for sale, years later, in 1836[290Li] was apparently brown [6], but it is possible that he was Carter's *Old Wax-work*.

In 1815[254Li], *Old Tom of Lincoln* was recorded as the sire of *Young Tom of Lincoln*, who in turn was the sire of a five year old black horse called *Farmer's Flower'*, advertised to cover (opposite), in Herefordshire.

Interestingly, *Farmer's Flower (who was apparently bred in Dorsetshire)* was owned by William Evans of Weobley (about 7½ miles south-west of Leominster, Herefordshire) who also owned *Young Gallimore* (**Table 1**, page 22 which he advertised at the same time in 1815[253]). There was, yet again, a Leicestershire connection as the dam of *Farmer's Flower* was said to have been by the *'Young Packington Horse'*.

> **1815.**
> **TO COVER THIS SEASON,**
> At One Guinea each Mare, and Half-a-Crown the Groom, the Money to be paid on or before the Twentieth of June, 1815,
>
> THAT beautiful and well-bred Black Wagon Horse, called THE FARMER's FLOWER, five years old, full Fifteen Hands Three Inches high, the property of William Evans, Birches, near Weobly, Herefordshire.
>
> The FARMER's FLOWER was got by Young Tom of Lincoln, whose Grandsire was Old Tom of Lincoln; his Dam a beautiful Black Wagon Mare, of great bone and strength, and remarkably active, she was got by the Young Packington Horse, which always covered at Five Guineas each Mare. The Farmer's Flower was bred in Dorsetshire; he obtained the Premium when he was two years old, and is supposed to be the best grown Wagon Horse in England. He has proved himself a sure Foal getter, his Stock is superior to any, and may be seen in Dorsetshire and part of Worcestershire.
>
> He will attend at the Talbot Inn, Kington, every other Wednesday during the Season; at other times he will wait on Gentlemen and Farmers in his own Neighbourhood

Storey - of Pinchbeck, Lincolnshire

A brown cart stallion, the property of John Storey, advertised (page 115) for sale in 1805[159Li], was said to have been got by the noted *Brown Horse*, which had belonged to Mr. Fisher of Weston In 1819[262Li] Thomas March of Swinstead (approximately five miles north-west of Bourne) advertised (opposite) his black stallion, rising 10 years old, for sale. He claimed that his stallion was sired by *'Mr. Storey's Black Horse of Pinchbeck*, which was sold for 300 guineas, when 12 years old'.
'Mr. Storey of Pinchbeck' was probably John Storey [c1748-1811].
Much later, in 1838 a brown stallion,

> To be SOLD by PRIVATE CONTRACT,
> A Capital BLACK STALLION, of the Cart kind, rising 10 years old, the property of Thos. March, of Swinstead, in the county of Lincoln. He stands full seventeen hands high, and for bone and shape is allowed by judges to be equal to any horse in the county. He was got by Mr. Storey's favorite Black Horse, of Pinchbeck, which was sold for 300 guineas, when 12 years old.
>
> He is a sure foal-getter, and his stock proves remarkably good.—For further particulars apply to Thos. March, the owner.   *Swinstead*, March 15th, 1819.

rising eight years old called *King William the Fourth* was advertised (in the Stamford Mercury, dated 6 April) to be sold or let for the season at Sutterton. He was said to have been got by Mr. Storey's horse and bred by Mr. Fisher, West of Pinchbeck (presumably Pinchbeck West, the small habitation about two miles south-west of Pinchbeck).
This Mr. Storey was probably John Storey [1781-1847], son of the earlier John Storey.
[Pinchbeck is a village about two miles north of Spalding. Sutterton is about halfway between Spalding and Boston, and close to Wigtoft].

Wiseman- of Fleet, Moulton and Whaplode, Lincolnshire ...... and Honest Tom

In 1819, a burst of advertising activity took place in Lincolnshire itself, with the first appearance of a reference to William Wiseman. An unnamed six-year-old cart stallion, rising six years old, dappled brown, was advertised (below) for sale in 1819[261Li] (*'got by 'Mr. Wiseman's Honest Tom of Whapload', and covered at two guineas a mare, and was sold for 400 guineas'*). In the same year 1819[264, 268] a brown stallion, rising five years old , was advertised for sale by Mr. Savage of Moulton which was also claimed to be '*by Wiseman's horse'*. Also in 1819[267Li], the stallion *Young Honest Tom* was advertised (below) to cover, the property of John Caswell, junior of Wigtoft. Described as being dark brown, rising six years old, it was claimed that he was got by '*the noted horse Honest Tom, property of Mr Wiseman of Whaplode'* which '*when six years old, was sold for Four Hundred Guineas'*.

To be SOLD,

A Valuable CART STALLION, rising six years old, stands 17 hands high, a dappled brown, (got by Mr. Wiseman's Honest Tom, of Whapload, who covered at two guineas a mare, and was sold for 400 guineas,) out of a capital mare, the property of John Tatam, Esq. of Moulton, whose dam had a foal sold for £60, which was Mr. Pepper's famous brown horse, of Walcot. From his size, color, and fine shape, he is superior to most horses; and is well worth the attention of any one who may wish to purchase.—For particulars enquire of Mr. Steel, at his livery-stables, Boston; or Mr. Briglin, horse-dealer, Lincoln.—All letters, post paid, will be duly attended to.   March, 1819.

261. **Stamford Mercury** - Friday 12 March 1819

http://www.britishnewspaperarchive.co.uk/viewer/bl/0000237/18190312/021/0001

At Two Guineas each Mare,
· **YOUNG HONEST TOM,**
Late the property of Mr. Sewards, of Quadring, and now the property of JOHN CASWELL, jun. of WIGTOFT.

He is a beautiful dark brown, stands sixteen hands and a half high, rising six years old, and has proved himself to be the best stock-getter in England. He was got by that noted horse called Honest Tom, the property of Mr. Wiseman, of Whaplode; which horse, when four years old, covered at Two Guineas and Half-a-Crown each mare; and, when six years old, was sold for Four Hundred Guineas. Young Honest Tom was bred out of a mare the property of Benjamin Harrison, of Quadring.

He will be through Gosberton and Surfleet, to the Bull at Pinchbeck, on Monday nights; from Pinchbeck, to the Horse and Jockey in Pinchbeck Fen, on Tuesday nights; at the White Swan Inn at Spalding on Wednesdays, and at the Bell Inn, Moulton, on Wednesday nights; from Moulton, through the Seas End, to the Old Saracen's Head, through Holbeach Marsh, to the New Inn at Fosdyke Wash, on Thursday nights; through Fosdyke, Algarkirk, and Sutterton, and home to Wigtoft, on Friday nights; through Bicker, Donington, and Quadring, on Saturdays and Sundays.

267. **Stamford Mercury** - Friday 26 March [& 2 April] 1819

http://www.britishnewspaperarchive.co.uk/viewer/bl/0000237/18190326/027/0004

Benjamin Harrison of Quadring [1773-1844], brother-in-law to William Wiseman (having married his sister Frances in 1796), owned the dam of *Young Honest Tom*.

Chivers [6] provided some detail of Wiseman's achievements and family background. William Wiseman [1780-1867] is credited with having been the breeder of the celebrated ancestral stallion *Honest Tom 1060*, although his father John Wiseman [1751-   ] could have bred this horse. Other candidates include his uncle, William Wiseman [1753-1797], and great-uncle William Wiseman [c1729-1803] (who both lived at Surfleet and Gosberton, in Lincolnshire), either of whom could have bred *Honest Tom*.

Depending on whether *Honest Tom 1062* was foaled in about 1796 or 1806, the earliest stallion of that name to appear in the first Stud-book was *Honest Tom 1060,* otherwise known as *Wiseman's Honest Tom.*

Honest Tom 1060 is said to have been sired in 1800, and according to Chivers, a year or two later William Wiseman bought some land at Fleet, near Holbeach. Wiseman was a beneficiary in the estate of his great uncle William, who died in 1803, and he may then have had the means to make this purchase [18].

Wiseman seems to have advertised using stud cards rather than newspapers. Chivers recorded the information which Wiseman gave on a stud card he used in 1812 to advertise his light brown horse *Young Honest Tom*, which he said was got by his horse *(Old) Honest Tom*. Interestingly, *Young Honest Tom* was said to be out of a mare sired by '*Mr. Fisher's* noted brown horse, *of Weston'*.

Evidently Mr. Fisher (page 114) had both a black horse and a brown horse.

William Wiseman had family connections in Surfleet and Gosberton, and according to Chivers had farms at Moulton, Whaplode and Weston. [Surfleet and Gosberton are villages just to the north of Spalding. Weston, Moulton and Whaplode are a few miles to the east of Spalding.]

An interesting point however is that William Wiseman himself, his sister Frances, his father John and his uncle William were all baptised in Bottesford, Leicestershire, not in Lincolnshire! There are Lincolnshire connections but the family seem to have had roots in Leicestershire, and in [Orston], Nottinghamshire.

Plate 15: *Welcher's Honest Tom*, foaled 1865. He was a celebrated 19th century stallion, and a direct descendant of *Wiseman's Honest Tom*.

The pedigree of *Honest Tom 1060* is unfortunately not well documented. His dam is unknown, and his sire is said to have been *Milton and Colley's Brown Horse of Bassingham*. Nothing is known about this stallion apart from that which was revealed by an old handbill advertising the auction, in 1825, of a ten year old horse called *Wellington* [6]. *Wellington* was said to have been by that 'noted brown horse *Honest Tom*, the property of William Wiseman'.

His grand-sire was also given as 'that capital brown horse *Old Honest Tom'*.

Milton and Colley's Brown Horse of Bassingham was therefore also called *Old Honest Tom*!

No individual with the surname Milton seems to have lived in Bassingham. A family by the name of Colley lived at neighbouring Carlton-le-Moorland, but not in Bassingham, and again, no individual of that name can be identified as having a role in producing this ancestral stallion. One can only speculate about the origin of *Honest Tom 1060*, but Bassingham is in the extreme west of Lincolnshire, near Newark, and less than 15 miles from Bottesford where William Wiseman was born. It is some considerable distance from William Wiseman's later home territory near Spalding and Holbeach. Perhaps *Honest Tom 1060* was not of Lincolnshire origin at all; he may have been sired in Nottinghamshire or Leicestershire!

Many stallions have been called *Honest Tom* – a name popular in Lincolnshire and neighbouring Fenland counties. Wiseman's stallion was not the first to be so named, leaving aside his sire, *Milton and Colley's Brown Horse of Bassingham* alias *Old Honest Tom*. The various cart horses named *Honest Tom* has led to much confusion and difficulty in distinguishing between different stallions bearing that name.

The earliest newspaper advertisements found to feature a stallion called *Honest Tom* are from Lincolnshire, and date from the 1790s.

In April 1792[113Li] *Honest Tom*, a <u>black</u> stallion stallion, rising three years old was advertised (opposite) by Mr. Perrin to cover for the season at Fiskerton (a village near Lincoln). What appears to be the same stallion was advertised in November 1792[120] to be sold by auction in the following January. It was said that he could be seen at the home of Mrs. Rice's, at Fiskerton. *Honest Tom* was then advertised for sale in the Stamford Mercury of 7th March 1794, and then again, in the same newspaper, dated 30th January 1795 [5]. He was still in the hands of Mrs. Rice at Fiskerton. The same *Honest Tom* was named, in an advertisement ten years later, in 1805[157] as the sire of a black cart stallion, rising three years which was to be sold by auction in Boston. *Honest Tom* was said to have been late the property of the Miss. Rices' of Fiskerton.

113. **Stamford Mercury** - Friday 6 April 1792
Image © THE BRITISH LIBRARY BOARD. ALL RIGHTS RESERVED
http://www.britishnewspaperarchive.co.uk/viewer/bl/0000237/17920406/014/0002

In 1810[213], another <u>black</u> stallion called *Honest Tom,* the property of M. Oxby of the Red Lion Inn (possibly at Swinderby, halfway between Lincoln and Newark) was advertised to cover for the season. In 1811[217Li], (opposite) this *Honest Tom* was owned by William Boulton and John Fenneley of Swinderby (a village six miles north-east of Newark), having lately been the property of Matthew Oxby. He was said to have been bred by Thomas Oxby of 'Auben' (Aubourn, a village about two miles north-east of Bassingham), and got by a noted black horse belonging to Mr. Pacey of Bassingham (page 115). [This may be a reference to *Pacey's Lame Horse (*alias *John Bull) 1702*, although the first Stud-book records his foaling date as 1811 [29].

217. **Stamford Mercury** - Friday 22 March 1811
Image © THE BRITISH LIBRARY BOARD. ALL RIGHTS RESERVED
http://www.britishnewspaperarchive.co.uk/viewer/bl/0000237/18110322/033/0004

Matthew Oxby [1760-1837] lived at Norton Disney, just about one mile south-west of Bassingham. Thomas Oxby [1769-1835] of Aubourn appears to have been Matthew Oxby's half-brother, and was the probable breeder of this *Honest Tom*. It is interesting that this stallion, with the name *Honest Tom* should have its origins in the Bassingham area at a similar time period as *Milton and Colley's Brown horse*. They must however, have been different horses, as this *Honest Tom* was <u>black</u>, not brown.

To add further to a complicated picture, a <u>brown</u> stallion called *Honest Tom*, rising 8 years old was advertised for sale in 1816[258] by John Thorp of Tilney with Islington, Norfolk. Could this horse have been *Honest Tom 1061*? The Stud-book [26] lists *Honest Tom 1061* as having been bred by Thorp, and foaled in about 1805. Thorp was living in the Fens, but in Lincolnshire, at Holbeach, not in Norfolk. However, given the lack of detail, and that the Stud-book contains errors, this stallion could have been *Honest Tom 1061*.

There is also possibly a link between the above *Honest Tom* and other *Honest Toms* offered for sale, as follows, three years later. An auction sale, advertised to take place in 1819[270], in Fen country, this time at Chatteris, in the Isle of Ely, Cambridgeshire, included two more stallions, each called *Honest Tom*. Lot 2 was the brown cart horse called *Honest Tom*, rising 8 years old. He was said to have been got by *Old Honest Tom*, the property of Mr. Freeman of Bodsey Toll, (just north of Ramsey) Huntingdonshire. Lot 3 was *Young Honest Tom*, rising three years old. He was said to have been got by *Old Honest Tom*, the property of Mr. Woods of Cottenham (a village just to the north of Cambridge). [Chivers [6] recorded Woods of Cottenham as having owned *Waxwork 2263*]. Also, Lot 1 in the sale was a black stallion, rising five years old, called *Farmer's Glory*. He was said to have been got by *Old Farmer's Glory*, owned by Mr. S. Bradley of Leverington, near Wisbech. [S. Bradley is likely to have been Stephen Bradley, recorded by Chivers [6] as being of Tydd St. Giles (near Leverington), Lincolnshire, and an important Shire breeder and owner.]

None of the various stallions referred to above could have been *Milton and Colley's Brown Horse of Bassingham* (otherwise the brown stallion called *Old Honest Tom*), and consequently nothing can be added to the pedigree details of *Wiseman's Honest Tom 1060*. The mystery remains!

Something of the legacy of *Wiseman's Honest Tom* can be seen within an auction sale advertised (opposite) to be held at Sandiacre, Derbyshire in 1874[307Li].

Lot 1 was the celebrated *Lincolnshire Lad*, (*Lincolnshire Lad* alias *Honest Tom 1196*). A direct descendant of *Wiseman's Honest Tom*, he was the sire of *Lincolnshire Lad II 1365*, who was in turn the sire of that famous stallion *Harold 3703* (**Plate 12**, page 82). Interestingly, Lot 2 was *Young Crown Prince,* said to have been by *Crown Prince,* his dam was by *William the Conqueror,* who was by *Leicestershire.* [*Leicestershire* was recorded also as the sire of *Leicester,* advertised (page 63) to cover in 1830[283Le].] The ancestry of *Young Crown Prince,* by contrast, was largely of Leicestershire rather than Lincolnshire origin, going back to the *Packington Blind Horse.*

BY MR. W. WRIGHT.

SANDIACRE, MIDWAY BETWEEN NOTTINGHAM AND DERBY.

HIGHLY IMPORTANT SALE OF FIVE ENTIRE HORSES.

WM. WRIGHT is instructed by Mr. JAMES BURROWS, of Risley Park Farm, to SELL by AUCTION, on TUESDAY, March 3rd, 1874, in a Paddock near the WHITE LION INN, Sandiacre, the following ENTIRE HORSES, viz. :—

LOT 1.—That celebrated Cart Horse, LINCOLNSHIRE LAD. Lincolnshire Lad is a good brown bay, rising seven years old, stands 17 hands high, on short legs, with immense bone and substance, good action, and sound in constitution. He has proved himself a sure foal getter. Lincolnshire Lad was got by Mr. Lister's Lincoln, Lincoln by Champion, and Champion by Honest Tom, which took the first prize in Louth, in 1850. Lincolnshire Lad's dam is the property of Mr. Bassett, of Willoughby, which took the first prize at Grimsby, in 1859, as the best two-year-old; at Horncastle, in 1860, as the best three-year-old; and at Horncastle, in 1860, as the best mare for breeding draught horses, beating 20 others. Lincolnshire Lad's sister took the first prize at Louth, open to all England. His stock are taking numberous prizes, viz. :—First and second at the Derby Agricultural Show, and first and second at the West Hallam Agricultural Show.

LOT 2.—That celebrated Cart Horse, YOUNG CROWN PRINCE. Young Crown Prince is a beautiful roan horse, eight years old. He stands over 17 hands high, possessing great muscular power, fine action, and a sound constitution. He has proved himself a sure foal getter. His Stock is large and good. Young Crown Prince took the prize at the Agricultural Show, Derby, in 1868; also in 1870; and first prize in 1872, when two-year-old colts by him took the second and third prizes; his stock also took the second prize at the Nottingham Horse Show, open to all England, and are now selling at very high prices. Young Crown Prince is by Crown Prince, his dam by William the Conqueror, by Leicestershire, which was got by Old Black Legs. Black Legs is a true descendant of the old Swebston horse, Mansetter, Old Kirby, and the Packington Blind Horse. Young Crown Prince is so well bred on both sides that he needs no further comment.

Boor and Bonner - of Bicker, Lincolnshire

In January 1819[259Li] an unnamed aged black stallion was advertised (below) to be sold at an auction in Donington, Lincolnshire. This horse, said to have been late the property of Mr. Franklin Bonner of Bicker, was at this time owned by Mr. John Casswell, senior of Hoffleet Stow, Wigtoft (page 112).

Later in 1819[266Li], *Young Farmer's Glory*, rising four years old, and got by '*that noted horse belonging to Messrs. Boor and Bonner, of Bicker*', was advertised (below) by John Casswell, junior of Wigtoft, to cover.

The '*noted horse*' which was the sire of *Young Farmer's Glory* was unnamed, but may have been the same aged black stallion advertised in (1819[259Li] (opposite) by his father, John Casswell, senior.

Following the death of John Casswell, junior an auction sale of his livestock and implements etc. was advertised to take place in 1821[272]. Included in the sale was a five year old black stallion which had been got by '*that noted horse, late the property of Messrs. Boor and Bonner, of Bicker*' - this black stallion was probably Casswell's *Young Farmer's Glory*.

Boor and Bonner of Bicker are recorded in the first Stud-book as the breeders of *England's Glory 707* [29].

Boor and Bonner's '*noted horse*' (above) may have been a stallion of quality and repute but was not *England's Glory 707*. *England's Glory 707*, a chestnut horse, and not foaled until 1820 must have been a product of their later work [29].

Ambrose Franklin Bonner [1773-1829] of Bicker is said to have been in partnership with 'Boor', although Bonner made no reference to his business partner in his will [15].

Mr. Boor was probably Jervis Boor [1773-1855]. He was baptised and buried in Lincolnshire at Holbeach, but seems to have resided at Bicker for a period of time. He and his wife had two daughters, both baptised at Bicker.

LINCOLNSHIRE.
To be SOLD by AUCTION,
By Lumby and Son,
At the Black Bull Inn in Donington, on Saturday the 13th day of February, 1819, at Four o'clock in the afternoon;

A Capital BLACK CART STALLION, aged, late the property of Mr. Franklin Bonner, of Bicker, and now of Mr. John Casswell, sen. of Hoffleet Stow, in the parish of Wigtoft. He is well known to be a good and sure foal-getter. He was shown at Boston market, and took the premium, when nearly thirty horses were shown against him.

Also, that capital BROWN CART STALLION, rising five years old, got by the noted Brown Horse of the aforesaid Mr. John Casswell, which covered by subscription at three guineas each mare, and is a good and sure foal-getter.

The horses may be seen at any time, by applying to

259. **Stamford Mercury** - Friday 29 January [& 5 February] 1819

At One Guinea and a Crown each Mare,
YOUNG FARMER's GLORY,
The property of JOHN CASSWELL, jun. of WIGTOFT.

He is rising four years old, and was got by that noted horse belonging to Messrs. Boor and Bonner, of Bicker, out of a famous black mare, the property of Mr. Harrison, of Quadring; and is allowed by judges to be superior to any horse in the kingdom.

He will be through Quadring and Fen, to the Five Bells, Gosberton Risegate, on Monday nights; on Sutterton Bank, through Fosdyke, to the Duke William at Frampton, on Tuesday nights; from Frampton, through Wyberton West End, to Boston, and Langrick Ferry, on Wednesday nights; by the Chapel Hill and Barley Sheaf, to the Harvest Men, Sutterton Drove, on Thursday nights; through Sutterton Drove and Algarkirk Fen, to the Wheel, Heckington Fen, and the Griffin Inn, Swineshead, on Friday nights; through Bicker Fen and Donington Northorpe, to the Bull Inn, Donington, and home to Wigtoft, on Saturday nights.

266. **Stamford Mercury** - Friday 26 March [& 2 April] 1819

Casswell - of Wigtoft, Lincolnshire

Members of the extensive Casswell family inhabited a number of villages in south Lincolnshire but only John Casswell, senior [1756-1820] of Hoffleet Stow, Wigtoft and his son John Casswell, junior [1793-1820] of Wigtoft are known to have been owners and breeders of

'Shire' horses. [Wigtoft is about six miles south-west of Boston and within two miles of Bicker.]

Chivers recorded John Casswell as the owner of the important ancestral stallion *Honest Tom 1062*, a horse also owned by Sewards of Quadring [6].

Casswell is said to have paid £300 for this stallion when it was the age of five. This celebrated horse, usually known as *Caswell's Honest Tom was* apparently also known as *Old Tom or Old David*. Another alias was *Little David,* which is interesting as Robert Bakewell had a horse of that name. Chivers argued that he had been foaled in 1796. Also, an article on 'The Rise of the Shire Horse' published in the Derby Mercury in 1891[309] stated that *Sewards Little David* was foaled in 1796. Chivers considered that the Stud-book's stated foaling date of 1806 for *Honest Tom 1062* (said to have been a chestnut horse), was incorrect.

CAPITAL STALLION HORSE.
To be SOLD by AUCTION,
By Mr. Jun.
On Thursday the 29th of July, on the MARKET-HILL, HOLBEACH, at 12 o'clock precisely,
THAT noted CART STALLION, HONEST TOM, the property of Mr. JOHN CASSWELL, sen. WIGTOFT. He has covered at great prices, is a sure foal-getter, his stock are equalled by few, and excelled by none: he is ten years old, and as to pedigree stands so high as to need no comment.
The premium of Three Guineas given by the Boston Agricultural Society in the year 1815, was awarded to him when thirty other horses were shown.
Twelve months' credit will be given on approved security.—The above sale is on account of Mr. Casswell

Evidence that John Casswell owned a horse called *Honest Tom* (presumed to have been *Honest Tom 1062*) is provided by by an advertisement (above) in 1819[269Li], in which John Casswell, senior also offered that '*noted Cart Stallion Honest Tom*' for sale by auction, at Holbeach. At ten years old this Honest Tom would been foaled in 1808 or 1809, not 1806, and certainly not 1796. Frustratingly no more information was given!

John Casswell, junior , also in 1819[267Li] (page 107) advertised *Young Honest Tom* as being available to cover. *Young Honest Tom*, a dark brown horse was advertised as rising six years old, and sired by *Wiseman's Honest Tom*, out of a mare belonging to Benjamin Harrison. This horse was also described as having been formerly owned by Sewards of Quadring, but as he was not foaled until 1813 he definitely was not *Honest Tom 1062*.

It is likely that the Casswells would have purchased more than one horse from Sewards (page 113) who was their near neighbour at Quadring (about three miles west of Wigtoft).

When John Casswell, junior advertised *Young Honest Tom*, he also advertised, in 1819[266Li] (page 111) his stallion *Young Farmer's Glory*. He was said to have been out of a black mare owned by Benjamin Harrison of Quadring, probably the same mare which was also the dam of *Young Honest Tom*. Also, on the same occasion, in 1819[265Li], John Casswell, junior advertised (page 113) a brown horse (unnamed), rising five years old, for sale, or to let, which he said had been sired by the *'famous horse Little David'*. *Little David* is considered to have been an alias of *Honest Tom'* 1062, but whether this was the same horse which John Casswell, senior advertised for sale in 1819[269Li] (above) is open to speculation. It would be odd if John Casswell, senior called his horse Honest Tom while his son called the same horse *Little David*!

In the auction sale in 1821[272] which followed the death of John Casswell, junior the horses he owned included, together with the five year old black stallion already mentioned (page 111), a three year old brown stallion got by that '*noted brown horse Honest Tom*'. This at least indicates that *Casswell's Honest Tom* was a brown horse.

In 1824[274], the late John Casswell's *Old David* was mentioned as the sire of the dam of a four year old chestnut horse offered for sale by Joseph Burtt of Welbourn.

[Welbourn is about 10 miles west of Newark, and five miles south-east of Bassingham.]

The first Stud-book [29] lists the Shire stallion *David 565*, foaled in 1818 as having been bred by Joseph Burtt, and owned by John Casswell of Wigtoft. *Honest Tom 1062* is named as his sire. Interestingly, in a much later advertisement (page 116), in 1844[292Li], for another horse called *Farmer's Glory'*, a pedigree was given which mentioned *Little David*. *Little David* was said to

have been got by *Fisher's Black Horse of Weston*. This is in agreement with what Chivers appears to suggest i.e. that *Fisher's Black Horse of Weston* (otherwise known as *John Bull*) was the sire of *Honest Tom 1062* (otherwise known as *Little David* or *Casswell's Honest Tom*). Chivers was of the opinion that *Honest Tom 1062* was foaled in 1796. This was based on the assumption that *Derbyshire 577,* sired by *Honest Tom 1062* was foaled in 1800 (and consequently *Blacklegs 142,* sired by *Derbyshire 577* was foaled in 1804) [29].
It was also recorded in an article on 'The Rise of the Shire Horse' (published

in the Derby Mercury in 1891[309]) that *Sewards Little David* was foaled in 1796. [It is however probable that the Stud-book was used as source material for this article.]
Honest Tom 1062 was mentioned in the pedigree details of the Shire stallion *Highflyer,* advertised to cover in 1893[310]. The advertisement stated that *Honest Tom 1062* foaled in 1806, and that he was sired by *John Bull* (*Fisher's Black horse*). Given that no evidence has been found of stallions being sired by *Fisher's Black Horse* (page 114) before 1800, a foaling date for *Honest Tom 1062* of, or near to, 1806 seems more likely.
Evidence is also lacking which supports the Stud-book's stated foaling dates for *Derbyshire 577* and *Blacklegs 142.* It is possible that each may have been foaled as much as ten years later. Alternatively, since a number of names or aliases have been given to what was apparently the same horse, and with the foaling dates of 1796 or 1806, the designation *Honest Tom 1062* may have been applied to more that one horse!
John Casswell, senior was selling his horses and retiring from the 'stallion business' in 1819, the same year in which his son John was very active in advertising his horses. This activity did not long continue as both father and son died within two months of each other, in 1820.

Sewards - of Quadring, Lincolnshire

The name of Seward (or Sewards) was regarded by Chivers [6] as an important one in Shire horse history.
Reference has already been made to an article on 'The Rise of the Shire Horse' published in the Derby Mercury in 1891[309] in which it was stated that *Sewards Little David* (thought to have otherwise been known as *Honest Tom 1062*) was foaled in 1796.
The first 'Seward', who is celebrated as having owned *Honest Tom 1062* (otherwise called *Sewards Little David*), and traded with John Casswell, senior can be identified as Samuel Sewards [c1758-1834] of Quadring. In his will he described Benjamin Harrison of Quadring as a friend, and appointed him as one of his executors [18].
Young Honest Tom, advertised (page 107) to cover by John Casswell, junior of Wigtoft in 1819[267Li] was said to have been formerly owned by Sewards of Quadring. This appears to be another stallion obtained from the Casswell family from Samuel Sewards.
Chivers also referred to an important contribution made by William Seward of Chatteris as the owner and breeder (in 1838) of a stallion called *Major 1447,* a greatly celebrated descendant of *Wiseman's Honest Tom.*
Samuel Sewards did have a son William who inherited some of his father's property at Quadring, but appears to have spent his life there. Chivers had implied some relationship, but this William Sewards is not the William Seward who lived at Chatteris.

Fisher - of Weston, Lincolnshire

Fisher's Black Horse of Weston, otherwise known as *John Bull* is revealed as the earliest known ancestor of a number of important 'Shire' stallions. Frustratingly, nothing is clearly known about his own ancestry. Weston is a village, just to the east of Spalding. According to Chivers, William Wiseman had a farm at Weston [6].

Chivers suggested that Fisher owned his *Black Horse* in the 1790s, although all the stallions he is said to have sired, and which are referred to here, were apparently foaled after 1800. *Fisher's Black Horse of Weston* was clearly a stallion of note in his day, with a number of ancestral lines leading back to him. He is celebrated as the sire of *Honest Tom 1062*, and therefore of *William the Conqueror 2343*, one of the most important Shire stallions.

No advertisements relating to *Fisher's Black Horse* have been traced before 1837[291] when a black cart stallion called *Young John Bull* was offered for sale. He was said to have been got by *Old John Bull*, William *Pacey's lame horse*, which in turn was got by *'a famous black horse, the property of Mr. Fisher of Weston'*.

In 1844[292Li], an advertisement (page 116) featuring a horse called *Farmers Glory* gave details of his pedigree which included a reference to *Mr. Caswell's David*, got by *Mr. Fisher's Black Horse of Weston*. Many years after, *Fisher's Black Horse* was still being named in the pedigree details of stallions advertised to cover. A cover advertisement (opposite) for *Matchless 1540* in 1883[308Li] stated that *Phenomenon 1711*, foaled in 1812, had been sired by *Mr. Fisher's Black Horse*. As late as 1893[310], pedigree details for a stallion called *Highflyer* were provided which went back to *Honest Tom 1062*, said to have been foaled in 1806, and in turn got by *John Bull, Fisher's Black Horse*. A stud card, used in 1812 by William Wiseman (page 107) to advertise his stallion *Young Honest Tom,* as already mentioned, made the claim that *Young Honest Tom* was out of a mare by *'Mr. Fisher's noted brown horse, of Weston'* [6].

A number of advertisements featured Mr. Fisher's brown horse. A brown cart stallion, rising three years old, advertised (page 115) for sale by John Storey of Pinchbeck in 1805[159Li], was said to have been got by *'that noted Brown Horse'*, late the property of Mr. Fisher of Weston. [A black stallion belonging to Mr. Storey of Pinchbeck was referred to in an 1819[262Li] advertisement (page 106).]

In 1806[173], a black stallion, rising three years old was offered for sale at Kirton Holme (four miles west of Boston). He was said to have been got by Mr. T. Fisher's *Brown Horse* of Whaplode.

"MATCHLESS" (1540),

Winner of First prize at Leicestershire A.S., 1878, will serve Mares at 30s. each, and 5s. the Groom. Groom's fee to be paid at the time of serving and the remainder as soon as proved to be In-foal. All mares sold to be paid for in full.

"Matchless" is a rich bay, rising 7 years old, stands 17½ hands high, on remarkably good legs and feet, he possesses immense power and substance, and for symmetry and action cannot be surpassed. He was bred by Mr. John James, near Huntingdon, sire "Thumper" (2136) Prizes:—First, Spalding; Second, Long Sutton, 1876; First, Peterboro'; First, Spalding, 1877.

G. sire "Waxwork" (2298). Prizes :—First, Peterboro', 1866; First Barton-on-Humber; Second, Huntingdon; Second, Cambridge, 1867.

G.G., sire "Matchless" (1500). G.G.G., sire "Active" (29). G.G.G.G. sire "Farmer's Profit" (873). G.G.G.G.G sire "Farmer's Profit," (Howard's), foaled in 1833. Dam's prizes :—Second, Peterboro', 1862; First, with foal at foot, 1863.

Dam's sire "Thumper" (2117). Prizes :—First, Peterboro' ; First, Grantham, 1857 ; Second, R.A.S.E., Warwick, 1859; by "Major" (144), by "Honest Tom" (1073), by "Honest Tom" (1067), by "England's Glory" (705). A winner at Lincoln twice, by "Honest Tom" (1060), foaled in 1800, by Milton and Colley's "Brown Horse."

G. dam by "Dragon" (600). Prizes :—First, Peterboro', 1848 ; by "Dragon" (599). First, Saffron Welden ; First, Huntingdon, 1839 ; First, Whittlesea ; First Peterboro', 1840 ; First, Peterboro', 1841 ; First, Whittlesea, 1842 ; by "Phenomenon" (1713), by "Phenomenon" (1712), by "Phenomenon" (1711), foaled 1812 ; by Fisher's "Black Horse."

The above horses will travel each week during the season alternately, as follows :—

MONDAY.—Leave Congerstone for Newton Regis, to bait, Wigginton for the night.

TUESDAY.—Leave for Elford, to bait, Fradley for the night.

WEDNESDAY.—Leave for Barton Turns, to bait, Overseal for the night.

THURSDAY.—Leave for Appleby, to bait, and home for the night.

For further particulars see cards.

308. **Tamworth Herald** - Saturday 7 April 1883

A brown stallion of the cart kind, rising four years old was advertised (above) for sale by auction at Wisbech in 1807[180Li], got by Mr. Thomas *Fisher's famous brown horse* of Weston. This advertisement usefully identified Mr. Fisher as Thomas Fisher.

In a further advertisement, in 1809[210] a brown cart stallion, rising four years old called *Grantham Lad* was offered for sale by auction in Grantham. He was also said to have been got by Mr. *Fisher's brown horse* of Weston, and out of a mare belonging to Mr. Johnson of Whittlesea (i.e. Whittlesey, just east of Peterborough). [Chivers [6] recorded Johnson of 'Whittlesea' as the breeder, in 1812 of *Phenomenon 1711*, a son of *Fisher's Black Horse* of Weston, as seems to be confirmed by the advertisement of 1883[308Li], page 115.]

The Stamford Mercury of 2 January 1824 recorded the death of Thomas Fisher, Gent, aged 70 who died at Whaplode, but was formerly of Weston. He was said to be the father of Mr. Fisher, a farmer of Billingborough [5].

Thomas Fisher [1753-1823] was married at Weston in 1781, and his son John was baptised at Weston in 1786. John Fisher was living at Billingborough from at least 1811 when he was married in that village. [Billingborough is about halfway between Sleaford and Bourne.]

Chivers stated that just two horses with Lincolnshire connections (about which we know little) are the true ancestors of the modern Shire Breed, the first being *Fishers Black Horse of Weston - John Bull*, as the ancestor of *Honest Tom 1062*, and the second being *Milton and Colley's Brown Horse of Bassingham (old Honest Tom)* as the ancestor of *Honest Tom 1060*.

It is to Bassingham we finally return in discussing Lincolnshire's role in the breeding of the Shire horse. Interestingly both of the above ancestral horses have played a part in this part of Lincolnshire.

Pacey – of Bassingham, Lincolnshire
Nicholas Brumby – of South Carlton, Lincolnshire
Marfleet – of Somerton Castle, Lincolnshire

Pacey's Lame Horse (alias *John Bull 1702*) was recorded by Chivers as being an early ancestor of *Lincolnshire Lad* (alias *Honest Tom 1196*). He is said to have been bred and owned by Pacey of Bassingham, having been foaled at Bassingham in 1811 [6]. [Bassingham is about eight miles from both Newark, Nottinghamshire and the city of Lincoln.]

The Derby Mercury article 'The Rise of the Shire Horse' published in 1891[309] also stated that Pacey's horse foaled in 1811. However, a horse called *Honest Tom*, advertised (page 109) to cover in 1811[217Li] was said to have been got by *'a noted black horse'* belonging to Mr. Pacey of Bassingham. If this was a reference to *Pacey's Lame Horse*, then he must have been foaled before 1811.

The sire of *Pacey's Lame Horse* is recorded as *Marfleet's Horse* of Somerton Castle [6]. An advertisement (opposite) in 1837[291Li] featuring a stallion called *Young John Bull*, contained pedigree information which made a reference to an earlier *John Bull* (identifiable as *John Bull 1160*). This horse was said to have been have been owned by Nicholas Brumby of South Carlton, near Lincoln. This was Nicholas Brumby [c1752-1811], or more probably his son Nicholas Brumby [1779-1845].

In an earlier cover advertisement, in 1824[274] Joseph Burtt of Welbourn had advertised his rising four years old chestnut horse, which was got by *Nicholas Brumby's horse*; his dam having been the late John Casswell's *Old David*. This must have referred to the younger Nicholas Brumby.

In the 1837[291Li] advertisement, Brumby's horse was in turn said to have been got by

CART STALLION.
To be SOLD by PRIVATE CONTRACT, THAT beautiful well-bred BLACK CART STALLION, YOUNG JOHN BULL, the property of Messrs. Foster and Elston. He is rising 7 years old, stands 15 hands 3 inches high, is clean in his legs, with remarkable substance, and good action; was out of a capital cart mare of Mr. Holmes', of Sturton; his dam was got by Mr. Bushe's horse, of Eagle Hall; his grandam by Mr. Skinner's old favourite horse, of Harby; and was got by that noted horse John Bull, late the property of Mr. Brumby, of Carlton, near Lincoln, which took the first five premiums for the best cart stallion shown at the agricultural meetings at Lincoln. He was got by that well-known lame horse Old John Bull, the property of Mr. Wm. Pacey, of Bassingham, which was bred by the late Mr. J. Marfleet, of Somerton Castle, and got by a famous black horse the property of Mr. Fisher, of Weston.—This excellent Stallion is well worth any person's attention, being known as a sure foal-getter, and is sold entirely on account of the owners dissolving partnership.—For further particulars and price apply to Mr. W. Foster, of Heapham, near Gainsburgh.

291. **Stamford Mercury** - Friday 3 March 1837
Image © THE BRITISH LIBRARY BOARD. ALL RIGHTS RESERVED
http://www.britishnewspaperarchive.co.uk/viewer/bl/0000237/18370303/031/0002

that '*well-known lame horse Old John Bull, the property Mr. Wm. Pacey of Bassingham*'. The advertisement went further by stating that *Pacey's lame horse* was bred by the late Mr. J. Marfleet of Somerton Castle, and got by a famous black horse, the property of Mr. Fisher of Weston. [Mr. Fisher's horse, of course was also called *John Bull*!]

The above account suggests that Mr. Pacey owned, but did not breed his '*lame horse*'. Also, contrary to the information supplied by Chivers [6], Mr. J. Marfleet was said to have bred him, but *Fisher's Black Horse of Weston* was said to have been the sire of *Pacey's horse*, rather than Mr. Marfleet's own horse.

An advertisement (opposite) in 1844[292Li], for yet another horse called '*Farmer's Glory*' provided similar information to the above. Horses owned by Mr. Brumby and Mr. Pacey were said to be in his pedigree. It was claimed that his sire was descended through Mr. *Caswell's David* from Mr. *Fisher's Black Horse of Weston*. His dam was said to be descended from Mr. *Brumby's horse* which had been got by Mr. *Pacey's horse of Bassingham*. However, in this instance, Mr. *Pacey's horse* was said to have been got by Mr. *Marfleet's Horse of Somerton Castle*. This is in agreement with Chivers [6], but does not agree with the (above) 1837[291Li] cover advertisement which claimed that *Pacey's horse* was sired by Mr. *Fisher's Black Horse of Weston*!

There was no mention of the sire of Marfleet's horse here. Perhaps what the

WILL arrive from Lincoln, and will be shown at W. HUTCHINSON'S STABLES, on SATURDAY next, MAY 4th, TO COVER THIS SEASON.
FARMER'S GLORY,
Dark Brown Horse, 16½ hands high, with short legs, rising 3 years old, bred by Mr. Israel Brice, of Risby, of the first breed in England, got by Mr. Wheatley's Farmer's Glory, which took the first prize at Lincoln three times. Mr Wheatley's Farmer's Glory was got by Mr. Caswell's David, who stood at home and covered at 3 guineas each Mare. Mr. Caswell's David was got by Mr. Fisher's Black Horse of Weston; Farmer's Glory's dam by Mr Marshall's John Bull Grandam, by Mr Pacey's Horse of Basingham, which horse was considered superior to any of his day. Mr. Marshall's John Bull took the first prizes in 1833 and 1834, at Otley, in Yorkshire, and was got by Mr. Brumby's horse of Carlton, which took the first prize four times at Lincoln. Mr. Brumby's horse, was got by Mr. Pacey's horse, Mr. Pacey's horse, was got by Mr. Marfleet's horse, of Somerston Castle.
FARMER'S GLORY, the property of Mr. WM. SMEED, of Monks Horton, near Hythe, will attend Canterbury and Ashford Markets, and will Cover at £1 5s. each Mare, and Half a Crown the Groom.

292. **Kentish Gazette** - Tuesday 30 April 1844
Image © THE BRITISH LIBRARY BOARD. ALL RIGHTS RESERVED
http://www.britishnewspaperarchive.co.uk/viewer/bl/0000396/18440302/039/0002

1837[291Li] advertisement was trying to communicate was that Mr. *Marfleet's horse* was sired by *Fisher's Black Horse of Weston*? If we accept that *Fisher's Black Horse* was the sire, or grandsire, of *Pacey's lame horse* a connection with Bassingham emerges. It is interesting that both of the two great ancestral sires i.e. *Milton and Colley's Brown Horse of Bassingham* [obviously!], and *Fisher's Black Horse* of Weston should have a link with Bassingham. William Pacey of Bassingham was probably William Pacey [1768-1851], or less likely, his nephew William Pacey [1793-1841].

The Marfleet family also formerly resided at Bassingham, but later lived at the ancient ruinous castle of Somerton, actually in the parish of Boothby Graffoe, but about two miles east of Bassingham. John Isaac Marfleet [1793-1867] had a malting business in nearby Newark, his father was Isaac Marfleet [1756-1826], and his grandfather was another John Marfleet [1724-1779]. The above advertisement of 1837[291Li] is therefore somewhat suspect in that John Marfleet had died in 1779. He could not have bred the '*lame horse*' which Pacey later owned (and according to Chivers [6] was foaled in 1811). Presumably this advertisement should have referred to his son Isaac Marfleet [1756-1826]; who leased, and then in 1812, purchased Somerton Castle.

Bingham – of Holbeach Marsh, Lincolnshire

With this reference to William Bingham [1755 -1824] we look towards the development of the modern breed of Shire horse.

[Holbeach Marsh lies to the north of the town of Holbeach and is an area of flat coastal land bordering The Wash.]

Chivers referred to the 'two glories of William Bingham', by which he meant *England's Glory 705* and *Farmer's Glory 816*, respectively son and grandson of Wiseman's Honest Tom 1060. These two horses, which Bingham owned were said by Chivers to be the most two influential stallions in the history of the Shire horse [6].

A sale of stock belonging to Bingham took place in April 1825 following his death [6]. Neither stallion was included in the sale; Chivers suggested this was because they were retained by Bingham's widow. The indications are, however, that they may have been already sold. The two stallions were offered for sale in an advertisement (opposite) in February 1825[276Li].

England's Glory, was said to be rising eleven years old (which is in agreement with the Stud-book record of 1814 as his year of foaling [29]). *Farmer's Glory* was said to be six years old. [*Farmer's Glory 816* is recorded as having been foaled in 1823, but based on this evidence, 1818 or 1819 would seem to be the correct date.]

276. **Stamford Mercury** - Friday 11 February 1825

Lincolnshire provides a fitting end-point to this account, being the county which claims to be the home of the ancestors of today's Shire horses, which are traced back to *Wiseman's Honest Tom*. Celebrated stallions such as *Harold* had Lincolnshire ancestry by descent through *Lincolnshire Lad II*, going back to *Wisemans's Honest Tom* [29], whose presumed origin was in the Lincolnshire Fens, although Honest Tom's dam is unknown and his sire, *Milton and Colley's Brown Horse of Bassingham* remains an enigma. Whatever the reality, Lincolnshire, notably in the fens around Spalding became prime Shire-breeding territory, producing many fine horses whose descendants are represented within the modern breed.

However, we should not dismiss the tradition of Shire breeding which had been established in other counties long before Lincolnshire's Shire breeders rose to prominence; they should not be considered an irrelevence today. Many men in Derbyshire, Staffordshire and Leicestershire made their contribution by breeding horses of quality which added to the genetic pool, notably the great Robert Bakewell whose considerable influence can never be known. They all had their part to play in the long history of this magnificent breed and we should recognise and celebrate their work.

Appendices

Appendix 1

A True & perfect Inventory of All the Goods Cattle & Chattells of
Samuel Gallimore late of Wotton in the Parish of Ellaston in the
County of Stafford Yeoman dec.[d] viewed & appraised the
day of   1750 by us whose names are now to Subscribed.

	Purse & Apparell	010	0	0
In the Geret	ffive heifers	017	10	0
	One Bull Two yearling Colts...............................	008	0	0
In the Brimshole	Two Segs Nine Oxen..	059	0	0
	One heifer	003	10	0
	Eight Ewes & Twelve Lambs	010	10	0
	ffour Colts	010	0	0
	One Bull	004	0	0
	ffour Yearling Colts	021	0	0
	One Three Year Old Colt	009	0	0
	Eleven Calves	009	12	6
At John Moretons	Wool	015	0	0
	ffour Tups	005	2	0
At Knaveholme	ffive Pigs	006	0	0
	Two Lame Cows	005	0	0
	Twenty four milking Cows	114	0	0
	One Bull	004	0	0
	One Yearling Colt	007	0	0
	Six heifers	021	0	0
	Twenty six Calves	022	15	0
In the Cow Close	Twelve stirks	016	10	0
	One Mare & ffole	007	0	0
In the Soflow	Ten Oxen	049	0	0
	Six stirks	012	0	0
	ffour Mares & Two ffoles	036	0	0
	Two ffilleys	010	0	0
In the Walk	ffour Yearlings	008	8	0
	One young Mare	006	6	0
	ffour hundred & Eighty Old Sheep & One hundred Seventy five Lambs ....}	275	0	0
At Wotton	Three stoned horses	021	0	0
	One stoned Colt at Ousley	005	0	0
	One other stoned Colt	007	0	0
	Six working Horses & One Mare for Rideing	022	0	0
	Twenty two Cows	077	0	0
	One Bull	004	0	0
	Three Calves	001	10	0
	One Turney head Heifer	001	0	0
	Eight Swine	006	05	0
Husbandry Ware	Two Waine	011	0	0
	One Cart	003	0	0
	One Waggon	006	0	0
	ffour pair of harrows & one Single Harrow	003	0	0
	Six plows & Irons	003	0	0
	Geering for Ten Horses	005	0	0
	Nine ox Chains	001	0	0
	Ten Ox Yolks	000	15	0

Brought over	957	8	6
	957	8	6
Three Packsaddles...	000	16	0
Twelve Bags & Two Packsheets	001	04	0
Nine hundred & Twenty Cheeses	094	10	0
Eight Packs of Wool	060	0	0
Two hundred Pounds of Lambs Wool	005	0	0
Beasts & horses sold by the Testator in his Life time which are not yet paid for ....}	189	0	0
Oates at Thorswood Sold at	080	0	0
ffour Ricks of hay	050	0	0
fforty five acres of Oates	101	0	0
ffour acres of Barley...	010	0	0
ffour acres of Wheat	012	0	0
Leaping money and Book Debts	100	0	0
ffor Ley of Beasts horses & Sheep	040	0	0
Muck	006	0	0
Lumber & things not seen	000	0	0
Household Goods	000	0	0
Afliattell Lease Sold by the Testator in his Life time & the money unpaid ....}	235	0	0
Lumber & things not seen	000	0	0

Tho. Orme

Samuel Finney

Comment: The above inventory lists a total of 38 horses of varying ages recorded at several places. In addition the inventory indicates that Samuel Gallimore owned other horses which he had sold during his lifetime; presumably not long before his death.

'The Geret' has not been identified.

'Brimshole' i.e. Brimsholme - was part of the Clownam or Abbotsholme estate of Thomas Orme, now the location of Abbotsholme public school, about one mile south-east of Rocester, Staffs.
[The village of Rocester is best known today as being the world headquarters of JCB]
Samuel Gallimore took out a 21 year lease on the Brimsholmes in 1736/37. References to Staffordshire Brimsholme and Derbyshire Brimholme suggests this land straddled the River Dove, which forms the boundary between the two counties [24].

[Thomas Orme's brother John married Edith Harrison, daughter of John Harrison of Combridge (page 79) Thomas Orme's grand-daughter, Lydia Orme was later to inherit the property, and in 1796, marry William Webb (page 76).] [19].

'John Moreton's house' - he lived at Clownham (page 122).

'Knaveholme' - a farm, approximately one mile south-west of Snelston, Derbyshire.

Both Clownam (also called Clownham) and Knaveholme are about five miles from Wootton.

'Cow Close, the Walk and Soflow' - are in Wootton, and part of a substantial area of land in the village leased from the owner Richard Davenport in a deed dated 1748 [31].
Samuel Gallimore also leased land at 'Thorswood' in Wootton [28].

Appendix 2

27th September 1753

These Exhihibants do upon their Oaths
declare that this Inventory doth _____
contain a true & Just Account of all
the Goods Cattle Chattells & personal
Estate of the within written Samuel
Gallimore deceased as ch since his
Death have come to their hands
Knowledge or pofsefsion. And do
further declare that if at any time
hereafter any other Goods or personal
Estate of the said Samuel Gallimore
should come to their Hands or pofsefsion
they will willingly charge themselves
therewith and add the same to this
Inventory. And these Exhihibitants
do upon their Oaths also declare that
that all the Goods & personal Estate
of the the sd Samuel Gallimore dece'd
were not sufficient at the time of
his death to pay and discharge
the just and lawful _____
Debts he then owed. And that they
these exhibitants have justly
and faithfully expended in the
execution of their Office as Executors
of his sd Will more money than his
the sd deceased personal Estate
was worth at his death or that they have actually
received ffor the same.

Wm Gallimore
Edwd How

The sd Edward Howe
and William Gallimore
were duly sworn
before me

Thos White Snr

A full just true plain and particular Inventory of all and . . .
singular the Goods and Chattels Rights and Credits of Samuel
Gallimore late of Wooton Under Weaver in the County of . .
Stafford yeoman deceased come to the possession, Custody or. .
knowledge of William Gallimore of Wooton Under Weaver
aforesaid, and Edward How of Tenford in the said County of Stafford
Yeoman, executors of the last Will and Testament of the said
Samuel Gallimore deceased upon the fifth day of June in the year
of our Lord one thousand seven hundred and fifty two.

[Note: This is not the full inventory. Items not related to horses have been removed. The remaining content records money collected which was due to Samuel Gallimore for leaping services by his stallions, and for the sale of his horses]

	1750 21st July	£	s	d.
24th July	Of George Smith of in Earnest for a Filley	0	3	0
30th	Received from John Massey of for one stoned Horse	47	16	6
....	From Luke Bacon of for a mare	0	19	6
4th Augt	Received from John Cope of for a Mare	2	19	6
18th	From Samuel Fynney of in part for a Mare and Foal .... }	4	10	0
20th	From John Clark of for a Mare..................	15	19	0
....	From Mr John Wheeldon of Caldon for a Mare	6	7	6
	For Cash received for a Colt sold at Stafford ffair	12	12	0
10th Septr 18th 19th	Received at Leek for leaping money due to Testator at his decease part was received from William Smith of Steel House In Bradnopp and a further part was received from William Gould of Westwood near Leek but from whom remainder was received Executers or Either of them cannot sett forth..}	2	6	0
	For Cash received at Uttoxeter for Leaping But from whom Executors cannot sett forth ....}	0	11	6
	From Francis Richardson of Bromshall for one Stoned Horse .... }	4	19	0
	From Thos Hiblin of Wooton for one year old Colt	2	15	0
27th	For Cash received for Orm's Mare sold at Ashbourne	5	17	0
	From Samuel Fynney of Wooton for two Cows and one Mare and Foal ....}	11	11	0
29th	From Robert Mellor of Wooton 2 Mares one Foal and Colt .... }	7	0	0
6th Oct.	From John Mafsey, Birchwood moor one Mare & Fole	8	17	6
7th	From Mr Cotton of Crack Marsh and his Servant for leaping .... }	1	9	0
13th	From John Smith of Wast for Leaping	0	5	0
Oct.	From Robert Robinson for Leaping	0	6	0
	From Richard Heath of Wooton for leaping and Straw	1	8	6
	From William Hopkin of Ousley for one Horse	3	2	0
	From Mr John Wheeldon of Caldon in part for two Filleys	8	12	0
	From John Gallimore of Wooton for one Filley	3	3	6
14th	From John Moreton of Clownam one mare and One year old Foal .... }	9	15	0
23d	From John Coxen, Snelston for one Fole	5	18	0
29th.......	Received from Paul Vicars of Oncoate due for leaping			
30th.......	two mares in Testator's Life time ....}	0	12	6
1st Novr	From Samuel Shelton of Oncoat for same	0	10	0

12th........	From James Olliver of Sheen for leaping money	0	4	0
	From John Forster, Bullsclough for same	0	7	0
	From George Titterton of Grindon for Do	0	15	0
17th.......	From John Gould of Elkstone for Do	0	5	0
27th.....	From John Salt, Knowles for Do	0	3	0
	From William Wardle, Stony Cliff for Do	0	9	0
	From Richard Gould, Hayside for Do	0	3	0
	From Moses Ash, Gunside for Do	0	7	0
	From James Bomford of Oncoat for Do	0	2	6
	From Widow Condlyffe of Hay Top for Do	0	4	0
	From William Needham of Elkstone for Do	0	7	0
	From Thomas Hays Hope for Do	0	4	0
	From Mr Blackwall of Gatham for Do	0	5	0
	From Mr Hawford of Calverly in Cheshire for Do	0	10	6
	From John Beech, Bentley for Do	2	12	6
	From William Holden of Thurvaston for Do	0	10	0
	From Mr Goodwin of Tissington for Do	0	10	0
	From Samuel Goodwin, Musden for Do	0	10	0
	From Mr Harding of Carston for Do	0	5	0
	From Mr Bloor, Ashbourne for Do	0	5	0
	From Mr Mould of Uttoxeter High Wood for Do	0	10	6
	From Mr Wooley of Booth for Do	0	9	0
	From Mr William Marston for Do	0	10	6
	From Mr Gilman, Bromley Hurst for Do	0	6	0
	From Thos Alkin of Agersley for Do	0	7	0
	From Mr Stone, Draycott in the Clay for Do	0	10	0
	From Sampson Parks, Waterfall for Do	0	10	0
	From Mr William Rogers, Oncoat for Do	0	7	0
	From Thomas Gould, Tissington for Do	0	15	0
	From Mr Ensor for Do. Executors know not where he lives He being not in Testators Book but brought the money on his own accord .... }	0	7	0
	From Thos Titley, Holley Wood for Do	0	4	0
	From William Godridge of Thorley for Do	0	2	6
	From Samuel Milward of Stanshope for Do	0	2	6
	From Thomas Bloor, Calton for Do	0	5	0
	From Henry Cooper of Hope for Do	0	2	6
	From Richard Mould of Ramsor for Do	0	2	0
	From Mr Hall of Ramsor for Do	0	3	0
	From Daniel Alcock of WildHay for Do	0	5	0
	From Mr Ensor of Bradley for Do	0	5	0
	From John Gerrard of Ellaston for Do	0	8	0
	From Matthew Smith of Farley for Do	0	5	0
	From Thos Woodward of Northwood for Do	0	5	0
	From Benjamin Barnett of Ellaston for Do	0	4	0
	From Edward Godridge of Denston for Do....................... From	0	5	0
	Robt Alsopp Junr of Rakes for Do.............................	0	5	0
	From Joseph Birch of Prestwood for Do..........................	0	5	0
	From Mr Taylor of Wetton for Do..................................	0	4	0
	From John Walker of Wooton for Do	0	5	0
	From Mr Taylor Junr of Wetton for Do............................	0	4	0
	From Mr Fynney of Callow for Do.................................	0	8	0
	From Samuel Philips of Alstonfield for Do........................	0	4	0
	From William Needham of Sheen for Do	0	4	0
	From Thomas Robinson of Calton for Do	0	5	0
	From Robt Dennis, Caldon Grange for Do	0	4	0
	From Thomas Rollin of Lady for Do	0	5	0
	From Richard Hall of Ellaston for Do	0	6	6
	From Edward Ratcliff of Sheen for Do	0	4	0

	From Tho⁵ Ward of Sheen for D°	0	5	0
	From John Gilman of Fawfield Head for D°	0	5	0
	From William Rushton of Cotton for D°	0	4	0
	From Mʳ Torr of Ford for D°	0	5	0
	From Timothy Myott, Longnore Edge for D°	0	5	0
	From Uriah Sutton of Blackbrook for D°	0	4	0
	From Thomas Brandon of Prestwood for D°	0	5	0
	From William Salt of Wooton for D°	0	4	0
	From John Chadwick of Blackbrook for D°	0	5	0
	From Richard Bolton of Caldon for D°	0	2	6
	From Robᵗ Brindley of Hays for D°	0	5	0
	From Thomas Pickering of Sheen for D°	0	4	0
	From Thomas Lea of Rudyard for D°	0	4	0
	From William Gould of Warslow for D°	0	5	0
	From Joseph Booth of Alstonfield for D°	0	5	0
	From John Marsh of Berresford for D°	0	3	6
	From George Wood of Fairfield Head for D°	0	5	0
	From Thomas Bently of Kingsley for D°	0	8	0
	From Mʳ Ratcliff of Rake's Head for D°	0	5	0
	From Thomas Pickering of Sheen for D°	0	5	0
	From Robᵗ Grub of Prestwood Moor for D°	0	5	0
	From Samuel Booth of Low for D°	0	5	0
	From Joseph Wooliscroft in Morridge for D°	0	4	0
	From Mʳ George Needham of Brund for D°	0	5	0
	From Andrew Knifton, Oakes Moor for D°	0	5	0
	From Mʳ Plant of Brandon Brook for D°	0	5	0
	From Jos. Birch of Prestwood for D°	0	5	0
	From Thomas Wood of Ellaston for D°	0	4	0
	From John Collis of Ellaston for D°	0	4	0
	From John Alcock of Kingsley for D°	0	5	0
	From George Berresford of Wooton Park for D°	0	4	0
	From Sampson Parks of Waterfall for D°	0	9	0
	From Trison Ratcliff of Wooton Park for D°	0	5	0
	From Robᵗ Grub of Prestwood Moor for D°	0	2	6
	From John Bagshaw of Harding Booth for D°	0	3	6
	From Mʳ Prince of Hilsdale for D°	0	5	0
	From Mʳ Hall of Stanshope for D°	0	2	6
	From Mʳ George Needham of Brund for D°	0	3	0
	From Charles Smith of Ellaston for D°	0	3	0
	From Thomas Brandon of Prestwood for D°	0	5	0
	From Robᵗ Grub of Prestwood Moor for D°	0	4	0
	From Benjamin Barnett of Ellaston for D°	0	4	0
	From John Wood of Denston for D°	0	9	0
	From Richard Smith of Ellaston for D°	0	6	0
	From John Gould of Warslow field for D°	0	3	0
	From Mʳ Mountford of Mixon Hay .....for D°	0	5	0
	From John Clewlow of Whitelee for D°	0	4	0
	From Philip Draycot of Oncoat for D°	0	5	0
	From Mʳ Fynney of Callow for D°	0	5	0
	From George Bloor of Cotton for D°	0	5	0
	From Mʳ Goodwin of Lees for D°	0	5	0
	From Robert Dennis of Caldon Grange for D°	0	4	0
	From Joseph Booth of Alstonfield for D°	0	3	0
	From Mʳ Ensor of Bradley for D°	0	5	0
	From Mʳ Warner of Bromshall for D°	0	9	0
	From Samuel Clark of Ellastone for D°	0	9	0
	From Edward Woodwif of Grindon for D°	0	5	0
	From Thomas Philips of Low fields for D°	0	9	0
	From Robᵗ Alsop junʳ of Rakes for D°	0	5	0

From John Chadwick of Blackbrook for Dº	0	4	0
From Thomas Horobin of Cotton for Dº	0	5	0
From Thomas Warner of Bromshall Park for Dº	0	5	0
From Thomas Bentley of Kingsley for Dº	0	4	0
From Thomas Rollin of Alstonfield for Dº	0	4	0
From Samuel Hudson of Wooton for Dº	0	5	0
From Thomas Plant of Blackbrook for Dº	0	4	0
From John Gould of Elkston for Dº	0	5	0
From Thoˢ Harrison of Calton for Dº	0	4	0
From Mʳ Froggat of Sheen for Dº	0	8	0
From Richard Stubbs of Butterton for Dº	0	5	0
From Thomas Salt of Elkstone for Dº	0	5	0
From Mʳ White of Hope for Dº	0	4	0
From James Mycock of Butterton for Dº	0	5	0
From John Cope of Hartington for Dº	0	5	0
From William Taylor of Wetton for Dº	0	5	0
From John Cope of Wooton for Dº	0	5	0
From Uriah Sutton of Blackbrook for Dº	0	4	0
From Joseph Deval of Cotton for Dº	0	5	0
From John Bagshaw of Newton Grange for Dº	0	5	0
From Mʳ Blackwall of Gatham for Dº	0	4	0
From Nicholas Mellor of Butterton for Dº	0	5	0
From John Smith of Alton Park for Dº	0	5	0
From Richard Hall of Ellaston for Dº	0	4	0
From Thomas Plant of Hurdlow for Dº	0	4	0
From William Rushton of Cotton for Dº	0	5	0
From Mʳ Goodridge of Farley for Dº	0	5	0
From Mʳ Spencer of Alstonfield for Dº	0	5	0
From Mʳ Cork of Butterton for Dº	0	5	0
From William Shemmilt of Wooton for Dº	0	5	0
From Mʳ Goodwin of Tissington for Dº	0	5	0
From William Crompton of Cheadle Grange for Dº	0	10	0
From Charles Smith of Ellastone for Dº	0	8	0
From Mʳ Hardy of Micilover for Dº	0	10	0
From Mʳ Brown of Thurvaston for Dº	0	8	0
From Revᵈ Stone of Draycot in Clay for Dº	0	8	0
From Thomas Sillito of Cheadle Grange for Dº	0	16	0
From William Orpe of Prestwood for Dº	0	17	0
From Joseph Smith of Riding for Dº	0	16	0
From Thomas Coxen of Snelston for Dº	0	10	0
From Mʳ Armishaw of Slade house for Dº	0	8	0
From Mʳ Poyser near Longnore for Dº	0	17	0
From John Tunnicliff of RakeWay for Dº	0	5	0
From John Goodwin of Fairfield Head for Dº	0	10	0
From Mʳ Rogers of Oncoat for Dº	0	10	0
From Benjamin Barnett of Ellaston for Dº	0	10	0
From Mʳ Hayne of Marston upon Dove for Dº	0	8	0
From William Maskery of Norbury for Dº	0	10	0
From John Wooley of Booth for Dº	1	1	0
From Samuel Goodwin of Musden for Dº	0	10	6
From Mʳ Froggat Sheen Lane End for Dº	0	7	0
From Esqʳ Davenport for Dº	0	10	0
From Joseph Booth of Alstonfield for Dº	0	5	0
From John Collis of Ellaston for Dº	0	10	0
From Mʳ Lyttleton, Marchington Woodlands for Dº	0	15	0
From Mʳ Gilbert of Waterhouses for Dº	0	10	0
From Edward Ratcliff of Sheen for Dº	0	7	0
From Samuel Masgreave of Mathfield for Dº	0	18	0
From George Oakes Of Ellastone for Dº	0	10	0

		£	s	d
	From Joseph Osborne of Loxley for D°	0	10	0
	From Samuel Forster of Snelston for D°	0	10	0
	From Mr Manifold of Morridge for D°	0	8	0
	From Robert Holliworth of Bradley for D°	0	11	0
	From Thomas Wood of Ellastone for D°	0	8	0
	From Mr Milward of Orchards for D°	1	1	0
	From Mr Eardley of Mathfield for D°	1	0	0
	From Ja^s Froggat, one at Sheen for D°	0	6	0
	From John Percival of Sheen for D°	0	7	6
	From Mr Orm of Scropton for D°	0	7	0
	From Mr Falkner of bratby for D°	1	0	0
	From William Mellor of Alstonfield for D°	0	7	6
	From Mr Greaves of Ingleby for D°	0	5	0
	From George Rogers of Mares Knowles for D°	0	10	0
	From Mr Buxton of Nowles for D°	0	10	0
	From John Hudson of Ash for D°	0	5	0
	From John Milward of Ilam moor Top for D°	0	7	0
	From John Osborne of Kinson for D°	0	5	0
	From Mr Hall of Brookhouse for D°	0	18	0
	From Richard Alsop of Bank Top for D°	0	5	0
	From Francis Bond of Bratby for D°	0	10	0
	From John Oakes of Ellaston for D°	0	10	0
	From John Adams of Silkmore for D°	0	10	6
	From James Gilman, over Booth low for D°	0	5	0
	A Man from Bratby Hall whose name Executors don't know for }	0	10	0
	From Mr Bowyer of Wardley for D°	1	0	0
	From John Masgrave of Norbury for D°	0	9	0
	From William Goosby of Ingleby for D°	0	10	0
	From Mr Wardle of Sheen for D°	0	7	6
	From William Smith of Mathfield for D°	0	8	0
	From John Gerrard of Prestwood for D°	0	17	0
	From William Needham of Sheen for D°	0	8	0
	From Thomas Harrison of Caldon for D°	0	8	0
	From Mr Turner, Pardwick for D°	0	10	0
	From John Coxen, Snelston for D°	0	10	0
	From William Jackson of Stanton for D°	0	10	0
	From Mr Moor of Fosson for D°	0	6	6
	From Simon Clark of Newton for D°	0	12	0
	From William Keeling of Hollington for D°	0	2	0
	From Thomas Shipley of Newton for D°	0	5	0
	From a widow at Newton whose name Executors don't know for D° }	0	4	0
	From Saml Hayns, Beamhurst for D°	0	3	0
	From Mr Ford of WillsLock for D°	0	10	0
	From Sampson Parks of Waterfall for D°	0	2	0
	From William Salt of Wooton for one Horse	3	19	0
	From Mr Wheeldon, remaining part of two Fylleys	3	3	0
	From Mr Wheeldon for John Lees 10 Sheep and one old mare }	2	6	8
	From George Heath of Wooton for one Mare	4	2	0
	From Jn.° Henshaw of Stubwood for 1 mare	3	13	0
11th Dec^r	From Thos Salt of Wooton for 1 mare one Load of malt 20 strikes of oats 1 Hog & one old cow }	8	14	0
3d Jan^r	From Geo Smith of Salley Moor for 1 year old Filley Winter Grafs of the High oft & the Hay Nursury and } Hay 2 Cows 10 Sheep & 1 Horse Allow'd by Edwd How of Tenford	31	5	9

	For 1 mare	2	9	0
26th.....	Reced for 5 Horses sold at Stafford ffair	52	0	0
2d Febr	From the sd Wm Gallimore			
1751.	.... for 2 ston'd Colts	22	0	0
26th Mar.	Reced from Thos Heath of Fenny Bentley			
	due to Testator for the use of his Stallion .... }	1	0	0
18th May	Do from Henry Gibson of Ousley for Do	0	5	0
	Do from Wm Turner of Tean for Do	0	10	0
	Do from Saml Pegg of SwinsCoe for Do	0	5	0
	Do from Thos Harvey of Prestwood for Do	1	1	0
	Do from Thos Rudge of Newton for Do	0	5	0
5th	Do from Mr Gallimore of Hollington for Do	0	7	0
Augt	Do from Mr Halford of ipr for Do	0	8	0
2d	Do from Wm Rogers of Stoney Cliff for Do	0	4	6
Apr	Do from John Lownds of Rocester for Do	0	19	0
1752				

Wm Gallimore
Edwd How

Appendix 3

Table showing location of 'customers' of Samuel Gallimore
who owed 'leaping money'; to be collected his executors.

Leaping Record					
Moderm place name	Place name in record, and variations	Times recorded	County	Map Ref. plotted	Alternative map ref.
Agardsley Park	Agersley	1	Staffs.	SK 135274	
Alstonfield		7	Staffs.	SK 131556	
Alton park		1	Staffs.	SK 080435	
Ash		1	Derbys.	SK 255333	
Ashbourne		1	Derbys.	SK 180465	
Bank Top		1	Staffs.	SK 118599	SK 129615 or SK 182497
Beamhurst		1	Staffs.	SK 060362	
Bentley Hall	Bentley	1	Derbys.	SK 178382	
Berresford		1	Staffs.	SK 125595	
Blackbrook	Brandon brook	6	Staffs.	SK 054572	
Booth		2	Staffs.	SK 043271	
Bradley		4	Derbys.	SK 225455	SK 059414
Bradnop	Bradnopp	1	Staffs.	SK 010550	
Bramshall	Bromshall	1	Staffs.	SK 061332	
Bramshall Park	Bromshall park	1	Staffs.	SK 072339	
Bretby	Bratby	2	Derbys.	SK 295232	
Bretby Hall	Bratby Hall	1	Derbys.	SK 300225	
Bromley Hurst	Bromley hurst	1	Staffs.	SK 088225	
Brookhouse		1	Staffs.	SK 118305	SJ 961512
Brund		2	Staffs.	SK 103613	
Bullclough		1	Staffs.	SK 060550	
Butterton		4	Staffs.	SK 075565	
Cauldon	Caldon	2	Staffs.	SK 077494	
Cauldon Grange	Caldon Grange	2	Staffs.	SK O85486	
Callow		2	Derbys.	SK 170470	SK 269520
Calton		3	Staffs.	SK 103503	
Calverly		2	Ches.		
Carsington	Carston	1	Derbys.	SK 251534	
Cheadle Grange		2	Staffs.	SK 027438	
Cotton		5	Staffs.	SK 066464	
Crakemarsh	Crack Marrsh	1	Staffs.	SK 093365	
Denstone	Denston	2	Staffs.	SK 010407	
Draycott in the Clay		2	Staffs.	SK 156385	
Elkstone	Elkston	4	Staffs.	SK 055591	
Ellastone	Ellaston	16	Staffs.	SK 117434	
Farley		2	Staffs.	SK 067443	
Fawfieldhead	Fair field Head	3	Staffs.	SK 075637	

Fenny Bentley		1	Derbys.	SK 175502	
Ford		1	Staffs.	SK 064540	
Foston	Fosson	1	Derbys.	SK 189318	
Gateham	Gathiam	2	Staffs.	SK 117567	
Grindon		2	Staffs.	SK 086543	
Gunside		1	Staffs.	SJ 982600	
Hardings Booth		1	Staffs.	SK 068644	
Hartington		1	Derbys.	SK 130604	
Hay Top		1	Derbys.	SK 175725	
Hayes	Hays	1	Staffs.	SK 081603	
Hayside		1		not known	
Hillsdale		1	Staffs.	SK 080554	
Hollywood	Holley Wood	1	Staffs.	SK 067377	
Hollington		2	Staffs.	SK 055391	
Hope		3	Staffs.	SK 125553	
Hurdlow		1	Staffs.	SK 022607	
Ilam Tops	Ilam Moor Tops	1	Staffs.	SK 139523	
Ingleby		2	Derbys.	SK 349271	
	ipr	1		not known	
Ipstones		2	Staffs.	SK 020500	
Kingsley		3	Staffs.	SK 009470	
Kingstone	Kinson	1	Staffs.	SK 060295	
Knowles	Nowles	1	Staffs.	SK 018614	
Ladyside	Lady	1	Staffs.	SK 091551	
Lees		1	Derbys.	SK 265373	SK 033472
Longnor		1	Staffs.	SK 088649	
Longnor Edge Top	Longnore Edge	1	Staffs.	SK 097647	
The Low	Low	1	Staffs.	SK 090628	
Lowfields	Low fields	1	Staffs.	SK 091376	
Loxley		1	Staffs.	SK 061320	
Marchington Woodlands		1	Staffs.	SK 115286	
Mareknowles	Mare knowles	1	Ches.	SJ 946658	
Marston upon Dove		2	Derbys.	SK 235296	
Mayfield	Mathfield	3	Staffs.	SK 158458	
Mickleover	Micilover	1	Derbys.	SK 315340	
Mixon Hay		1	Staffs.	SK 030575	
Morridge Side	Morridge	2	Staffs.	SK 022544	
Musden		2	Staffs.	SK 125513	
Newton		5	Derbys.	SK 152545	
Newton Grange		1	Derbys.	SK 165535	
Norbury		2	Derbys.	SK 128411	
Northwood Farm	Northwood	1	Staffs.	SK 121439	
Oakamoor	Oakes Moor	1	Staffs.	SK 097637	
Oncote	Oncoate or Oncoat	6	Staffs.	SK 050550	
The Orchards	Orchards	1	Staffs.	SK 154472	
Ousley		1	Staffs.	SK 117447	
Over Boothlow	over Booth Low	1	Staffs.	SK 167637	
Padwich	Pardwick	1	Staffs.	SK 013526	
Pointhorne	Printhorn	1	Staffs.	SK 075393	

Prestwood		9	Staffs.	SK 103425	
Rakes		2	Staffs.	SK 119598	
Rake's Head		1	Staffs.	SK 063662	
Rakeway	Rake Way	1	Staffs.	SK 025420	
Ramshorn	Ramsor	2	Staffs.	SK 083453	
Riddings	Riding	1	Staffs.	SK 090398	SK 173394
Rocester		1	Staffs.	SK 110395	
Rudyard		1	Staffs.	SJ 952578	
Scropton		1	Derbys.	SK 193302	
Sheen		12	Staffs.	SK 113615	
Sheen Lane End		2	Staffs.	SK 110606	
Silkmore		1	Staffs.	SJ 932218	
Slade House	Sladehouse	1	Staffs.	SK 107511	
Snelston		3	Derbys.	SK 153434	
Stanshope		2	Staffs.	SK 127542	
Stanton		1	Staffs.	SK 126462	
Stoney Cliffe	Stony Cliff	2	Staffs.	SK 009603	
Swinscoe		1	Staffs.	SK 127483	
Tean		1	Staffs.	SK 010397	
Throwley Hall	Thorley	1	Staffs.	SK 110525	
Thurvaston		2	Derbys.	SK 242377	SK 138385
Tissington		3	Derbys.	SK 176523	
Uttoxeter		1	Staffs.	SK 090335	
Uttoxeter Highwood		1	Staffs.	SK 096320	
Waldley	Wardley	1	Derbys.	SK 125370	
Warslow	Warslow Field	2	Staffs.	SK 087587	
Westwood Hall, Leek	westwood, Leek	1	Staffs.	SJ 966562	
Waste Farm, Wootton	Wast	1	Staffs.	SK 098434	
Waterfall		3	Staffs.	SK 082516	
Waterhouses		1	Staffs.	SK 085502	
Wetton		3	Staffs.	SK 109555	
White Lee Farm	Whitelee	1	Staffs.	SK 029564	
Wildhay		1	Staffs.	SK 119453	
Willslock		1	Staffs.	SK 076307	
Wootton	Wooton	6	Staffs.	SK 107451	
Wootton Park	Wooton park	2	Staffs.	SK 090445	

PREPAID FEES TO
CIPPENHAM HARVESTER (41375).

	£	s.	d.
Members	2	15	0
Annual Subscription to the Society ...		5	0
Non-Members	3	10	0
Assisted Nominations	1	15	0

Groom-in-charge - H. W. Smith.

Assisted Nominations (which are strictly limited) may be had to this Horse on application to the Hon. Secretary.

The Members of the Meynell Hunt will offer a Champion Silver Cup for Competition for Foals sired by the Uttoxeter Society's Stallion at Uttoxeter Foal Sale, and Cash Prizes will also be given.

Foals sired by this Horse are eligible for the Peterboro' Produce Stakes.

The Society will not be responsible for any damage or loss that may occur, but every care will be taken.

For Nominations, before sending Mares, apply to the Hon. Secretary.

W. H. Smith's Printing Works, Uttoxeter.

President : Major E. GERALD THOMPSON, M.V.O., J.P.

THE UTTOXETER & DISTRICT
SHIRE HORSE SOCIETY
Have Hired for SEASON 1938
CIPPENHAM HARVESTER
41375

Photo by Orr & Sons.

Travelling Season - April 6th to July 16th.

High Street,
Uttoxeter.

Telephone No. 44.

C. J. BLORE,
Hon. Sec.

Cippenham Harvester (41375)
BROWN.   FOALED 1932.

(The Property of Messrs. REINHOLD & FRESHNEY.)

Sire—PENDLEY HARVESTER 40368.

Dam — 11800 CIPPENHAM MARJORIE, by CIPPENHAM DRAUGHTSMAN 38109.

G. Dam—88531 FENNY MENESTREL DOLLY, by NORBURY MENESTREL 23543.

G.G. Dam—48992 PEAK DOLLY, a big winner—including 1st and Junior Champion and Reserve, Supreme Champion S.H.S., London, and 1st Ashbourne.

Wonderful breeding, and a real class young horse.

Cippenham Harvester has won the following Prizes :

1932—Two Firsts Royal Counties ; 1st Peterborough ; 1st and 2nd Tring ; 2nd R.A.S.E. ; 7th Peterborough Produce Stakes.

1933—5th S.H.S., London.

PENDLEY HARVESTER is out of 99582 PENDLEY LADY that celebrated Mare, who won 1st and Reserve, S.H.S., London, and was the Winner of more Prizes than any other Shire Mare—her Dam 72149 SNELSTON LADY, was the famous Mare who was Reserve Champion, S.H.S., London, three times ; and was sold at the Pendley Sales for 2,200 guineas.

88531 FENNY MENESTREL DOLLY is also the Dam of His Grace the Duke of Devonshire's noted Stallion, CIPPENHAM FRIAR.

This Horse holds Ministry of Agriculture Licence for 1938, and is subject to the Rules and Regulations of the Ministry of Agriculture and Fisheries.

ROUTE FOR 1938.

Cippenham Harvester (41375)
will be stabled the week-end at the " Greyhound " Inn, Balance Street, Uttoxeter, and will travel the following Route, which may be subject to slight alterations :—

MONDAY.

Leave Uttoxeter at 8.0 a.m. through Bramshall to Mrs. Meakin's, Nobut, to bait ; on through Leigh, to Mr. Brandrick's, Heybridge, for the night.

TUESDAY.

Leave Heybridge for Mr. Hulme's, Draycott-in-the-Moors, to bait ; and on through Tean and Hollington, to Rocester, to Mr. T. C. Bailey's, for the night.

WEDNESDAY.

Leave Rocester for " Greyhound " Inn, Balance Street, Uttoxeter, for the Day.

THURSDAY.

Leave Uttoxeter via Loxley Green, to Woodcock Heath, Kingstone, to bait ; and on through Blythe Bridge, Booth, Newton, to Bagots Arms, Abbots Bromley, for the night.

FRIDAY.

Leave Abbots Bromley to Mr. J. Leadbetter's, Tomlinson's Corner, Newborough, to bait ; and on through Marchington Woodlands to Houndhill, for the night.

SATURDAY.

Leave Houndhill via Sudbury Station and Mackley, to Harehill, to bait ; leaving at 12 noon for Uttoxeter for week-end.

This route is subject to slight alteration.

NO BUSINESS ON SUNDAYS.

PREPAID FEES TO
RAANS RECORD (40796)

	£	s.	d.
Members	3	15	0
Annual Subscription to the Society ...		5	0
Non-Members	6	6	0
Assisted Nominations	2	15	0

Groom-in-charge - ~~H. Schofield~~ J. Davies.

Assisted Nominations (which are strictly limited) may be had to this Horse on application to the Hon. Secretary.

The Members of the Meynell Hunt will offer a Champion Silver Cup for Competiton for Foals sired by the Uttoxeter Society's Stallion at Uttoxeter Foal Sale, and Cash Prizes will also be given.

Foals sired by this Horse are eligible for the Peterboro' Produce Stakes.

The Society will not be responsible for any damage or loss that may occur, but every care will be taken.

For Nomination, before sending Mares, apply to the Hon. Secretary.

W. H. Smith's Printing Works, The Library, Uttoxeter.

President : Major E. GERALD THOMPSON, M.V.O., J.P.

THE UTTOXETER & DISTRICT
SHIRE HORSE SOCIETY

Have Hired for Season 1939

RAANS RECORD (40796)

Photo by G. H. Parsons

Travelling Season - April 12th to July 15th.

High Street,
Uttoxeter.
Telephone No. 44.

C. J. BLORE,
Hon. Sec.

RAANS RECORD (40796)
BAY. FOALED 1929.

(The Property of Messrs. Reinhold & Freshney.)

Sire—Cippenham Recorder 39866.
Dam—114353 Gunby Autumn Briar Rose, by Normanby Briar King 32672.
G. Dam—103407 Gunby Autumn Tints, by Champions Cup Bearer 32215.

Wonderful Breeding, and a real class horse.

Raans Record has won the following Prizes :
1931—Second Royal Lancs.
1932—Third S.H.S., London ; First and Reserve for S.H.S.
1933—Third S.H.S., London ; (Gold Medal, R.A.S.E.)
1936—Third S.H.S., London.
1937—Second and Reserve Senior Champion, S.H.S., London.
1938—Second and Reserve Senior Champion, S.H.S., London.

The only sire to win the Cup outright for siring winning foals at the Peterborough Stakes, too well-known to require any description. Sire of Raans Record Wave 41506, a great prize-winner, and of 127882 Margaret of Chippinghurst, First and S.H.S. Gold Medal, Peterborough Produce Stakes, 1934 ; First and Champion S.H.S., London, 1935 ; First, Junior Champion and Reserve for Champion, S.H.S., London, 1936 ; also of 127115 Raans Lady Record, First, S.H.S. Gold Medal and Reserve for Challenge Cup, Peterborough Produce Stakes in 1933 ; Lechhampstead Reward 42696, First and Gold Medal Peterborough Stakes, 1936 ; Record Breaker 42747, Second two-year-old Stallion, S.H.S., London, 1938 ; Broken Record (Vol. 60) 5th Yearling Colt, S.H.S., London, 1938 ; and a great many other winners at all the principal Shows. At last London Show he sired the Second, Third and Seventh prize Yearling Colts and Fifth prize two-year-old besides.

"Raans Record" is ten years old, and is as clean and new in his limbs as a two-year-old. The best sire to-day of the most correct and wearing type. His dam is 17 years of age, sound, clean of limb, and still breeding.

This Horse holds Ministry of Agriculture Licence for 1939, and is subject to the Rules and Regulations of the Ministry of Agriculture and Fisheries.

ROUTE FOR 1939.

RAANS RECORD (40796)
will be stabled the week-end at the "Greyhound" Inn, Balance Street, Uttoxeter, and will travel the following Route, which may be subject to slight alteration :—

MONDAY.
Leave Uttoxeter at 8.0 a.m. through Bramshall to Mrs. Meakin's Nobut, to bait ; on via Park Hall to Mr. Hulme's, Draycott-in-the-Moors, for the night.

TUESDAY.
Leave Mr. Hulme's, Draycott-in-the-Moors, and on through Tean and Hollington, to Rocester, to Mr. T. C. Bailey's, for the night.

WEDNESDAY.
Leave Rocester for "Greyhound" Inn, Balance Street, Uttoxeter, for the Market, leaving again 3.30 p.m. to Mr. A. J. Bettson's, Woodcock Heath, Kingstone, for the night.

THURSDAY.
Leave Woodcock Heath, Kingstone, through Blythe Bridge, Booth, Newton, to Baggots Arms, Abbots Bromley, for the night.

FRIDAY.
Leave Abbots Bromley to Mr. J. Leadbetter's, Tomlinson's Corner, Newborough, to bait ; and on through Marchington Woodlands to Houndhill, for the night.

SATURDAY.
Leave Houndhill via Sudbury Station and Mackley, to Harehill, to bait ; leaving at 12 noon for Uttoxeter for week-end.

This route is subject to slight alteration.

NO BUSINESS ON SUNDAYS.

THE LICHFIELD SHIRE HORSE SOCIETY

will not be responsible for any accident to Mares whilst being tried or served.

ALL MARES sent to Stud Horse at Owners' Risk.

No Mare served twice within 10 days
(see Rules of the Society).

NO BUSINESS ON SUNDAYS.

FEES.

	£	s	d
Members	3	0	0

Non-Members (10/- in addition to fee)

Members' Annual Subscription ... 5/-

ALL FEES must be paid prior to Service.

£6 in CASH PRIZES will be given in 1935, for FOALS by "Raans Clansman" 41267, and £4 for Mare served by "Raans Clansman" 41267 in 1934.

The Stud Horse will arrive on April 9th, 1934, and stand at the Smithfield Hotel, Lichfield, and will travel the route.

ALL COMMUNICATIONS to be addressed to the Secretary.

F. D. WINTERTON,

S. Mary's Chambers,

Telephone : Lichfield 32. **LICHFIELD.**

A limited number of Assisted Nominations to Owners of Mares residing in the district, Members of the Society (being *bona-fide* farmers) farming under 100 acres—Half the Fee. Apply to the Secretary.

MEACHAM, PRINTER, LICHFIELD.

Lichfield Shire Horse Society
SEASON 1934.

"RAANS CLANSMAN"
41267.

The Property of James Forshaw and Sons.

"RAANS CLANSMAN" 41267

Black, foaled 1931.

PRIZES.
1932—1st Winslow. 1934—2nd London.
Reserve for Junior Championship.

It is no exaggeration to say he was the most promising young horse at the London Show and especially liked by breeders from the North.

Sire THEALE RICHARD 40179.
A winner and sire of some good stock.

G. Sire BASILDON CLANSMAN 36277.

Dam 118821 RAANS ACTRESS.
(A most excellent mare of up-to-date type) by Sundridge Nulli Secundus 24253, that famous sire.

G. Dam 111678 FRANT ACTRESS
(A big good mare) by Champion's Goalkeeper 30296.

"Raans Clansman" is a promising young horse fully 17-2 hands, big, natural, unforced, and well-bred, great crest, deep middle with short back on extraordinary big deep blue feet, excellent pasterns and a hind leg that has the breadth, a hock broad and deep that stallions that leave good stock must have.

Being of the Champion Clansman, Blaisdon Draughtsman and Champion's Goalkeeper blood, helps to make his stockgetting propensities more certain.

Take the opportunity now he is here.

SEASON 1934.

"RAANS CLANSMAN" 41267

will stand at
THE SMITHFIELD HOTEL, LICHFIELD,

and travel the following route
(subject to alterations).

MONDAY, 10 a.m.—Leave Lichfield for Mr. Weston's, **Stychbrook,** through **Elmhurst** to Mr. Smallwood's, **Handsacre,** to bait ; then through **Hill Ridware,** to Mr. W. Froggatt's **Hill Ridware** for the night.

TUESDAY, 10 a.m.—Leave Mr. Froggatt's through **Blythbury, Hamstall,** to Mr. C. Lees's, **Cowley Hill Farm,** to bait ; to **Morrey, Yoxall,** and to Mr. Jeffries', **Eastfields, Kings Bromley,** for the night.

WEDNESDAY, 10 a.m. — Leave Eastfields, to **Alrewas** (Mr. P. Mallaber's) then to **Fradley** (Mr. W. Shaw's) to bait ; **Hillyard's Cross** to **Lichfield** for the night.

THURSDAY—Stands at Lichfield.

FRIDAY, 10 a.m.—Leave Lichfield through **Fisherwick Park** to **Elford Lowe** (Mr. F. Hidderley's) to bait ; then to **Mere Pits, Wigginton and Syerscote** (Mr. W. Walker's) for the night.

SATURDAY, 10 a.m. — Leave Syerscote, through **Coton, Hopwas, Bodnetts,** through Mr. Kinson's farm for Mr. W. Taylor's, **Bangley,** to bait ; then through **Hints, Weeford,** to **Lichfield.**

Stands at Lichfield for the week-end.

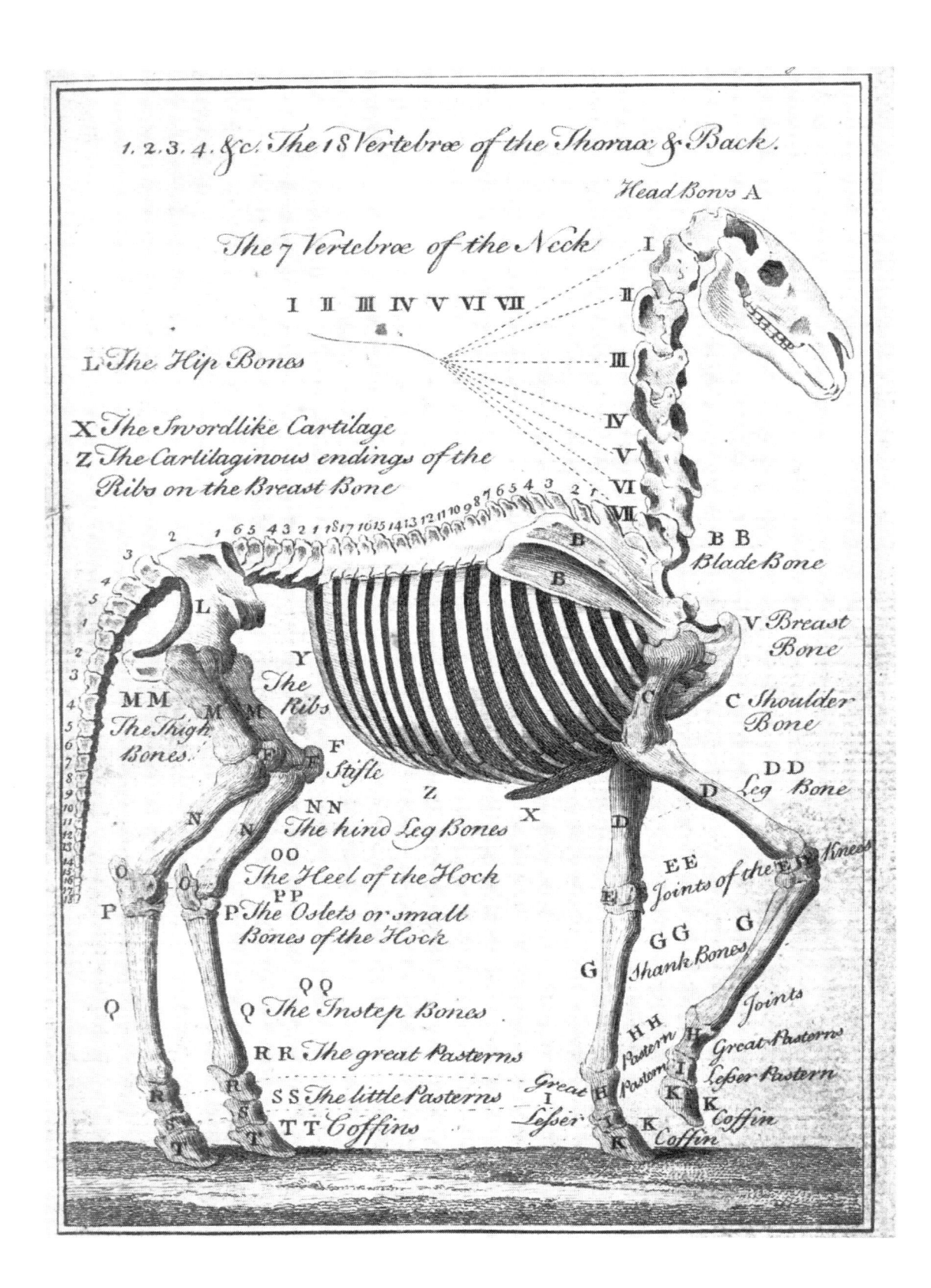

1. 2. 3. 4. &c. The 18 Vertebræ of the Thorax & Back.

Head Bones A

The 7 Vertebræ of the Neck

I II III IV V VI VII

L The Hip Bones

X The Swordlike Cartilage
Z The Cartilaginous endings of the
Ribs on the Breast Bone

I
II
III
IV
V
VI
VII

B
B

BB Blade Bone

V Breast Bone

C Shoulder Bone

DD Leg Bone

Y The Ribs

MM
M M
The Thigh Bones

F
F F

F Stifle

NN
The hind Leg Bones

OO
The Heel of the Hock

PP
P The Oslets or small Bones of the Hock

QQ
Q The Instep Bones

RR The great Pasterns

SS The little Pasterns

TT Coffins

Z

X

D

EE Joints of the Knees

GG G
Shank Bones
G

Joints

HH H Great Pasterns
Pastern
Pastern Lesser Pastern

Great
Lesser
Coffin

K Coffin

References:

[1] Annals of Agriculture & other Useful Arts Vol. 21 p 494-501
An account of the sale of the capital live stock belonging to Thomas Paget
Esq. of Ibstock, Leicestershire which was sold on 14th November (and the
following days) 1793.   www.books.google.co.uk

[2] Beastall, T.W.   History of Lincolnshire Vol VIII Agricultural Revolution
                  in Lincolnshire   History of Lincolnshire Committee for the
                              Society of Lincolnshire History & Archaeology 1978.

[3] Biddell, Herman et al   HEAVY HORSES - BREEDS AND MANAGEMENT
                  From: LIVE STOCK HANDBOOKS   NO III,
                  Edited by James Sinclair   Vintner & Co. London 1894
           http://www.archive.org/stream/cu31924051110306#page/n27/mode/2up

[4] Burgess, Peter The Horse and Ox as Agricultural and Industrial Draught Animals
                  Cave & Quarry 6   2011   Wealdon Cave and Mining Society
                  http://www.wcms.org.uk/cgi-bin/wcmsnewsletter.pl?issueref=CQ6

[5] The British NEWSPAPER Archive

                              http://www.britishnewspaperarchive.co.uk/

Newspaper Advertisements and Notices:

http://www.britishnewspaperarchive.co.uk/viewer/

1757[1De]	Derby Mercury - 25 March & 1 April 1757 bl/0000189/17570325/015/0004
1757[2Le]	Derby Mercury - 8 April 1757 bl/0000189/17570408/012/0004
1758[3]	Derby Mercury – 31 March [& 14 April] 1758 bl/0000189/17580331/017/0004
1758[4De]	Derby Mercury - 7 April 1758 BL/0000189/17580407/008/0003
1758[5]	Derby Mercury – 16 June 1758 bl/0000189/17580616/023/0004
1759[6De]	Derby Mercury - 20 April 1759 bl/0000189/17590420/015/0004
1761[7]	Derby Mercury - 27 March 1761 bl/0000189/17610327/005/0001
1762[8Le]	The Leicester and Nottingham Journal - Saturday 17 March & Saturday 3 April 1762
1762[9]	Derby Mercury - 16 April 1762 bl/0000189/17620416/011/0003
1763[10Le]	The Leicester and Nottingham Journal - Saturday 16 April 1763
1764[11Le]	The Leicester and Nottingham Journal - Saturday 17 November 1764
1765[12]	Derby Mercury – Friday 12 April 1765 bl/0000189/17650412/006/0004
1765[13Le]	Derby Mercury – Friday 19 April 1765
1765[14Le]	The Leicester and Nottingham Journal - Saturday 23 November 1765
1765[15De]	Derby Mercury - 21 Mar 1766 bl/0000189/17660321/018/0004
1766[16Le]	Derby Mercury - 11 April 1766 /bl/0000189/17660411/008/0004
1767[17]	Derby Mercury - Friday 24 April 1767 bl/0000189/17670424/004/0004
1768[18Li]	Stamford Mercury - Thursday 31 March 1768 bl/0000254/17680331/014/0004
1769[19Le]	Derby Mercury 17 March [& 31 March] 1769 BL/0000189/17690317/007/0004
1768[20]	The Leicester and Nottingham Journal - Saturday 16 March 1768
1769[21]	Derby Mercury - Friday 31 March 1769 bl/0000189/17690331/004/0001
1769[22De]	Derby Mercury - Friday 7 April 1769 BL/0000189/17690407/004/0004
1769[23Le]	The Leicester and Nottingham Journal - Saturday 15 April 1769
1770[24]	Derby Mercury - Friday 30 March 1770 BL/0000189/17700330/018/0004
1770[25]	Derby Mercury - Friday 30 March 1770 BL/0000189/17700330/018/0004
1770[26]	Derby Mercury - 6 April [& 13 April] 1770 BL/0000189/17700406/006/0004
1770[27]	Derby Mercury - 27 April 1770 BL/0000189/17700427/006/0004

1770[28Le]	Derby Mercury - 27 April [& 11 May] 1770 BL/0000189/17700427/006/0004
1770[29]	Derby Mercury - 27 April 1770 BL/0000189/17700427/006/0004
1771[30Le]	Derby Mercury - 22 March 1771 bl/0000189/17710322/007/0004
1771[31Le]	Stamford Mercury - Thursday 28 March 1771 bl/0000254/17710328/026/0004
1771[32]	Derby Mercury - 5 April 1771 bl/0000189/17710405/004/0004
1771[33]	The Leicester and Nottingham Journal - Saturday 6 April & 13 April 1771
1771[34]	Derby Mercury - Friday 12 April 1771 BL/0000189/17710412/024/0004
1771[35]	Derby Mercury - Friday 19 April 1771 bl/0000189/17710419/007/0004
1771[36De]	Derby Mercury - Friday 19 April 1771 bl/0000189/17710419/007/0004
1771[37Le]	Derby Mercury - Friday 19 April 1771 bl/0000189/17710419/007/0004
1772[38De]	Derby Mercury - 17 April 1772 BL/0000189/17720417/007/0004
1772[39De]	Derby Mercury - 17 April 1772 BL/0000189/17720417/007/0004
1772[40]	Derby Mercury - Friday 20 April 1772 BL/0000189/17720320/013/0004
1772[41]	Derby Mercury - 24 April 1772 bl/0000189/17720424/008/0004
1772[42]	Derby Mercury - 24 April 1772 bl/0000189/17720424/008/0004
1772[43De]	Derby Mercury - Friday 8 May [& 15 May] 1772 BL/0000189/17720508/025/0004
1773[44]	Derby Mercury - Friday 30 April 1773 BL/0000189/17730430/019/0004
1774[45]	The Leicester and Nottingham Journal - Saturday 5 March 1774
1774[46]	Derby Mercury - Friday 18 March 1774 bl/0000189/17740318/003/0004
1774[47]	Derby Mercury - Friday 25 March 1774 bl/0000189/17740325/005/0004
1774[48]	Derby Mercury - Friday 18 March [& 25 March] 1774 bl/0000189/17740318/003/0004
1774[49]	Derby Mercury - Friday 25 March 1774 bl/0000189/17740325/005/0004
1774[50]	The Leicester and Nottingham Journal - Saturday 2 April 1774
1774[51De]	Derby Mercury - 8 April 1774 bl/0000189/17740408/005/0004
1774[52]	Oxford Journal - Saturday 23 April 1774 bl/0000073/17740423/008/0004
1774[53]	Derby Mercury - 18 November [& 25 November] 1774 bl/0000189/17741118/004/0004
1774[54]	Derby Mercury - 2 December 1774 bl/0000189/17741202/005/0004
1775[55]	Derby Mercury - 10 February 1775 bl/0000189/17750210/005/0004
1775[56]	Derby Mercury - Friday 7 April 1775 bl/0000189/17750407/005/0004
1775[57]	Derby Mercury - 14 April 1775 BL/0000189/17750414/004/0004
1775[58]	Derby Mercury -14 April 1775 BL/0000189/17750414/004/0004
1775[59]	The Leicester and Nottingham Journal - Saturday 15 April & Saturday 22 April 1775
1775[60Le]	The Leicester and Nottingham Journal - 20 April & 27 April 1775
1776[61]	Northampton Journal - 25 March 1776 bl/0000317/17760325/010/0003
1776[62]	Derby Mercury - Friday 29 March 1776 bl/0000189/17760329/004/0004
1777[63]	The Leicester and Nottingham Journal - 15 March 1777
1777[64De]	Derby Mercury - 28 March 1777 bl/0000189/17770328/004/0004
1777[65]	Derby Mercury - 28 March 1777 bl/0000189/17770328/004/0004
1777[66]	Derby Mercury - 28 March 1777 bl/0000189/17770328/004/0004
1777[67Le]	Derby Mercury - Friday 4 April 1777 bl/0000189/17770404/006/0004
1777[68]	The Leicester and Nottingham Journal - 19 April 1777
1777[69]	Derby Mercury - Friday 2 May 1777 bl/0000189/17770502/004/0001
1778[70Le]	Derby Mercury - 10 April 1778 bl/0000189/17780410/004/0004
1778[71]	The Leicester and Nottingham Journal - 11 April & 18 April 1778
1778[72]	The Leicester and Nottingham Journal - 18 April & 25 April 1778
1778[73St]	Derby Mercury - Friday 24 April 1778 BL/0000189/17780424/013/0004
1778[74]	Derby Mercury - Friday 24 April 1778 BL/0000189/17780424/013/0004
1778[75Le]	The Leicester and Nottingham Journal - 2 May 1778
1779[76]	Stamford Mercury - Thursday 11 March 1779 bl/0000254/17790311/016/0003
1780[77]	Derby Mercury - Friday 14 January 1780 bl/0000189/17800414/003/0004
1780[78]	Derby Mercury - Friday 14 April 1780 bl/0000189/17800414/003/0004
1781[79St]	Derby Mercury - Thursday 5 July 1781 BL/0000189/17810705/004/0003
1782[80Le]	Derby Mercury - Thursday 4 April 1782 BL/0000189/17820404/004/0001
1783[81De]	Derby Mercury - 17 April 1783 bl/0000189/17830417/008/0002
1783[82De]	Derby Mercury - Thursday 8 May 1783 BL/0000189/17830508/011/0003
1783[83]	Derby Mercury - 29 May 1783 bl/0000189/17830529/004/0004
1784[84De]	Derby Mercury - Thursday 15 April 1784 bl/0000189/17840415/005/0004

1785[85]	Derby Mercury - Thursday 24 March 1785 BL/0000189/17850324/013/0004
1785[86]	Derby Mercury - Thursday 7 April 1785 bl/0000189/17850407/004/0003
1785[87]	The Leicester and Nottingham Journal - 9 April & 16 April 1785
1785[88Le]	Stamford Mercury - Friday 15 April 1785 bl/0000237/17850415/021/0001
1786[89St]	Derby Mercury - Thursday 23 March 1786 bl/0000189/17860323/006/0001
1786[90]	Derby Mercury - 30 March 1786 bl/0000189/17860330/007/0001
1786[91]	Derby Mercury - 27 April 1786 bl/0000189/17860427/006/0004
1786[92]	Derby Mercury - Thursday 18 May 1786 bl/0000189/17860518/007/0004
1787[93]	Derby Mercury - 12 April 1787 bl/0000189/17870412/007/0001
1787[94]	Derby Mercury - 12 April 1787 bl/0000189/17870412/007/0001
1787[95Le]	Derby Mercury - 12 April 1787 bl/0000189/17870412/007/0001
1788[96]	Derby Mercury - Thursday 20 March 1788 bl/0000052/17880320/006/0004
1788[97]	Derby Mercury - Thursday 3 April 1788 BL/0000052/17880403/021/0004
1788[98]	Derby Mercury - Thursday 3 April 1788 BL/0000052/17880403/021/0004
1788[99]	Derby Mercury - Thursday 3 April 1788 bl/0000052/17880403/008/0001
1788[100St]	Derby Mercury - Thursday 10 April 1788 bl/0000052/17880410/005/0004
1789[101Le]	The Leicester and Nottingham Journal - 24 April 1789
1789[102]	Derby Mercury - Thursday 14 May 1789 BL/0000052/17890514/006/0003
1790[103]	The Leicester and Nottingham Journal - 2 April & 9 April 1790
1790[104]	The Leicester and Nottingham Journal - 16 April 1790
1791[105]	Stamford Mercury - Friday 25 March 1791 bl/0000237/17910325/015/0004
1791[106]	Derby Mercury - Thursday 7 April 1791 BL/0000052/17910407/018/0004
1791[107]	Derby Mercury - Thursday 7 April & 14 April 1791 bl/0000052/17910414/003/0001
1791[108St]	Derby Mercury - Thursday 12 May 1791 bl/0000052/17910512/003/0004
1792[109]	Derby Mercury - Thursday 9 February 1792 BL/0000052/17920209/005/0002
1792[110]	The Leicester and Nottingham Journal - 24 February 1792
1792[111Le]	Northampton Mercury - Saturday 25 February 1792 bl/0000317/17920225/011/0002
1792[112]	Derby Mercury - Thursday 22 March 1792 bl/0000052/17920322/003/0001
1792[113Li]	Stamford Mercury - Friday 6 April 1792 bl/0000237/17920406/014/0002
1792[114]	Northampton Mercury - Saturday 7 April 1792 bl/0000317/17920407/012/0001
1792[115]	Derby Mercury - Thursday 12 April 1792 bl/0000052/17920412/003/0001
1792[116]	Northampton Mercury - Saturday 14 April 1792 bl/0000317/17920414/019/0003
1792[117]	Northampton Mercury - Saturday 14 April 1792 bl/0000317/17920414/019/0003
1792[118Le]	Northampton Mercury - Saturday 14 April 1792 bl/0000317/17920414/019/0003
1792[119]	The Leicester and Nottingham Journal - 20 April 1792
1792[120]	Stamford Mercury - Friday 23 November 1792 bl/0000237/17921123/017/0002
1793[121]	Stamford Mercury - Friday 25 January 1793 bl/0000237/17930125/018/0002
1793[122Le]	The Leicester and Nottingham Journal - 1 March 1793
1793[123Li]	Stamford Mercury - 8 March 1793 bl/0000237/17930308/013/0002
1793[124]	Northampton Mercury - 6 April 1793 bl/0000317/17930406/017/0002
1793[125Le]	Derby Mercury - Thursday 11 April 1793 bl/0000052/17930411/004/0001
1793[126]	Northampton Mercury - 30 March 1793 bl/0000317/17930330/019/0003
1793[127Le]	Northampton Mercury - 20 April 1793 bl/0000317/17930420/027/0003
1793[128]	The Leicester and Nottingham Journal - 12 April 1793
1793[129]	Northampton Mercury - Saturday 13 April 1793 bl/0000317/17930413/019/0001
1794[130]	Derby Mercury - Thursday 17 April 1794 bl/0000052/17940417/007/0004
1794[131]	Derby Mercury - Thursday 1 May 1794 bl/0000052/17940501/005/0003
1794[132]	Derby Mercury - Thursday 13 November 1794 bl/0000052/17941113/003/0001
1795[133Sh]	Chester Courant - Tuesday 6 January 1795 bl/0000388/17950106/024/0003
1797[134]	The Leicester and Nottingham Journal - 24 February 1797
1797[135]	Oxford Journal - 25 February 1797 bl/0000073/17970225/007/0002
1797[136]	Derby Mercury - 9 March 1797 bl/0000052/17970309/006/0003
1797[137]	Derby Mercury - Thursday 6 April 1797 BL/0000052/17970406/003/0001
1797[138Li]	The Leicester and Nottingham Journal - 7 April 1797
1797[139Li]	Northampton Mercury - 6 May 1797 bl/0000317/17970506/030/0003
1799[140]	Stamford Mercury - Friday 15 February 1799 bl/0000237/17990215/024/0004
1798[141St]	Staffordshire Advertiser - Saturday 21 April 1798 bl/0000215/17980421/015/0001

1799[142]	Derby Mercury - Thursday 25 April 1799 bl/0000052/17990425/005/0001
1799[143]	Chester Courant – Tuesday 16 April 1799 bl/0000388/17990416/023/0003
1800[144]	Northampton Mercury - Saturday 3 May & 17 May 1800 bl/0000317/18000517/024/0004
1802[145De]	Derby Mercury - Thursday 29 April 1802 bl/0000052/18020429/002/0001
1802[146]	The Leicester and Nottingham Journal - 30 April 1802
1803[147]	Stamford Mercury - Friday 11 March 1803 bl/0000237/18030311/015/0001
1803[148St]	Derby Mercury - Thursday 7 April 1803 bl/0000052/18030407/005/0002
1803[149De]	Derby Mercury - Thursday 14 April 1803 bl/0000052/18030414/002/0001
1803[150]	Derby Mercury - Thursday 14 April 1803 bl/0000052/18030414/002/0001
1803[151]	Derby Mercury - Thursday 5 May 1803 bl/0000052/18030505/002/0001
1804[152De]	Derby Mercury - 29 March 1804 bl/0000052/18040329/002/0001
1804[153]	The Leicester and Nottingham Journal - 20 April 1804
1804[154]	Salisbury and Winchester Journal - Monday 23 April 1804 bl/0000361/18040423/019/0001
1804[155St]	Derby Mercury - Friday 12 April 1804 bl/0000052/18040412/009/0003
1804[156De]	Derby Mercury - Thursday 3 May 1804 bl/0000052/18040503/002/0001
1805[157]	Stamford Mercury - Friday 15 February 1805 bl/0000237/18050215/023/0003
1805[158]	Stamford Mercury - Friday 8 March 1805 bl/0000237/18050308/013/0001
1805[159Li]	Stamford Mercury - Friday 22 March 1805 bl/0000237/18050215/023/0003
1805[160St]	Derby Mercury - Thursday 14 March 1805 bl/0000052/18050314/002/0001
1805[161Le]	Derby Mercury - Thursday 4 April 1805 bl/0000052/18050404/002/0001
1805[162]	Derby Mercury - Thursday 4 April 1805 bl/0000052/18050404/002/0001
1805[163]	Derby Mercury - Thursday 4 April 1805 bl/0000052/18050404/002/0001
1805[164]	Derby Mercury - Thursday 4 April 1805 bl/0000052/18050404/002/0001
1805[165]	Northampton Mercury - Saturday 6 April 1805 bl/0000317/18050406/019/0001
1805[166]	Northampton Mercury - Saturday 6 April 1805 bl/0000317/18050406/019/0001
1805[167]	Derby Mercury - Thursday 25 April 1805 bl/0000052/18050425/002/0001
1805[168]	Derby Mercury - Thursday 25 April 1805 bl/0000052/18050425/002/0001
1805[169]	Derby Mercury - Thursday 25 April 1805 bl/0000052/18050425/002/0001
1805[170]	Derby Mercury - Thursday 25 April 1805 bl/0000052/18050425/002/0001
1805[171De]	Derby Mercury - Thursday 25 April 1805 bl/0000052/18050425/002/0001
1805[172Le]	Northampton Mercury - Saturday 27 April 1805 bl/0000317/18050427/017/0001
1806[173]	Stamford Mercury - Friday 31 January 1806 bl/0000237/18060131/015/0003
1806[174St]	Derby Mercury - Thursday 3 April 1806 bl/0000052/18060403/002/0001
1806[175]	Derby Mercury - Thursday 10 April & 17 April 1806 bl/0000052/18060417/002/0001
1806[176]	Derby Mercury - Thursday 17 April 1806 bl/0000052/18060417/002/0001
1806[177De]	Derby Mercury - Thursday 17 April 1806 bl/0000052/18060417/002/0001
1806[178]	Derby Mercury - Thursday 17 April 1806 bl/0000052/18060417/002/0001
1806[179]	Derby Mercury - Thursday 17 April 1806 bl/0000052/18060417/002/0001
1807[180Li]	Stamford Mercury - Friday 13 February 1807 bl/0000237/18070213/015/0003
1807[181]	Chester Chronicle - Friday 6 March 1807 bl/0000341/18070306/016/0001
1807[182]	Northampton Mercury - Saturday 11 April 1807 bl/0000317/18070411/016/0001
1807[183]	Derby Mercury - Thursday 16 April 1807 bl/0000052/18070416/002/0001
1807[184St]	Derby Mercury - Thursday 16 April 1807 bl/0000052/18070416/002/0001
1807[185]	Derby Mercury - Thursday 16 April 1807 bl/0000052/18070416/002/0001
1807[186]	Northampton Mercury - Saturday 18 April 1807 bl/0000317/18070418/026/0004
1807[187]	Northampton Mercury - Saturday 18 April 1807 bl/0000317/18070418/026/0004
1807[188St]	Staffordshire Advertiser - Saturday 25 April 1807 bl/0000215/18070425/013/0001
1807[189St]	Staffordshire Advertiser - Saturday 25 April 1807 bl/0000215/18070425/013/0001
1807[190]	Staffordshire Advertiser - Saturday 25 April 1807 bl/0000215/18070425/013/0001
1807[191]	Derby Mercury - Thursday 30 April 1807 bl/0000052/18070430/002/0001
1807[192St]	Derby Mercury - Thursday 14 May 1807 bl/0000052/18070514/003/0001
1807[193]	Staffordshire Advertiser - Saturday 5 December 1807 bl/0000215/18071205/028/0001
1808[194Le]	Derby Mercury - Thursday 7 April 1808 bl/0000052/18080407/002/0001
1808[195]	Derby Mercury - Thursday 7 April 1808 bl/0000052/18080407/002/0001
1808[196]	Derby Mercury - Thursday 14 April 1808 bl/0000052/18080414/008/0003
1808[197]	Derby Mercury - Thursday 14 April 1808 bl/0000052/18080414/008/0003
1808[198]	Northampton Mercury - Saturday 23 April 1808 bl/0000317/18080423/026/0004

1808[199]	Northampton Mercury - Saturday 23 April 1808 bl/0000317/18080423/026/0004
1808[200]	Derby Mercury - Thursday 28 April 1808 bl/0000052/18080428/002/0001
1808[201]	Derby Mercury - Thursday 28 April 1808 bl/0000052/18080428/002/0001
1808[202De]	Derby Mercury - 9 June 1808 bl/0000052/18080609/002/0001
1809[203]	Hereford Journal - 29 March 1809 bl/0000398/18090329/024/0003
1809[204]	Derby Mercury - Thursday 13 April 1809 bl/0000052/18090413/002/0001
1809[205]	Derby Mercury - Thursday 13 April 1809 bl/0000052/18090413/002/0001
1809[206]	Derby Mercury - Thursday 13 April 1809 bl/0000052/18090413/002/0001
1809[207]	Derby Mercury - Thursday 13 April 1809 bl/0000052/18090413/002/0001
1809[208]	Derby Mercury - Thursday 13 April 1809 bl/0000052/18090413/002/0001
1809[209]	Stamford Mercury - Friday 24 November 1809 bl/0000237/18091124/022/0003
1809[210]	Stamford Mercury - Friday 17 November 1809 bl/0000237/18091117/022/0004
1810[211]	Derby Mercury - Thursday 22 February 1810 bl/0000052/18100222/004/0002
1810[212]	Stamford Mercury - Friday 23 March 1810 bl/0000237/18100323/027/0004
1810[213]	Stamford Mercury - Friday 13 October 1810 bl/0000237/18100413/017/0002
1811[214Le]	Derby Mercury - 28 February 1811 bl/0000052/18110228/001/0001
1811[215]	Derby Mercury - Thursday 14 March 1811 bl/0000052/18110314/006/0003
1811[216]	Derby Mercury - Thursday 14 March 1811 bl/0000052/18110314/006/0003
1811[217Li]	Stamford Mercury - Friday 22 March 1811 bl/0000237/18110322/033/0004
1811[218]	Hereford Journal - Wednesday 27 March 1811 bl/0000398/18110327/022/0004
1811[219]	Derby Mercury - Thursday 2 May 1811 bl/0000052/18110502/002/0001
1811[220]	Derby Mercury - Thursday 2 May 1811 bl/0000052/18110502/002/0001
1811[221]	Derby Mercury - Thursday 2 May 1811 bl/0000052/18110502/002/0001
1811[222St]	Derby Mercury - Thursday 2 May 1811 bl/0000052/18110502/002/0001
1811[223]	Derby Mercury - Thursday 2 May 1811 bl/0000052/18110502/002/0001
1811[224]	Derby Mercury - Thursday 2 May 1811 bl/0000052/18110502/002/0001
1811[225]	Derby Mercury - Thursday 2 May 1811 bl/0000052/18110502/002/0001
1812[226]	Derby Mercury - Thursday 30 January 1812 bl/0000052/18120130/003/0002
1812[227Li]	Stamford Mercury - Friday 27 January 1812 bl/0000237/18120327/017/0002
1812[228]	Hereford Journal - 18 March 1812 bl/0000398/18120318/018/0003
1812[229]	Derby Mercury - Thursday 16 April 1812 bl/0000052/18120416/002/0001
1812[230]	Derby Mercury - Thursday 16 April [& 23 April] 1812 bl/0000052/18120416/002/0001
1812[231Le]	Derby Mercury - Thursday 16 April 1812 bl/0000052/18120416/002/0001
1812[232]	Derby Mercury - Thursday 23 April 1812 bl/0000052/18120423/001/0001
1812[233St]	Derby Mercury - Thursday 23 April 1812 bl/0000052/18120423/001/0001
1812[234De]	Leicester Journal - 21 August 1812 bl/0000205/18120821/018/0001
1813[235]	Derby Mercury - Thursday 14 January 1813 bl/0000052/18130114/004/0002
1813[236]	Derby Mercury - Thursday 11 March 1813 bl/0000052/18130311/002/0001
1813[237]	Leicester Journal - Friday 23 April 1813 bl/0000205/18130423/026/0002
1813[238]	Derby Mercury - Thursday 29 April 1813 bl/0000052/18130429/003/0001
1813[239]	Derby Mercury - Thursday 29 April 1813 bl/0000052/18130429/003/0001
1813[240]	Derby Mercury - Thursday 6 May 1813 bl/0000052/18130506/002/0001
1813[241]	Derby Mercury - Thursday 6 May 1813 bl/0000052/18130506/002/0001
1813[242]	Derby Mercury - Thursday 6 May 1813 bl/0000052/18130506/002/0001
1814[243]	Hereford Journal - Wednesday 23 March 1814 bl/0000398/18140323/022/0004
1814[244]	Hereford Journal - Wednesday 13 April 1814 bl/0000398/18140413/021/0003
1814[245]	Chester Chronicle - Friday 15 April 1814 bl/0000342/18140415/027/0002
1814[246St]	Chester Courant - Tuesday 26 April 1814 bl/0000388/18140426/024/0004
1814[247Le]	Derby Mercury - Thursday 28 April 1814 bl/0000052/18140428/005/0002
1814[248]	Derby Mercury - Thursday 5 May 1814 bl/0000052/18140505/002/0001
1814[249]	Derby Mercury - Thursday 5 May 1814 bl/0000052/18140505/002/0001
1814[250]	Derby Mercury - Thursday 5 May 1814 bl/0000052/18140505/002/0001
1814[251Li]	Stamford Mercury - Friday 24 June 1814 bl/0000237/18140624/027/0002
1815[252]	Stamford Mercury - Friday 3 March 1815 bl/0000237/18150303/027/0004
1815[253]	Hereford Journal - Wednesday 5 April 1815 bl/0000398/18150405/020/0004
1815[254Li]	Hereford Journal - Wednesday 5 April 1815 bl/0000398/18150405/020/0004
1815[255St]	Leicester Journal - 7 April [& 14 April] 1815 BL/0000205/18150407/028/0001

1815[256]St	Derby Mercury - Thursday 11 May 1815 bl/0000052/18150511/003/0001
1815[257]	Derby Mercury - Thursday 11 May 1815 bl/0000052/18150511/003/0001
1816[258]	Cambridge Chronicle and Journal - Friday 08 March 1816 bl/0000420/18160308/020/0002
1819[259]Li	Stamford Mercury - Friday 29 January [& 5 February] 1819 bl/0000237/18190129/025/0002
1819[260]	Hereford Journal - Wednesday 10 March 1819 bl/0000398/18190310/019/0003
1819[261]Li	Stamford Mercury - Friday 12 March 1819 bl/0000237/18190312/021/0001
1819[262]Li	Stamford Mercury - Friday 19 March 1819 bl/0000237/18190319/028/0004
1819[263]	Stamford Mercury - Friday 19 [& 26 March] 1819 bl/0000237/18190319/028/0004
1819[264]	Stamford Mercury - Friday 19 [& 26 March] 1819 bl/0000237/18190319/028/0004
1819[265]Li	Stamford Mercury - Friday 26 March 1819 bl/0000237/18190326/027/0004
1819[266]Li	Stamford Mercury - Friday 26 March [& 2 April] 1819 bl/0000237/18190326/027/0004
1819[267]Li	Stamford Mercury - Friday 26 March [& 2 April] 1819 bl/0000237/18190326/027/0004
1819[268]	Stamford Mercury - Friday 2 April 1819 bl/0000237/18190402/026/0004
1819[269]Li	Stamford Mercury - Friday 23 July 1819 bl/0000237/18190723/024/0001
1819[270]	Cambridge Chronicle and Journal - Friday 30 December 1819 bl/0000420/18191203/029/0001
1821[271]	Stamford Mercury - Friday 2 March 1821 bl/0000237/18210302/028/0003
1821[272]	Stamford Mercury - Friday 23 March 1821 bl/0000237/18210330/021/0001
1823[273]	Worcester Journal - Thursday 3 April 1823 bl/0000150/18230403/002/0002
1824[274]	Stamford Mercury - Friday 27 February 1824 bl/0000237/18240227/028/0002
1824[275]	Stamford Mercury - Friday 19 March 1824 bl/0000237/18240319/025/0002
1825[276]Li	Stamford Mercury - Friday 11 February 1825 bl/0000237/18250211/016/0001
1827[277]	Hereford Journal - Wednesday 14 March 1827 bl/0000398/18270314/014/0002
1829[278]Le	Leicester Journal - 27 March 1829 bl/0000205/18290327/030/0002
1829[279]	Derby Mercury - Wednesday 27 May 1829 bl/0000052/18290527/001/0001
1830[280]	Leicester Journal - Friday 15 January 1830 bl/0000205/18300115/038/0002
1830[281]	Hereford Journal - 18 August 1830 bl/0000398/18300818/015/0002
1831[282]	Norfolk Chronicle Saturday 5 March 1831 bl/0000244/18310305/040/0004
1831[283]Le	Staffordshire Advertiser - 23 March 1831 bl/0000252/18310423/038/0004
1832[284]De	Derby Mercury - Wednesday 25 March 1832 bl/0000052/18320425/007/0002
1832[285]	Leicester Journal - Friday 6 April 1832 bl/0000205/18320406/048/0003
1833[286]De	Derby Mercury - Wednesday 17 April 1833 bl/0000052/18330417/010/0002
1835[287]	Hereford Journal - Wednesday 28 January 1835 bl/0000398/18350128/019/0002
1835[288]De	Derby Mercury - Wednesday 22 April 1835 bl/0000052/18350422/006/0002
1836[289]	Staffordshire Advertiser - Saturday 26 March 1836 bl/0000252/18360326/054/0001
1836[290]Li	Stamford Mercury - Friday 1 April 1836 bl/0000237/18360401/029/0002
1837[291]Li	Stamford Mercury - Friday 3 March 1837 bl/0000237/18370303/031/0002
1844[292]Li	Kentish Gazette - Tuesday 30 April 1844 bl/0000396/18440302/039/0002
1846[293]	Hereford Times - 11 April 1846 bl/0000396/18460411/067/0001
1847[294]	Derby Mercury - Wednesday 17 March 1847 bl/0000052/18470317/002/0002
1849[295]St	Derby Mercury - Wednesday 14 February 1849 bl/0000052/18490214/011/0002
1850[296]	Hereford Times - 9 March [& 16 March] 1850 bl/0000396/18500309/053/0001
1849[297]	Hereford Times - 10 [& 17 March] 1849 bl/0000396/18490310/063/0004
1849[298]	Hereford Times - Saturday 29 September 1849 bl/0000396/18490929/077/0004
1854[299]	Hereford Times - 18 March 1854 bl/0000396/18540318/089/0005
1855[300]	Hereford Times 7 July [& 14 July] 1855 bl/0000396/18550707/081/0001
1862[301]	Hereford Times - 8 March [& 15 March] 1862 bl/0000396/18620308/142/0005
1862[302]	Hereford Times Saturday 29 March 1862 bl/0000396/18620329/084/0004
1862[303]	Hereford Journal - 27 September 1862 bl/0000398/18620927/053/0001
1863[304]	Hereford Journal - 18 January 1863 bl/0000398/18630131/051/0001
1863[305]	Derby Mercury - Wednesday 1 April 1863 bl/0000052/18630401/001/0001
1867[306]	Hereford Journal - 23 February 1867 bl/0000398/18670223/037/0001
1874[307]Li	Derby Mercury - Wednesday 11 February 1874 bl/0000052/18740211/001/0001
1883[308]	Tamworth Herald - Saturday 7 April 1883 bl/0000484/18830407/082/0004
1891[309]	Derby Mercury Wednesday 4 March 1891 bl/0000052/18910304/018/0005
1893[310]	Western Gazette - Friday 31 March 1893 bl/0000406/18930331/100/0001

[6] Chivers, Keith   The Shire Horse - A history of the Breed, the Society and the Men
J. A. Allen & Co. London 1976   ISBN 0 85131 245 4
Abridged edition by: Futura Publications Limited, London 1976 ISBN 0 7088 1373 9

[7] List of electors for the southern division of the county of Derby, shewing how they
voted ... Jan. 20th and 21st 1835.   Melbourne Polling District: Twyford & Stenson
Stych, William, Jun. ...: Stenson   Stych, William   ...: ditto
www.books.google.co.uk

[8] Farey, John   General View of the Agriculture and Minerals of Derbyshire:
With Observations on the Means of Their Improvement Volume 3 1817
Section III Horses p150-155   www.books.google.co.uk

[9] The Farmer's Magazine: Volume the Fifth   July to December 1836 p. 214-215
19, Old Boswell Court, Strand, London
www.books.google.co.uk

[10] The Farmer's Magazine: Volume the Eighth   January to June 1838 p. 93
24, Norfolk Street, Strand, London
www.books.google.co.uk

[11] The Friesian horse   http://en.wikipedia.org/wiki/Friesian_horse

[12] Gilbey, Sir Walter The Great Horse or The War Horse: From the time of the
Roman Invasion till its development into the Shire Horse.
Vintner & Co. London 1899

[13] Gilbey, Sir Walter Concise History of the Shire Horse
[Originally published as The Great Horse or Shire Horse 1889]
3rd Edition Revised by J Barnes Nimrod Press, Alton, Hants. 1990
ISBN 1-85259-109-9

[14] Stephen Glover's Directory of the County of Derby 1827-29
Repton & Gresley Hundred   Swarkeston:
Smith William, Esq. (a celebrated breeder of rams) Agent to Sir
George Crewe, bart. Farms: Swarkstone-Lows, Foremark Park and Dishley
http://freepages.genealogy.rootsweb.ancestry.com/~brett/glo29i1.htm

[15] Howitt, Mary   An autobiography
[Edited by her daughter Margaret Howitt] 1889
Isbister & Co. Ltd, 15 & 16 Tavistock Street, Covent Garden, London
http://archive.org/stream/maryhowittautobi00howi#page/n7/mode/2up

[16] The Knowles family of Nailstone
http://www.amostcuriousmurder.com/Knowles.htm

[17] The Record Office for Leicestershire, Leicester & Rutland.
Long Street, Wigston Magna, Leicester, LE18 2AH
http://www.leics.gov.uk/recordoffice
Leicester & Nottingham Journal 1759-1810
[The British NEWSPAPER Archive does not include these dates]
• Will of John Capp of Loughborough, 1775
• Will of John Capp of Loughborough, 1780
• Will of John Donnisthorpe of Packington, 1774

- Will of Hastings Garner of Packington, 1798
- Will of Edward Hackett of Naileston, 1806
- Will of William Hart of Culloden House, Norton Juxta Twycross 1812
- Will of John Hood of Packington, 1796
- Will of William Hood of Packington, 1807
- Will of John Knowles of Odstone, 1770
- Will of William Knowles of Nailstone, 1784
- Will of Thomas Knowles of Castle Dunington, 1707
- Will of Thomas Oldacres, Peatling Magna, 1809
- Will of Thomas Ward of Odstone Hill, 1787
- Will of Samuel Wyles of Coton, 1798

[18] Lincolnshire Archives

St Rumbold Street, Lincoln, LN2 5AB
http://www.lincolnshire.gov.uk/residents/archives/

- Will of Ambrose Franklin Bonner, Bicker 1829/34
- Will of John Caswell (senior), Hoffleet Stow, Wigtoft 1820/46
- Will of John Caswell (junior), Wigtoft 1821/65
- Will of Thomas Fisher of Billingborough, Whaplode 1824/94
- Will of Benjamin Harrison, Quadring 1844/162
- Will of Samuel Sewards, Quadring 1834/231
- Will of William Wiseman, Gosberton 1797/ii/105
- Will of William Wiseman, Gosberton 1803

[19] Lichfield Record Office

Lichfield Library, The Friary, Lichfield, Staffordshire WS13 6QG
http://www.staffordshire.gov.uk/leisure/archives/homepage.aspx

- Will of John Bancroft, Barrow on Trent, Derbyshire 1826
- Will of Isaac Bennet, Bramshall, Staffordshire 1825
- Will of Paul Caulton, Duffield, Derbyshire 1822
- Will of George Chadwick, Grindon, Staffordshire 1801
- Will of John Chadwick, Grindon, Staffordshire 1833
- Will of William Chadwick, Draycott in the Moors, Staffordshire 1844
- Will of John Coxon, Atlow, Derbyshire 1781
- Will of William Edge, Leek, Staffordshire 1810
- Will of Thomas Faulkner, Bretby, Derbyshire 1781
- Will of Samuel Gallimore, Ellastone 1750 (together with
-         inventory and executors accounts which contain 'leaping' record)
- Will of Joseph Glossop, Chesterfield, Derbyshire 1825
- Will of John Hambleton, Blore, Staffordshire 1807
- Will of John Harrison, Rocester, Staffordshire 1772
- Will of Thomas Hartshorn, Ashbourne, Derbyshire 1822
- Will of Lionel Henley, Edgmond, Shropshire 1812
- Will of John Massey, Swarkstone, Derbyshire 1740
- Will of John Massey, Hilton, Derbyshire 1814
- Will of Thomas Wharton Orme, Doveridge, Derbyshire
- Will of James Perkin, Stafford, Staffordshire 1833
- Will of William Perkin, Stafford, Staffordshire 1823
- Will of Samuel Tateham, Tibshelf, Derbyshire 1804
- Will of John Wagstaff, Atlow, Derbyshire 1774
- Will of John Webb, Stafford, Staffordshire 1771
- Will of Joseph Webb, Marston, Staffordshire 1803
- Will of Joseph Webb, Stafford, Staffordshire 1839

- Consistory Court Cause Papers B/C/1752/140-155 (describing circumstances relating to suicide of Samuel Gallimore).
- Consistory Court Papers B/C/5/1826/19   2 October 1826
  Joseph Glossop, coal master -
  Gilderoy Glossop (brother), acting executor of Joseph Glossop of Stonegravels in Newbold, Chesterfield.
  (Reference to auction of goods at Loundesley Green colliery, including steam engine, pit ropes and head gear.)

[20] London Gazette 10th July 1866
John Stych, cattle and horse dealer, and cattle & sheep salesman, dealer and chapman –declared bankrupt 3rd July 1866
http://www.london-gazette.co.uk/issues/23135/pages/3963/page.pdf

[21] Marshall, William The Rural Economy of the Midland Counties: Including the Management of Livestock in Leicestershire and its Environs: p.305-315
Published 1790 for G. Nicol, Pall Mall, London
http://archive.org/stream/ruraleconomymid00marsgoog#page/n331/mode/2up

[22] The MOORES of Shirleywich
http://freepages.genealogy.rootsweb.ancestry.com/~simpsont/MOORE_Staffs_line.htm

[23] Museum of English Rural Life [MERL] Special Collections and MERL: Chivers Collection
University of Reading, Redlands Road,Reading RG1 5EX
http://www.reading.ac.uk/merl/

[24] The National Archives: Online Collections: Wills

- Will of Robert Bakewell of Dishley with Thorpe Acre, Leicestershire 1795
- Will of John Mynors Bulstrode, Gentleman of Worthington, Leicestershire 1804
  http://www.nationalarchives.gov.uk/records/wills.htm

  Deeds relating to the Abbotsholme Estate ,Rocester
- (i)   D 1529/86   1736/37   The Brimsholmes & Lord's Meadow
  Lease for 21 years Samuel Pole/ Samuel Gallimore
- (ii)   D1529/131   1804 Re. Staffordshire Brimsholme and Derbyshire Brimsholme
  http://apps.nationalarchives.gov.uk/a2a/records.aspx?cat=169-d1529&cid=-1#-1

[25] Pitt, William   General view of the agriculture of the county of Leicester:
With observations on the means of their improvement. p. 282-289 1809.
University of Leicester Special Collections Online
http://cdm16445.contentdm.oclc.org/cdm/ref/collection/p15407coll6/id/792

[26] Pitt, William   A topographical history of Staffordshire 1817
including its agriculture, mines ....p. 303-305 -
describes Mr. Moore's saltworks at Shirleywich
http://books.google.co.uk/books/about/A_Topographical_History_of_Staffordshire.html?id=JNpCAAAAIAAJ&redir_esc=y

27] Staffordshire General & Commercial Directory, 1818
Compiled by Messrs W Parson & T Bradshaw. Published in Manchester, 1818
in three parts: Part II, including Uttoxeter:
Summerland Mrs Sarah, Carter Street
Summerland, William, butcher, grazier, & mule dealer, Carter Street

[28] Staffordshire Record Office

Eastgate St, Stafford ST16 2LZ
https://www.staffordshire.gov.uk/leisure/archives/contact/sro/home.aspx

- Bartholomew Massey, plaintiff v Thomas Ellot, defendant. Stafford Assizes. 26 Mar 1778 Dispute re terms for sharing an estate called Boosley Farm, Alstonefield, leased from Sir Henry Harpur: briefs for defendant   DocRefNo D3359/12/1/75
- Affairs of Sir Walter Blount in Staffordshire, including agreement for Stych to lease Bellamour   1767-1776, 1779   DocRefNo D538/C/13/7
- Leases for parcel called Thorswood in Wootton, parish of Ellastone Shrewsbury to Gallimore to Hodgkinson 1747-1750   DocRefNo D240/D/290/1-2

[29] The English Cart horse Stud-book [i.e. Shire Horse Stud-book] Volume 1

The First Volume –containing the pedigrees of stallions foaled previous to January 1st 1877 (compiled by R.S. Reynolds) It also contains a Genealogical Table of the more immediate descendants of the Packington Blind Horse.

A 'History of the English Cart-Horse' supplied by R.S. Reynolds M.R.C.V.S.
is also published within this volume.
Printed for the Society by Cassell, Petter & Galpin, La Belle, Sauvage Yard, E.C., LONDON 1880

[30] Swinscoe, David   Calton is My Dwelling Place

Published by Churnet Valley Books, Leek, 2006
ISBN 10: 1904546404 / ISBN 13: 9781904546405

[31] University of Manchester - The John Rylands University Library:

Special Collections - Bromley-Davenport Muniments
Deed dated 1 July 1748: Richard Davenport of Calveley, Co. Chester leases for 99 years to Samuel Gallimore of Wootton yeoman a messuage commonly called Bagnalls farm, and other lands in Wootton.

http://www.library.manchester.ac.uk/rylands/

[32] White's 1857 Directory of Derbyshire

http://freepages.history.rootsweb.ancestry.com/~claycross/246-259.htm

[33] Wykes, David. L. Robert Bakewell (1725–1795) of Dishley: farmer and livestock improver

The Agricultural history Review: British Agricultural History Society
http://www.bahs.org.uk/AGHR/ARTICLES/52n1a3.pdf

[34] Young, Arthur General View of the Agriculture of the County of Lincolnshire

W. Bulmer and Company, 1799.

Index to Horses [not including horses named in **Table 2**]

Flower 47 72
Gaer Conqueror 4 [Plate 1]
Gallemore 5 15 41
Gallemore 903 18 19 22 53 56 57 59 74 78 91 92 93
Gallemore 904 18 24 73 74 78 79 91 93
Gallemore 905 79 100
Gallemore 906 19
Gallemore 908 19
Gallimore 18 19 20 21 23 24 33 41 42 50 52 55 57 59 60 65 86 91 92 96
Gallimore (Old) 18 19 20 21 22 23 39 52 53 54 56 57 60 74 75 77 78 79 86 91 92 93 94 97 98
Gallimore (Young) 18 19 20 23 24 52 78 79 92 93 98 103 106
Gallimore (Young) (Trumper's) 19
Gallimore Biill's) 23
Gallimore (Earl of Oxford's) (Lord Oxford's) 19 20 22 23
Gallimore (Jones's) 23
Gallimore (Knowles's) 21 23
Gallimore Massey's) 18 20 21 39 41 52 87 92 98
Gallimore (Moore's) 19 22 92 96 97
Gallimore Perkin's) 18 19 22 23 78 79
Gallimore (Trumper's) 23
Gallimore (Watkin's) 24
Gallymoore (old horse) (Glossop's) 21 52 98
Galymoor (Gallymoor) 5 18 21 50 65 81 86 87 88
Geaton (Gayton) Brown Horse 68 81
G (or Gee)(Old) Bakewell's 24 38 42 43 44 45 56 68 74 75 81 83 88 89 103 104
G890 (Bakewell's) 42 44 45 70 87
G (Massey's) 77 87 88
Gee (Young) 21 24 103
General 59 74
George 83
Grantham Lad 115
Grey Spark 43426 8 [Plate 3]
Grinn Horse 48 88
Hacket's Horse of Nelson 50 86
Hanley's (Handley's) brown horse of Pave Lane 83
Harley's mare 102
Harold 3703 16 73 82 [Plate 12] 110 118
Harrison's Old Bumper 73 76 79 80
Harrison's Old horse of Combridge 79 80
Hart's Horse of Culloden 61 94 95 96
Hean's (Haynes) Horse 65 66
Hercules 19 23
Highflyer 113 114
Honest Ben 1046 72 75
Honest Ben 1049 72
Honest John 76
Honest Tom 105 107 108 109 110 111 115
Honest Tom (Old) 107 108 109 110
Honest Tom (Young) 107 112 114
Honest Tom (Wiseman's) 108 110 112 113 118
Honest Tom of Whapload (Wiseman's) 107
Honest Tom (Old) (Wiseman's) 111
Honest Tom 1060 101 103 107 108 110 114 115 117 118
Honest Tom 1061 109
Honest Tom 1062 (alias Little David) 71 105 107 112 113 114 115
Honest Tom (Caswell's) 112 113
Honest Tom (Welcher's) 108 [Plate 15]
Invincible 72
Invincible - Mr. Hinckley's Brown Horse 72
Invincible 1138 71
Isley Walton old Horse 40 57 58
John Bull 109 113 114 116
John Bull (Young) 114 116
John Bull (Marshall's) 116
John Bull 1160 116
K. (Bakewell's) (Dishley K.) 43 47 89

King (Old) 105
King (Old) of the Levels 104
King (Young) 104
King Charles 54
King Charles 1206 88
King Tom (Pave-Lane Horse) 74 77 83
King Tom 74
King Tom 1260 76 83
King William the Fourth 106
Kirby (Kerby) 36 38 39 55 56 57 59
Kirby (Old) 23 37 52 53 55 59 61 63 78 79 94 95 110
Kirby (Young) 57
Kirby (Kettle's) 57
Kirby (Oldacre's) 36 59 100
Kirby 1286 18 55
Leicester 63
Leicester 1313 63
Leicestershire 63 110
Leicestershire (Old) 63
Leicestershire 1312 63
Leicestershire 1321 63
Leicestershire Hero 63
Lignum Vitae 83
Lincolnshire Lad 37 110
Lincolnshire Lad (alias Honest Tom 1196) 110 115
Lincolnshire Lad II 1365 110 118
Lion 43
Lister's Lincoln 110
Little David 112 113
Little David (Bakewell's) 104
Little David (Sewards) 112 113
Little David 1397 76
Little John 56 57 60 70 71 75 76
Little John (Chadwick's)
Little John (Oldacres') 55 57 100
Little John (Young) 105 114 116
Little John 1398 76
Little John 1401 75
Lockwood 60 76 77 83
Lockwood G 1418 77
London Horse 44 45
Lord Byron 76
Major 1447 114
Mansetter (Oldacres) 22 37 47 53 54 55 56 57 60 61 63 74 92 93 94 95 96 97 100 110
Mansetter 1476 18 37 54 82
Mansetter 1477 81
Mansetter 1479 81
Marfleet's Horse of Somerton Castle 116
Marston (or Marson) 59 60 73 74 75 77 83
Marston (Young) 74 77
Marston 1486 73 74 76 83
Marston 1488 75
Marstone 75
Massey (Bulstrode's old bald Horse) 59 100
Massey's Horse of Birchall-Moor 42 81 88
Massey's old horse of Birchwood Moor 80 87
Match'em 66
Matchless 1540 114
Mellor's horse of Cawlow 74
Merriman 59
Merryman 38 39 41 42 45 48 58 60 61 70 71 74 75 83 89
Merryman (Bakewell's) 42 52
Merryman (Old) 23 68 74 77
Merryman (Old), Cap's sort, of Loughborough 48 68 90
Merryman (Massey's old horse) 70 71 75
Merryman 1548 48 75 81 82
Merryman 1552 70
Mettle 21 52 98
Milton and Colley's brown horse of Bassingham (Old Honest Tom) 103 108 109 110 114 115 117 118

Index to Breeders and Owners (by county of residence)

Derbyshire

Abbot, John, of Spondon   26 54 93 94
Abbot, Mr., of Spondon   19 53 62 63
Abbot, William, of Mapperley   54
Abbott Mr., of Borrowash   22 91 92 93 97
Abbott, Henry, of Mapperley
Adams, Thomas, of Etwall   36 39
Allestry, Mr., of Alvaston   39
Arnold, John, of Radbourne (Radburne)   26
Ashby, Luke [1757-1818], of Eggington   26 92 94 95 97
Bancroft, John [1743 - 1826], of Synfin   95
Bancroft, John [1771 -   ], of Sinfin   95
Bancroft, John [1801 - 1848], of Sinfin   96
Bancroft, John of Sinfin, near Derby   26 61 94 95
Bancroft, Mr., of Synfin   72 95
Bancroft, William [1767 -1847], of Sinfin   95
Bancroft, William, of Barrow   27
Barker, William, of Tupton   49
Beard, John, of Ashover, Chesterfield   63
Bennet, Isaac [c1748 - 1825], of Over Haddon   19 53 60 91 93
Blunston, John, of Risley, near Derby   26
Bond, Francis, of Bretby ('Bratby')   90
Bott, Thomas, of Toadhole Furnace   41 42
Bowmer, Joshua, of Shottle   39 49
Bowyer, Thomas [1759 -1824], of Waldley   27
Bowyer. Mr., of Waldley   27
Broome, Mr., of Osmaston ('Ormiston')   62
Brownhill, Mr., of Aston, Derbyshire   40
Bull, Mr., of Newton Solney   91
Cantrell, William, of Stanslow, Ashbourne   42 80 81 88
Caulton, Paul [1750 -1822] of Shottle   48 58 99
Chadwick, John, of Shottle   48 88
Chesterfield, 4th Earl of, [Philip Dormer Stanhope] [1694-1773]   13 14 90
Chesterfield, 5th Earl of, [Philip Stanhope] [1755 -1815], of Bretby Park ('Bradby Park')   26 27 90
Clarke, Job , of Repton   26
Cockayne, Mr., of Walton, near Burton-upon-Trent   26
Cooly, William, of Alvaston   86
Cowlishaw ('Cowlyshire'), of Tupton   86
Coxon, John [1717 -1781], of Atlow   48 88
Crewe, Sir George, Bart.   95
Devonshire, Duke of, Chatsworth House   26
Edge, Mr. of Quarndon, near Derby   26
Faulkner, Mr., ('Falkner' or 'Falconer'), of Bretby ('Bratby' or 'Bradby')   14 18 19 22 40 90 91 92 93
Faulkner, Thomas [-1780], of Bretby   90
Faulkner, John [c1740 -1824], of Bretby   91 92
Faulkner, John [1771 -1845], of Bretby   91 92
Gibbs, Richard [1758 -1841], of Tissington   76
Glossop, Francis [1743 -1835], of Upper Haddon   21 98
Glossop, Joseph [1748 -1824], of Stonegravels, Chesterfield   18 21 52 98
Greaves, Robert Charles, of Ingleby   27
Hardy, Mr., of 'Winshall' (Winshill)   63
Harpur Crewe, Sir Henry, Bart. of Calke   27
Harpur-Crewe, of Swarkestone & Calke   86
Harrison, Richard, of Ash, Sutton on the Hill   26
Harrison, William, of Little Eaton   49 87
Hartshorn, Thomas [1741 -1822], of Ashbourne   65 66 71
Hassall, Thomas, of Hartshorn   26
Hawksworth, Mr., of Stanton by Bridge   74
Hodgkinson, Mr., of Kniveton   76
Holmes, Paul [1765 -1849], of Newton Solney   19 22 92
Hudson, Thomas [1746 - 1838], of Rowland, Bakewell   97
Johnson, Thomas, of Derby   36 37 38
Kendall, Jonathan, of near to Toadhole Furnace   41 42 51

Leicester, Mr., of Hartshorn   96
Lister, John [1762 - 1813], of Amberley Farm, Pentrich   69
Malin, George, of Duffield   36 37 38 58
Manfold, Thomas, of Winshill   94
Marsden, Thomas, of Hilton   39 89
Massey, Bartholomew [1739 -1803], of Birchwood Moor   27 80 87
Massey, John [1709 -1799], of Birchwood Moor   18 20 21 37 86 87 88
Massey, John [1744 -1814], of Cockshuthill   36 38 39 49 86 87
Massey, John [c1671 -1740], of Norbury & Swarkestone   86
Massey, Sampson [1723 -1764], of Swarkestone   27 50 86
Massey, Sampson [1780 - 1860], of Swarkestone   88
Massey, Thomas [1721 -   ], of Little Ireton   18 20 21 50 81 86 88 98
Mellor, Mr., of Cawlow   74
Moore (or Moor), Mr., of Winshill   18 19 92 93 94
Moore, Daniel [1770 - 1849], of Winshill   22 26 93 94
Moore, John [1767 - 1838], of Winshill   19 22 26 53 57 93 94
Morley, Joseph of Draycot, near Derby   26
Oakey, Mr., of Doveridge   93
Orpe, William [1782 -1859], of Birchwood-Moor   26 27
Plimley, Walter of Styd Hall, Shirley   26
Porter, John, of Sandiacre, Derby   85
Radford , Francis [1745 -1801], of Little Eaton   95 98
Radford, Charles [1766 -1853], of Denby   53 61 92 94 96 97
Radford, John [1737 -1798], of Denby   39 49 50 96 97
Radford, Mr., of Little Eaton   46 59 92 95 97
Redfern, William, of Mickleover, near Derby   43 58 91
Robinson, John, of Weston-on -Trent   26
Roper, Daniel of Toadhole Furnace   51
Salt, Mr., of Newton   40
Scott, Mr., of Newton   40
Shepherd, Thomas, of Newton Solney   26
Sims, John [1766 -1843], of Stanton by Bridge   20 21 54 60 63 64 87 88 91 92
Sitwell, Sir Sitwell, Bart., Renishaw, Chesterfield   26
Smith Joseph, of Lullington
Smith, Edward, of Draycot, Derby   26
Smith, James, of Aston, Sudbury   26
Smith, John, of Coton, near Burton-upon-Trent   26
Smith, John, of Sawley, near Derby   26
Smith, Joseph, of Lullington   26
Smith, Mr., of the Ash, Sutton on the Hill   39
Smith, William, [c1768 -1843], of Foremark Park & Swarkestone Lowes   26
Soresby, Mr. of Brailsford   97
Stych, John [1815 -1868], of Stenson   71 73
Stych, William [1807 -1839], of Stenson   71
Stych, William [c1768 -1853], of Bellamore, & Barton-under-Needwood (Staffordshire) & Stenson   70 71 72 73 75
Tateham, Samuel [1726 - 1803], of Tupton   51 85 89
Twig, Joseph, of the Common, Marston Montgomery   26
Wagstaff, John [1767 -1836], of Atlow   56 62 89 90
Wagstaff, John, [1740 - 1796], of Atlow   38 39 43 48 51 56 58 85 88 89 90 97
Walker, Gilbert , of Kirk Hallam   85
Wall, John, of Brassington Moor   69
Walls, George, of Barton Fields, Longford   73
Ward, John, of Lullington   26
Webster, Joseph, of Birchin Fields, Bradley Hall   41
Wild, Richard, of Burchill, Bakewell   21 52
Winson, Thomas, of Shottle   97
Wright, Anthony [1777 -1852], of Wheston Hall   79 99
Wright, Joseph [1758 -1838], of Wheston Hall   99 100
Wright, William [1822 -1893], of Wheston Hall   99
Wright, William, of Matlock Bridge   100

Lincolnshire

Andrews, Mr., of Kyme   21 103
Bellamy, John, of Wainfleet   102
Bingham, William [1755 -1824], of Holbeach Marsh   117
Bonner, Ambrose Franklin [1773 -1829], of Bicker   111 112
Boor, Jervis [1773 -1855], of Bicker   111 112
Boulton, William, of Swinderby   109
Brice, Israel [1777-1854], of Risby   116
Brumby, Nicholas [1779 -1845] ,of South Carlton   116
Brumby, Nicholas [c1752 -1811], of South Carlton   116
Buck, Mr., of Billingborough   104
Burtt, Joseph, of Welbourn   112 113 116
Carter, John [1776-1861], of Dunsby   105
Casswell, John, junior [1793-1820], of Wigtoft   107 111 112 113
Casswell, John, senior [1756 -1820], of Wigtoft   111 112 113
Castle, Mr., of Dousby   105
Cox, Mr., of Pinchbeck   105
Coy, John, of Billinghay   105
Fenneley, John, of Swinderby   109
Fisher, Thomas, of Weston   107 114 115 116
Fisher, Mr., of Pinchbeck West   106
Harrison, Benjamin [1773 -1844], of Quadring   107 112
Jacques, Thomas, of Rippingale   105
Johnson, Richard [1752 -1792], of Culverthorpe   21 103
March, Thomas, of Swinstead   106
Marfleet, Mr., (J.) of Somerton Castle   116
Marfleet, Isaac [1756 -1826], of Somerton Castle   117
Marsden, T., of Stamford   52
Oxby, Matthew [1760 -1837], of Norton Disney   109
Oxby, Thomas [1769 -1835], of Aubourn   109
Pacey, William [1768 -1851], of Bassingham   109 115 116 117
Pacey, William [1793 -1841], of Bassingham   116 117
Palmer, Robert, of Toft, near Bourne   105
Pepper, Mr., of Walcot   107
Pycroft ('Bycroft' or 'Bycraft'), Mr., of Donington   103 104
Pycroft, William [1761-1812], of Donington   104
Reynolds, Mr., of Dunsby   105
Rice, Misses, of Fiskerton, Lincoln   109
Rockcliffe, Mr., of West Ashby, Horncastle   104
Rose, Nicholas [1726 -1784], of Denton   102
Rose, T. of Tallington   52
Savage, Mr. ,of Moulton   107
Savidge, John [1772 -1835], of Carlton Scroop   103
Sewards, Samuel [c1758 -1834], of Quadring   105 107 112 113
Sharp, Mr., of Sleaford   103
Simpson, Mr., of Moulton   115
Storey, John [1781 -1847], of Pinchbeck   106 114 115
Storey, John [c1748 -1811], of Pinchbeck   106 114 115
Storey, Mr., of Pinchbeck   106 114 115
Trimnell, Charles ('Trimland' Mr.) [1789 -1814], of Bicker Fen   103 104
Wiseman, William [1780 -1867], of Fleet, Moulton, Weston & Whaplode   107 108 112 114
Younger, John, of Wainfleet   102

Cambridgeshire

Bradley, S., of Leverington, near Wisbech   110
Freeman of Bodsey Toll, Ramsey   110
Johnson, Mr. of Whittlesea   115
Patrick, John of Thorney Fen   39 104
Seward, William, of Chatteris   113
Woods, Mr., of Cottenham   110

Cheshire

Downs, John, of Sheppenhall, Nantwich   84
Jones, Samuel, of Poulton, near Chester   74
Kettle, Samuel, of the Marsh, Acton, Nantwich   57
Occleston, Thomas [1759 -1826], of Bollen Hall, Wilmslow   67

Herefordshire

Evans, John [1746-1833], The Birches, Weobley   22 24
Evans, William [1784-1815], The Birches, Weobley   22 24 106
Hemmings, Mr., of the Vineyard, Ledbury   24
Jones, George, The Birches, Weobley   23 24
Jones, Mr., of Lyonshall   23
Merrick, Mr., of Fenhampton, Weobley   23
Oxford, Earl of (Lord), Edward Harley [1773 -1848], of Brampton Bryan   19 20 22 23
Price, Edwin Alfred, of Ross   24
Rogers, Robert, of Walterstone, Longtown   23
Smythies ('Smithies' Mr.), John R. Rev. [1778 -1852], of Lynch Court, Pembridge   24
Stephens, James [1762 - 1830], of Hollington, Holme Lacy   19
Trumper, William [1764 -1822] of Pembridge   19 23
Watkins, John, of Crasswell, Clodock   23 24

Monmouthshire

Parry, Thomas, of Llanvetherine, Abergavenny   24
Watkins, John, of Abergavenny   19

Norfolk

Thorp, John, of Tilney with Islington   109

Northamptonshire

Bland, George, of Maidwell   44
Colman, W. of Murcott, Long Buckby, Northampton   55

Nottinghamshire

Challenor, Mr., of Nether Thorp, near Worksop   25

Oxfordshire

Salmon, Mr., of near Banbury   69

Rutland

Sisson, Thomas, of Pickworth, Rutland   42

Warwickshire

Brown, Mr. (Zephaniah) [-1801], of Stretton under Fosse   52 53 97
Hill, Abijah, [-1796], of Offchurch Grounds   36
Hill, Mr. of Stretton   40
Lythal, J., of Redford, Warwick   69
Powers, Mr., of Stretton-upon-Foss   69
Salisbury, Thomas, of Higham, near Nuneaton   39
Slingsby, William, of Foleshill, Coventry   56 57 100
Wagstaff, Daniel, of Nuneaton   39

Wiltshire

Francis, Walter [1749 -1784], of Ramsbury   69
Francis, Walter, of Wiltshire   67 69
Shipley, Thomas [1733 -1794], of Zeals   69

Yorkshire

Shirt, Robert, of Beighton, near Sheffield   26

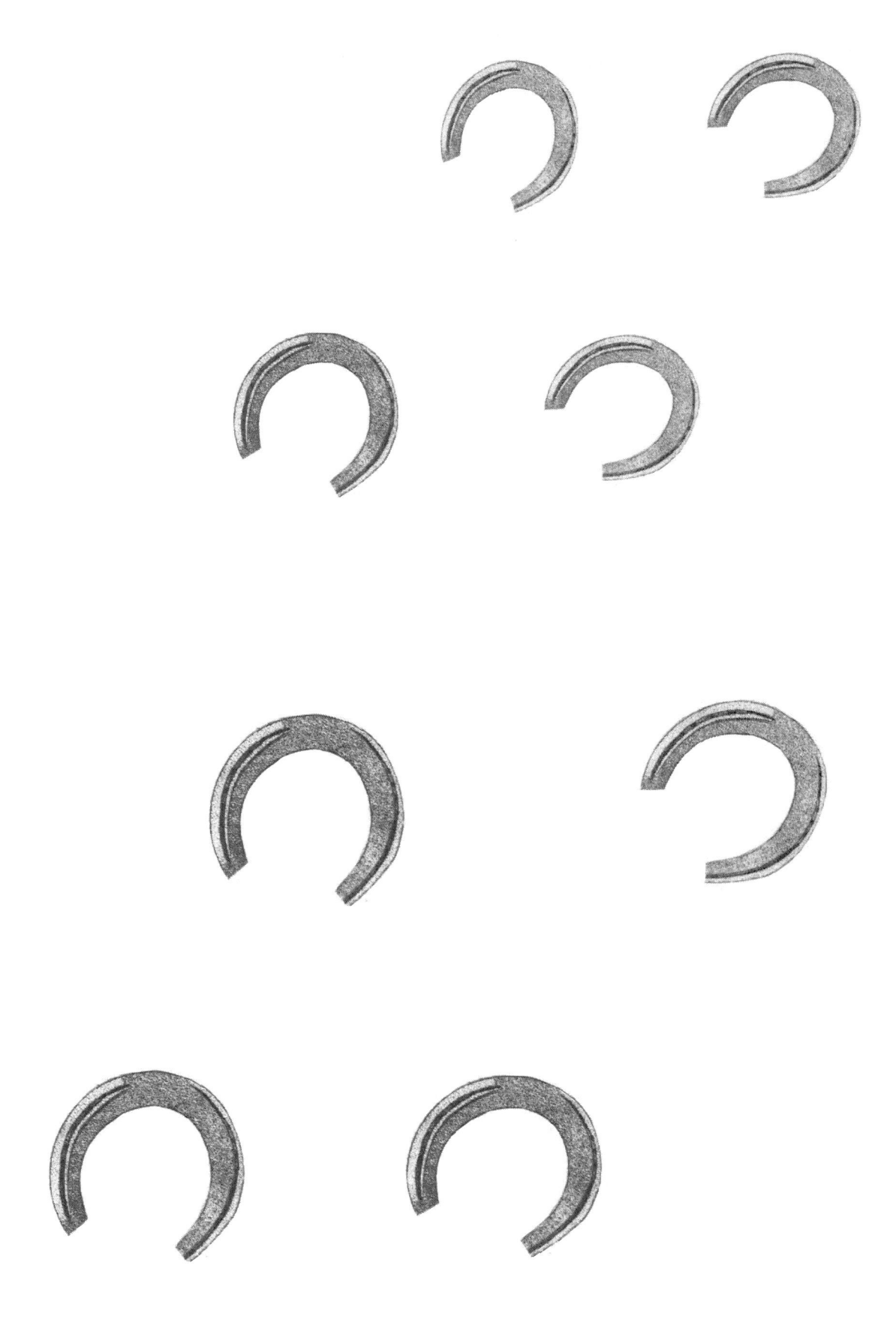

Printed in Great Britain
by Amazon